WAITING

for the

ALBINO DUNNOCK

Also by Rosamond Richardson

Britain's Wild Flowers (for the National Trust)
Meeting Dante
The Zen of Horseriding

WAITING

for the

ALBINO DUNNOCK

HOW BIRDS CAN CHANGE YOUR LIFE

ROSAMOND RICHARDSON

Illustrations by Carry Akroyd

WEIDENFELD & NICOLSON

First published in Great Britain in 2017
by Weidenfeld & Nicolson

1 3 5 7 9 10 8 6 4 2

Text © Rosamond Richardson 2017
Illustrations © Carry Ackroyd 2017

Grateful thanks to Faber and Faber Ltd for permission to reproduce
excerpts from 'Little Gidding' from *Four Quartets* by T. S. Eliot,
and 'The Hawk in the Rain' by Ted Hughes

A CIP catalogue record for this book
is available from the British Library.

ISBN 978 1 4746 0300 3

Typeset at The Spartan Press Ltd,
Lymington, Hants

Printed and bound by CPI Group (UK) Ltd,
Croydon, CR0 4YY

Weidenfeld & Nicolson
The Orion Publishing Group Ltd
Carmelite House
50 Victoria Embankment
London, EC4Y 0DZ

An Hachette UK Company

www.orionbooks.co.uk

*Waiting for birds is like waiting for God, but I don't
think I'd wait three hours for God.*

Priest, poet and birdwatcher R. S. Thomas,
on waiting for a sighting of an albino dunnock

Contents

Contents

For James

Prologue

I came to birdwatching late, and immediately loved being away from the noise and busyness of the world. Waiting for birds became a favourite pastime. Not that it has much to do with the passing of time, because the clock stops in the silences of wild places, and when they come, encounters with birds can be timeless.

My complete ignorance of ornithology would have been humiliating had not my friendly birdwatching mentor made sure it wasn't. I wasn't particularly interested in finding rarities or in counting like a twitcher (although later, seeing twenty thousand lapwings on the Ouse Washes, or a ring ouzel on passage in a nearby field, were to prove unforgettable thrills). I wanted to know more about 'ordinary' birds, never having really looked at or listened to them before. They'd always been there, of course, but I'd never stopped to notice how beautiful they were or appreciate their mystery. As I did so, I became aware of exploring a disappearing world, as human populations encroach on habitats fast becoming unsustainable for winged creatures which evolved millions of years before we turned up. Every bird became an elegy.

The compelling science and natural history of birds— migration facts, anatomical facts, historical facts, every fact I could lay my hands on—absorbed me. But all that was an added extra to what birds came to mean to me. I came across the word 'ornitheology', and found its meaning in the nowness of looking at a yellowhammer, or catching a glimpse of a bittern flying over reedbeds, or watching the first fieldfares as trees changed colour in November, or seeing a red-throated diver at dusk on the sea: in the absorption of those moments, 'eternity'.

A bit of a loner and with a habit of silence, the glove fitted: I discovered that I could sit for hours in wild places, alone, in stillness, and there was nothing more I could want. Except then the birds turned up, a kind of divine intervention or so it seemed. A sudden song, a flight formation or a detail of plumage awakened a sense of something I couldn't name. The moments when I first saw a crane, or a ptarmigan, or a wood warbler, all sense of time and self dissolved. However freezing the feet and hands, the potency of the experience was more than the sum of its parts: as Victorian nature writer and mystic Richard Jefferies wrote, *the soul finds itself in beautiful things.* Like a mirror, the birds reflected back something of themselves. Standing in the bleak wastes of the Fens or the oakwoods of Wales or the mountains of Macedonia, the alchemy of landscapes worked their magic on me too. Aldo Leopold, the American author, philosopher and ecologist, describes this as the noumenon of the phenomenon, and explains noumenon as *imponderable essence.* The experience of each encounter burned into my mind's eye, imprinting on the darkroom of memory: so I decided to write pictures about them.

*

What providence was at work one day in 2009 when a fellow traveller at Mycenae suggested a tortoise-hunting expedition? We'd been picnicking under the monolithic walls where wild cyclamen grow among boulders, he watching some distant birds from time to time and remarking that they must be migrants on their way to Africa for the winter. I thought, how does he know that? He mentioned there might be wild tortoises in the hills, and that did sound thrilling to me, so we set off, my friend stopping constantly to point out birds I would never have noticed. When he came to a full stop and cried, 'There's a woodchat shrike!' I looked at him in bewilderment. I'd never even heard of one. Patiently he showed me where to look, and what to look for, and again I thought, how can he possibly know all this? (He had been doing it since he was six years old, I later discovered.) We continued, pausing for butterflies and wild flowers (where I was more in my comfort zone), scrambling and sliding over scrubby scree slopes looking for tortoises. As we clambered down over the slippy stones I realised I'd lost my sunglasses and also realised I didn't care. He was concerned and wanted to retrace our steps but I said let's just keep looking for tortoises. We found none, but I felt radiant with happiness as we returned, as if I'd fallen in love again. I had: with natural history, an early love neglected for years—and with a new love, of the avian variety. A window had opened on my life, and I had no idea that day how much it would change as the birds flew in.

JULY

Norfolk's Brecklands, north-west Essex

walking

Through that window lay *the solitude of horizons*, as coined by J. A. Baker in 'The Peregrine', unspoiled places where nature is left largely to itself. I've always been a walker, loving to be out in open countryside, and at one point I took up running, relishing the movement, the freedom, the exhilaration of flying along at speed. But the process of waiting for and looking at birds made me slow down and see things in new ways. My inability to be still, to wait and watch (more than challenged in a restless age) was gradually overridden by a new habit of stopping, listening and looking. I began to explore the world of birds. I became more of a saunterer, a word that comes from the medieval word for pilgrims to *la Sainte Terre*, the Holy Land: *sainterreurs*. Waiting for birds in their habitats did indeed evolve into a kind of holy land as the birds and their beauty awakened a sense of something more. I became wrapped in the mystery I sensed in wild birds, discovering in their simple presence, in their innate beauty, just by being themselves as they have been for millions of years, a place of absorption. Another world.

In the beginning, the world of birds appeared so vast I didn't know where to start. There are over ten thousand species worldwide, and I knew next to nothing of most of them, nothing about ornithology, nor of the impact of birds on our cultural life and imagination, let alone how to identify birds.

But luckily I sensed there was no hurry: *N'allez pas trop vite,* as Proust said. For the world is too interesting to skip over the slightest detail (as Marcel himself went on to prove in one of the world's longest novels). The man in the fur coat who spent years in his cork-lined bedroom with the curtains drawn, suffering, writing, was a man with time to think about time: the passing of time, *temps perdu, temps retrouvé,* timelessness and the timeless moment—and the complex detail of the commonplace. All of which are pertinent to watching birds. This new world would take time to explore, and I absorbed his further advice, that *the real voyage of discovery consists not in seeking new lands but seeing with new eyes.*

Life consists with wildness, wrote Henry David Thoreau. *The most alive is the wildest. Not yet subdued to man, its presence refreshes him.* Thoreau, writer and rebel, philosopher and ever the individualist, built himself a wooden hut near Concord in the wilds of Massachusetts, where he lived for two years in the mid-1840s. Here he became acquainted with the local wildlife, sauntered, read a lot and wrote a famous essay on walking which contains one of his most quoted dictums—*In Wildness is the preservation of the World.* His credo, *I believe in the forest, and in the meadow,* came from the experience of having plenty of both, living on the edge of Walden Pond where he was surrounded by miles of dense, unspoiled nature. He came to love the birds, his encounters with them changed him, they taught him to look more closely, to listen more intently, leading him into their world just as they have done for others and were beginning to do for me: at a time of need, taking me down unexplored paths to new places. Where waiting for birds in wild places would be transformative.

Thoreau conflates the wild with the good: *In short, all good*

things are wild and free ... Give me a wildness whose glance no civilisa-
tion can endure, to which I would migrate. Tameness, he declares,
is synonymous with dullness.

The following summer, James my Mycenae friend and I ven-
tured out into the Brecks as the sun was setting. Norfolk, windless at twilight in high summer. Venus rose over the treeline in
a cloudless sky, bright and bleached of colour. It was just after
ten o'clock, a pine forest clearing on sandy heathland punctuated with silver birch. We stopped and listened in the dusk,
inhaling damp smells of late evening. Wild flowers scrambled
underfoot—wild mignonette, lady's bedstraw, toadflax. Viper's
bugloss gleamed blue in the half-light, yarrow glowed ivory. A
stone curlew called, clear in the stillness, a rare sound from a
threatened bird: the call of the Norfolk Plover as they call it
there, ringing over the Brecks at nightfall.

It wasn't long till the churring started. Then again, a long-
winded, soft, musical trill. We waited. After a while, the wing-
clap of a male nightjar resounded into the stillness. Suddenly,
we saw him in silhouette flying out of the trees, circling in our
direction, soundless, sharp winged, swerving and tilting, ivory
wingtips flicking in the gloom, white flashes on the outer tail
feathers. Traced against the pale sky, he glided on raised wings,
wheeling, twisting, turning, tail feathers fanning. Unearthly his
streamlined beauty, a bird the size of a small hawk, spectral,
elegant and mysterious.

Somewhere not far from where we stood, a female nightjar
would spend the daylight hours of summer in an unlined

scrape on the ground, sphinx-like on her eggs, camouflaged by the dead-leaf cross-shading of her plumage. Her mate, dozing lengthwise on a branch, would be watching through narrow slits, his mottled feathers merging with lichens and tree bark and dappled leaf-shade, eyes screwed, almost closed (the Hopi Indian name for nightjar means 'the sleeping one'). The nineteenth-century poet and naturalist John Clare describes the nightjar as *a beautiful mottld bird variously shadowd with the colors of black and brown it appears of the hawk tribe its eye is keen its bill hookshapd and its mouth very wide with bristle like hairs growing at each corner*... He noted the nightjar's weird folklore, how it gets its specific name *Caprimulgus europaeus* from the word meaning goat-milker, since country people believed that, because it flew among livestock, the nightjar stole goats' milk. The spirits of unbaptised children, said others, went into night-jars, hence their eerie calls—and ghostly they are, with notes emitted at between thirty and forty per second (a Norfolk name is Razor Grinder). Some country people called it Jenny-Spinner because of the machine-like sound it makes, others Nighthawk (as it's widely known in the USA), Fern Owl or Moth Owl.

Nightjars are extraordinary creatures. Crepuscular and noc-turnal, they are often seen flying with bats, strange, moth-like, otherworldly. Silent night-fliers, gracefully gliding on long narrow wings, short beak agape to catch night-flying insects, nightjars are birds of the shadows and the dimness of dusk, thus one of the world's least known. But male nightjars are inquisitive and can be attracted by the flap of a tissue. They think the flash of white comes from the wingtips of a rival male: James tried it and it worked. Another nightjar flew up out of the treetops: on tapered wings he moved with swift wingbeats, then disappeared. A rival male? The courtship wing-clap of the first male, made by clapping his wings over his back, resumed, the cracking followed each time by a short melodious song to attract the female. For more than half an hour we listened and watched as, between long churrings, the male nightjar emerged spectral from darkening trees, swooping, floating, agile. The intense rattle seemed sustained on an unending breath, with only the briefest of pauses (the fact that sound recordists have been able to analyse nineteen hundred notes to the minute highlights the limitations of our human hearing).

The far-carrying churr would have been heard on summer nights by a shepherd in his wooden wagon leaning derelict at the edge of the glade, a hut where he tended orphaned lambs, sleeping them with his sheepdog under the bench-plank that served as his bed. Summer after summer he would wake to look out on a green world through a mist of cow parsley, woken by birds hopping over the barrelled roof which echoed like a drum when rain fell, or by the drilling of a woodpecker, or the scrabbling of rabbits, or the drone of wasps. The iron wheels of the wagon had sunk into nettles, obscured by rosebay willowherb. The timbers had rotted, the corrugated tin roof was disintegrating, the stovepipe eaten away by rust. But every summer, year after year, in his makeshift home, this shepherd heard the nocturnal song of the nightjars until the time came for them to fly back to Africa for the winter.

The next time I returned to the forest clearing the wagon had gone.

*

Known to Aristotle, nightjars were first recorded in Britain in the tenth century, having been around for forty million years, ten times longer than we have: through strata of history and memory, predating our gods, birds connecting us to geological time. *I have ever tried to isolate the invisible substance of time,* said Proust. It took him twelve volumes to investigate how the involuntary memory of a distant time and place, triggered by sensory experience (the taste of a madeleine dipped into tea, in his case), is extra-temporal, beyond measurement of time. Equally, seeing a particular bird in a particular landscape, or hearing sudden birdsong, may awaken in us something *ever ancient and ever new*, as St Augustine has it, something archetypal in the winged creatures which have been on the planet as far back as 150 million years, intersecting with us in our lives today through layers of time—here, now, the same as ever, fragments of ancestral memory.

Ernst Haeckel's Palaeontological Tree of Vertebrates of 1879 shows how, shortly after reptiles evolved back in the Carboniferous Period three hundred million years ago, two branches split off. At the top of one branch of his engraving sit the birds, at the top of the other, man. From shared reptile ancestors, beings with equal footing now look at each other atop their evolutionary branches. On one, man surveys what he regards as his world and still wishes, after millions of years, that he could fly. On the other, the birds, closer to heaven than to earth, show no tendency to emulate the exploitative barbarisms of *Homo sapiens*. Time will tell who falls off their branch first.

Sensing, at one stage in his evolution, the continuity of created things, mankind came up with the notion of a Great Chain of Being: how everything has its own place in the scheme of things. From the lowest orders to the highest, in a hierarchy reflecting an ecological pyramid, everything is connected (Leonardo da Vinci said he saw actual lines connecting objects in a kind of visible geometry). From minerals to soil to plants to reptiles to invertebrates to insects to fish to birds to wild animals to man to angels to God, a chain of interdependence: that was the medieval Western angle. The Eastern point of view, summed up by the second-century Buddhist philosopher Nagarjuna, was that *things derive their being and nature by mutual dependence.*

Einstein (who once said that God was the garden and the gardener and that all his life he had been trying to catch him at his work) considered a culture that separates humanity from nature to be deluded. *A human being is part of a whole, called by us the 'Universe', a part limited in time and space.* [Yet] *he experiences himself, his thoughts and feelings, as something separated from the rest—a kind of optical delusion of his consciousness.*

The Great Chain of Being. Known today as ecology.

I've always been a scribbler, and after the evening in the Brecks with the nightjars, I wrote a piece about them. I showed it to James and he encouraged me to write more. That was the beginning of a new direction for me. I was at one of life's crossroads, lost and uncertain which way to go. Suddenly it became clear what I should do. Discovering birds became a lifeline at a time when I was unhappy and confused, they led me into the wild landscapes of their lives, showing me as much about the world inside as the world outside. The bird world opened up new avenues: I discovered habitats I'd never imagined I would, both local and further afield. I met, and read about, people whose lives have been changed by birds, past and present. In a time of need, writers and artists who loved birds opened up new places in my imagination. They expressed qualities of birds I saw but couldn't articulate—including those moments when 'timelessness' becomes an experience, when beauty offers a glimpse of something more, something of the vastness out there, of what we do not and cannot know.

That summer, harvest was late. Most of the roses in my cottage garden were over, deadheaded and waiting for their autumn flush. A few nasturtiums were peeping out of the crowded border among verbascum, clematis, lavender. There's a raggedness about a July garden: valerian dying back, a hardy geranium bursting into magenta flower, an everlasting sweet pea, dazzling white, scrambling untidily over the rose-arch by the bird table. Apples were ripening on the Bramley, the lawn was brown from drought, long grasses under the tree in fescue glory. Bees and butterflies were busy around a repeat-flowering daphne, heavy with scent at twilight.

The village lay quiet. Lying twenty miles south of Cambridge, it's cradled in a dip along a tributary of the River Cam called Wicken Water, a stream crossed by bridges to a row of thatched cottages infilled with newer houses. They nestle between fields in the heartland of East Anglia's industrial arable farms, where the only 'wild' places left are a number of old bridleways and byways, patches of woodland, and a network of footpaths, some of which retain mature hedgerows. The village has a population of a few hundred people: its feudal manor house (long rebuilt) was mentioned in the Domesday Book, and the cottage where I've lived for three decades was built for generations of stablemen who looked after the working horses (in 1925 the incumbent had six children in the two-bedroom cottage, a cooking range in the inglenook and an outside privy). Like most villages within fifty miles of London today, it's mainly a commuter community, with a church, a pub and a village hall— and three farms. The shop and the school are but memories.

A nearly full moon rose low in the sky, gauze-white. A skylark was perched on the telegraph wire beyond the yew hedge, crest outlined against the washed-out sky, streaked breast feathers discernible as he flew off weaving and fluttering, all graceful lines and dipping flight. Dusk was gathering. I walked over the crest of the hill to where a tall hedgerow, remnant of old woodland, shields the top field from the north wind. The barley, ripening over the weeks from soft golden-green to bronze, was now bleached to blond and brittle whiskered. Some wild flowers had resisted the toxic onslaught of the farming year: buttercups shone from the edge of the footpath, busy with insects, and a few late butterflies fluttered into the sunshine: hedge browns, red admirals.

I stopped and listened. Skylarks were singing midsummer evensong as William Blake's 'mighty angels' filled the sky with liquid sound. An exultation of larks was spiralling upwards, hovering high over the field, filling the air with polyphony, pouring out a rain of notes (thirty-six notes to the second when slowed down) for several relentless minutes before dropping like winged pebbles into the barley. I walked slowly back down the sloping field. Two skylarks perched in profile on the fence-posts. The barley rippled behind them in the evening breeze, silver in the late light.

The lark and the light are one, wrote Richard Jefferies of the minstrel of our fields that carries its song to the heavens. *There is sunshine in the song.* Thomas Bewick, Northumbrian wood-engraver who at the turn of the nineteenth century wrote and illustrated the precursor to all bird guides, 'British Birds', noted how the skylark *rises in the air almost perpendicularly and by successive springs, and hovers at a vast height,* soaring as high as a thousand feet and becoming a dot in the sky as it sings its full-throated song. Gerard Manley Hopkins describes how *from his height he gives the impression (not to me only) of something falling to the earth and not vertically quite but tricklingly or wavingly, something as a skein of silk ridged by having been tightly wound on a narrow card or a notched holder.* Somehow, even in the intensive agribusiness of the fields around me, doing exactly that as they nest and breed, skylarks survive, year after year, the chemical drenching and the early harvest, some of them singing through even the severest of winters.

The time had come to cut the barley. All week the combine harvester had been trundling through the village, giant omnivore with roaring jaws that can mow the hillside in a single night. From my garden I watched the monster machine crawling over the crops, mincing the ground-nests of the blithe spirits of the fields. Later I walked up the naked footpath, inhaling the straw smell of stubble, sensing the shocked silence of fields after harvest. A few skylarks were skimming over shorn stalks where the combine had reaped their ground-nests. On one side of the path was a crop of as yet uncut oilseed rape: nervously they darted in and out, finding cover in an alien field. One skylark high above in the heavens was singing its heart out in what sounded like an elegy. Others were fluttering in and out along the path, confused by the obliteration of their habitat, looking for home. As I returned down the lane I watched them scattering out of the hedge and flitting up from the ditch where they'd taken cover.

Skylarks declined by seventy-five per cent between 1972 and 1996, just one statistic in the loss of biodiversity that, according to the United Nations, *is so crucial to our security, health, wealth and well-being.* But who cares? When, in 2010, members of the public were asked what biodiversity is, eighty per cent of them replied, 'some kind of washing powder'. *O the world! Ah the world!* cries Ishmael in 'Moby-Dick'. The rebel in Thoreau had much to say about that, writing a discourse on the duty of civil disobedience and the necessity of protest against conformity to rules made by the wicked, famously declaring in his master-piece, 'Walden', that *the mass of men lead lives of quiet desperation.*

Given our island climate, there aren't many evenings in July when completely calm blue skies and mellow temperatures invite you to walk for miles, watching the light change over the stubblefields. Wild grasses growing among ragwort and yarrow border the hedgerows, palest mauve scabious trembles in a slight breeze as the sun sinks. A wren hops out of the verge into the safety of scrub. Sunset lingers over the land. *It requires a direct dispensation from Heaven to become a walker*, says Thoreau. *You must be born into the family of the Walkers.* It's the old adage *solvitur ambulando*, which roughly translates as 'you can sort it out by walking'. Especially as you become aware of birds. Unknotting the tangled skeins of the mind, soothing the soul. *I think that I cannot preserve my health and spirits*, continues Thoreau, *unless I spend four hours a day at least,—and it is commonly more than that,—sauntering through the woods and over the hills and fields, absolutely free from all worldly engagements.* Walking as thinking time, mending time, learning time: *You must walk like a camel,* he says, endearingly, *which is said to be the only beast which ruminates when walking.*

I felt increasingly at home wherever birds were. Walking in search of them began to open out the maps of my east-of-England homeland, widening its horizons as the row of Ordnance Surveys on the bookshelf grew longer. I discovered wildlife reserves, bridle paths and footpaths all over west Essex, east Suffolk and north Norfolk, including many previously unexplored ones close to home. I was drawn to record something of what I found: Matsuo Basho, seventeenth-century master of the Japanese haiku, coined a fitting phrase in 'Records of a Travel-worn Satchel':

> To talk casually
> About an iris flower
> Is one of the pleasures
> Of the wandering journey

Or in my case, to talk—write—about birds: the pleasures of my wandering journey.

An early morning walk is a blessing for the whole day, declares Thoreau. So I embarked on one where the River Stort winds languidly out of Bishop's Stortford, its calm waters seemingly oblivious to planes flying overhead out of Stansted Airport. After a mile of outer-town wasteland the towpath passes a nature reserve, enchantingly (and optimistically, being bordered to the east by a busy road) called Rushy Mead. Here you are plunged into the emerald light of meadows, reedbeds and spreadeagled trees—alder, oak and willow mostly, with hazel and black poplar growing among acres of nettles and bramble. The trees look happier and healthier than their counterparts lining the nearby roads, or punctuating the surrounding arable fields where they struggle with half a century of herbicides and pesticides. These trees, often standing in hedgerows flailed at the wrong time of year, in fields ploughed too close to too-narrow verges, are nourished on a fallout of agrochemicals. They look sick and about to give up, but those in the reserve by the river, protected by their location and a few good-willed naturalists, have grown full and lush into leafy canopies full of birdsong.

You enter a world of green where a grassy path tunnels through scrambling undergrowth past several ponds, opening into glades where stream banks are alive with dragonflies and wild flowers, where purple comfrey flourishes, hogweed stands tall, wild carrot, ragwort and teazel grow freely, and nettles tangle with bramble. A wooden plank crosses one of the brooks, choked with rushes, where an elderly pollarded willow sprouts withies from a gnarled and knotted base. A dead oak stands alone in a meadow, nettles growing from the hollow trunk charred long ago by a lightning strike.

I was standing by the river bank when a kingfisher flew up into a willow and perched on a cascade of weeping branches. In profile, he had the sun on his back, shimmering blue, dazzling, iridescent. I could see the orange-rust front, the snow-white neck patch, the dagger that is his bill. He was watching, listening, turning his head from time to time. After a while, with a deft hop, he turned to face away from me, jewelled flash of azure and sapphire. Eventually he took off for the bank and landed on a slender reed stem that bent under his minimal weight (a kingfisher weighs less than two ounces) curving into an arch over the water. Like an acrobat he turned again on the almost non-existent balance line of the reed. He remained there watching, listening, waiting, revolving his head from side to side, scouting for fish before making a lightning dive, turquoise torpedo disappearing momentarily into the water with a plop, then out again on to a willow branch, fish in beak.

The kingfisher is the halcyon bird, bird of the Greek gods who hurled a thunderbolt at Alcyone's lover and killed him, upon which she drowned herself for grief. Repentant, the gods turned the lovers into a pair of electric-blue birds who built a floating raft of fishbones on which to lay their eggs. The gods saw to it that the winds and the water were calm enough for the incubation period, ensuring that new life could emerge: halcyon days. Days to make the most of, for kingfishers are short lived. One year may be their allotted span. As they laser through our vision with flash of cerulean light, these ephemeral beings remind us by their beauty that *Creation is the primary and most perfect revelation of the divine,* as St Thomas Aquinas put it. *Ice and sapphire conjure flame,* wrote the Norfolk poet Peter Scupham of the king of fishers who can catch up to a hundred fish a day while feeding their young—and they can have two or three broods of up to ten, in a good year, so that's a lot of fish. John Clare observes the bird at work, how it *sits on a branch of a tree that hangs over a river for hours on the watch for any small fish that passes bye when it darts down and seizes its prey in a moment—they make there nests in holes on banks sides by the water . . .*

Kingfishers were spirits of good luck in bird folklore, yet that didn't use to deter Top-Predator *sapiens* who doesn't generally appear to make full use of the brain capacity granted him: shore-shooters on the Norfolk Broads used to get one shilling a piece for a kingfisher's skin. *Too brilliant to be real,* wrote the pioneering photographer and ornithologist Emma Turner in the early 1900s, *a tiny statue bedecked with precious stones of sapphire, turquoise, ruby—and scarlet feet*. One of surprisingly few female nature writers (why is this, where are they?), Emma Turner considered writing about birds tantamount to interviewing an archangel. I decided to find out more about this woman.

The kingfisher shot off from its branch, rapier-fast streak of lapis and flash of rust, flying dead straight along the middle of the river, and disappeared around a bend like a missile, piping, a fleeting streak of bright blue searing the water to land somewhere out of sight. My heart felt lighter. That's all it took, I needed only one bird a day to lift my spirits as I walked: *I have two doctors,* said the historian G. M. Trevelyan, *my left leg and my right leg.* Walking, absorbing myself in birds, in tiny details of the natural world, proved more powerful medicine than any drug. I had embarked on this new path during July, the middle of the year, month of high summer, metaphor of the cycle of any life. I was alone, grieving the sudden ending of one of the closest relationships of my life. Where my entry into the avian world would lead me I had no idea, but something told me that birds were involved. I obeyed that voice.

While I was watching birds, time disappeared and self dissolved. *I felt a calmness birds can bring to people,* writes Barry Lopez in 'Arctic Dreams' about being out in wild places with wildlife: *quieted, I sensed here the outlines of the oldest mysteries: the nature and extent of space, the fall of light from the heavens, the pooling of time in the present, as if it were water.* Walking in the woods and fields of East Anglia I began to notice things I'd not seen before: opening my eyes and ears for birds was sharpening my awareness of the beauty around me. Whether in the arable prairies of eastern England, or on the flat and mysterious Fens, or walking tracks through Thetford Forest in the 'broken lands' of Breckland, or along the windswept north Norfolk coast, the *solitude of horizons* became my favourite habitat. *Above all, do not lose your desire to walk,* Søren Kierkegaard instructed his niece. *Everyday, I walk myself into a state of well-being & walk away from every illness. I have walked myself into my best thoughts, and I know of no thought so burdensome that one cannot walk away from it . . . Thus if one just keeps on walking, everything will be alright.* I believed him.

The birds of the air are unconditionally joyful, wrote Kierkegaard in one of three devotional discourses called 'The Lily of the Field, the Bird of the Air', a sensibility akin to Gerard Manley Hopkins' *Sun and stars . . . glorify God, but they do not know it* (which he underlines). *The birds sing to him,* wrote the priest-poet in his journal, *they make him known, they tell of him, they give him glory, but they do not know that they do.* The Jesuit who wrote one of the best-loved poems of the canon about the kestrel, 'The Wind-hover', also wrote one for the kingfisher, beginning: *As Kingfishers catch fire, dragonflies draw flame,* his lines erasing the delusion of separateness, capturing the enigma of beauty that is not the measure of words. The priest-poet's kingfisher reveals how

> Each mortal thing does one thing and the same
> . . . myself it speaks and spells
> Crying What I do is me: for that I came.

While I walked in the evenings under calm July skies, they paled to palest of blues and faded pinks. An orange glow nimbed the sinking sun. I remembered something that Roger Deakin, environmentalist, writer and close observer of nature, wrote in his journal: *It's when I do all my thinking—when I'm walking*. Wild flowers lining the hedgerows and fields were spent now, those late-summer flowers of thistle and mayweed, bindweed and burdock. The only sound was the crunch of cut straw under my feet as I walked. Crossing tramlines, sliding on silky stems of stubblestalks, I inhaled the smell of ripened wheat. Sunset cloaked the fields in the colours of its changing light. A sparrowhawk chipped its alarm call, and a green woodpecker flew swooping and dipping into a copse where a stag oak impaled the sky. Gradually the evensong of the birds faded into silence. The sun sank over the silent land as the reaped fields fell quiet.

I became greedy for everything avian, determined to absorb as much information as I could take in. I hadn't known James for long, but we'd clicked immediately. He too was a writer, of nature-travel books and books on birds and art, and we had much in common including a similar sense of humour. He was a great mentor. His husband was a musician, a singer with a fine tenor voice, a sweet funny man I came to adore. James knew little about my private life and didn't ask. I preferred it that way: I think he sensed my sadness, but we kept the two worlds separate and I was glad of that. Among his mnemonics for bird ID were 'the black and white bird with a carrot in its mouth' (oystercatcher), 'the sound of jangly keys' (corn bunting) and 'hairy armpits' (how to tell a golden plover from a grey plover in flight: the former with white patches under the wing near the body, the latter black). Looking back, I still don't know what prompted him to take me metaphorically by the hand and lead me into the bird world, a world he knew so well and in which I was a total novice. But he did, generous with his time and more than patient as I slowly tried to pick my way through what seemed a mountain of visual and factual information. I forgot as much as I remembered, despairing that I would ever begin to master such a huge subject. But loving every moment—and laughing, sometimes a lot.

The birds of the air are unconditionally joyful. 'Joy' is one of John Clare's most commonly used nouns, which might seem enigmatic for a man who was incarcerated in Northampton General Lunatic Asylum for the last twenty-two years of his life. Diagnosed as mad, today he would have been treated with drugs: but then the world would have missed out on the late poems of his madness, some of the most powerful and moving in the English language. Landworker and jobber who lived from 1793 to 1864, Clare was largely self-educated, and desperately poor. Though he was condescended to by the literary establishment as a 'peasant-poet', time has proved him to be in a class of his own, a rare combination of true naturalist with a unique and authentic poetic voice. He was also an unwitting prophet of environmentalism. The point for Clare was that, in spite of his inner anguish, joy was all around him in the fields and woods, in the wild flowers and trees and birds and small creatures. *For everything I felt a love / The weeds below, the birds above.* He discovered, as did Kierkegaard, that *this joy is achieved by being in the moment . . . Joy is the present tense, with the whole emphasis upon the present.* Thoreau got that too: *Above all, we cannot afford not to live in the present.*

*

Otherwise known as meditation.

Beyond the verbiage (ever ancient and ever new) about meditation, this age-old practice has a simplicity that makes it universal. *Meditation ... can take place when you are walking in the woods full of light and shadows ... It is when the heart enters into the mind ... it cannot be learned from another.* Thus world-teacher Jiddu Krishnamurti, who spent much of his free time walking alone in wild places. Wherever he went as he travelled the globe, teaching, he would seek out the hills and woods to be alone, to walk, to empty himself of thoughts, and commune with what was around him. To connect. To pay attention. Most of the time we are oblivious to the detail of what is around us, we don't even see what we're looking at. *Meditation is a state of total attention,* he wrote, *and in that attention there is no frontier, there is no center, as the 'me' who is aware or attentive. That attention, that silence, is a state of meditation.*

I soon recognised that the attention required to watch birds was a form of meditation: the stillness and absorption it required took me out of myself. Waiting for birds, observing birds, I lost myself in what Krishnamurti calls the immensity of the present. He spoke of how meditation is never in time: it is freedom from thought, the ending of experience, the action of silence. Meditation, he goes on, is the seeing of what is, and going beyond it—which became my experience of watching birds, where the spirits are lifted, when time and self are irrelevant—*and that which has no time is the everlasting,* as he says. Thoreau, alone in the woods near Walden Pond, would agree: he had found a kind of heaven under his feet. It wasn't somewhere else, or some time in the future. It was right here and now.

JULY

Krishnamurti kept a journal for seven months in 1961, recounting his experiences of walking, mostly alone, in places as various as his home in Ojai in California, London, Gstaad, Paris, Rome and all over India. He describes a *strange light that you see not only with your eyes but with your heart, [when] the heavens are very close to the earth, and you are lost in the beauty... The beauty... seemed to be everywhere—about you, inside you, over the waters and in the hills. Meditation is this.*

There's a feel of fulfilment in the countryside in July with its long days. Waving grasses and tall nettles repose in untidy old age. Hogweed presides over hedge woundwort and spikes of lemon-yellow agrimony. Self-heal makes a splash of imperial purple, knapweed glows amethyst in the darkening foliage of high summer. The smell of harvest filled the evenings as I walked up the footpath behind my cottage. Instead of watching my feet, wrapped in my thoughts, or gazing without seeing, as I would have done before, now I was looking out for birds. I spotted yellowhammers perched on fenceposts near the top of the hill, this year's youngsters, plump, fresh canary yellow and tawny. I caught sight of buzzards circling over the treetops, sometimes with their young, shimmering in the late light, floating on thermals. I heard a parent skylark singing high above its nest in a patch of unharvested wheat now ripened to old gold, the seeds cracking and popping. One of its fledglings was attempting to balance on top of one of the ears, looking around, unsure, on its maiden flight perhaps, as if wondering what to do next.

AUGUST

North-west Essex, Suffolk, the Fens

beginner's mind

It used to be respectable to collect birds' eggs. Oologist, egg collector, from the Greek *oion* meaning egg. Regarded as a valid scientific pursuit, it was an approved way to learn about avian life cycles and bird behaviour before the days of binoculars and scopes, let alone electronic tagging and tracking. Shooting birds was regular practice in the cause of ornithology, as was collecting their eggs. Today it's illegal except under special licence. For all his love of birds and passion for the countryside, John Clare as a boy was an inveterate egg collector and bird-nester, although later he repented his ways and left them alone.

Clare, a prolific scribbler, compared himself to the yellowhammer, known as Scribble Lark since its eggs are marked with scribble patterns (according to the Welsh, whose name for the yellowhammer translates as 'servant of the snake', the scribblings warned snakes of impending danger). Close observer of small things, Clare describes how his children found, in a gooseberry bush in the garden, a yellowhammer's nest with five eggs in it: it is a *bold bird [which] builds its nest on the ground & in low bushes of dead grass & twitch & lines it with horse hair layes five eggs of a fleshy ash colour streaked all over with black crooked lines as if done with a pen & for this it is often called the 'writing lark'*.

Clare was still incarcerated in Northampton Asylum when Gerard Manley Hopkins was a young boy. *All the world is full of inscape,* wrote the latter, the word expressing for him what he regarded as God's immanence through created things. Although he never called it that, Clare would have understood what the priest-poet meant: at face value 'inscape' implies that inner and outer worlds reflect each other, as in the way every landscape is a condition of the soul. But inscape is more than that, too, it's a perception of the isness of things. In that creation never repeats itself, ever. Nature's fingerprint is unique and specific: no one snowflake is ever the same as another, nor has ever been. No bird either. The mystery of matter was to Hopkins a mark of sanctity. A century or so later, the quantum physicist Niels Bohr pointed out that the universe is not only stranger than we think, but stranger than we *can* think. Every individual identity acted out dynamically in a life was, for the Jesuit Hopkins, a reflection of the stamp of Creation. *Imago Dei.*

Only months after my bird-epiphany I caught sight of a flock of yellowhammers without knowing what they were. It was spring, and as I was walking along a grassy path beside a ditch, a sprinkling of sulphur-yellow sprayed out of the hedge and dissolved again into the thicket ahead of me. I walked slowly on, and the yellow birds whose name I didn't yet know gained ground again and again, dispersing in a burst of gold each time, before disappearing into scrub behind the hedge. Even before that, in the middle of the winter, I'd disturbed a flock of citrine-bellied birds which came fluttering out of the hedge down into the brassicas where they fed for a while before skittering up again, flying close to me, splashes of gold on a leaden February day, fixing a snapshot in my memory. Yellowhammers.

By the time it came to the following August, I knew what these lovely birds were and could recognise a yellowhammer's song. Their music took me off-piste one damp afternoon, down a lane towards a copse. Cloud shadows crept over the fields and it began to rain, lightly, the grey sky darkening above lines of trees and hedgerows that stretched into the distance. The patter of raindrops on leaves. Two yellowhammers flew out of the woodland edge with a flash of sunshine-yellow, disappearing with long jerky undulations—and fast, but not before I could clearly see the bright canary head, olive-brown back dashed with yellow, the chestnut flanks, the longish tail with white tail-corners. They called urgently, a sharp *tsit tsit* as they fled. I sheltered for a while and waited. The drizzle stopped. From the silent wood they started up their song, the wheezy ditty of tinkling notes ending in a nasal *tseeeeeeeee*. 'A little bit of bread and no cheeeeeese.' Richard Jefferies loved it: *There is sunshine in the song*, he wrote. *I remember the yellowhammers most, whose colour, like that of the wild flowers and the sky, has never faded from my memory.*

One day at the end of the month, walking along a footpath I'd not discovered before, I came across another flock of yellow-hammers. Alerted by the sound, I focused my binoculars on a young ash tree where several dozen had spilled on to the branches, canary yellow against a dull sky. That elegant shape, long tail, dash of chestnut, dark eyed. They took off across the path like drops of sunlight and disappeared, leaving me with a smile. I was reminded of the ballerina Lydia Lopokova's remark, *When I am on the Downs in the morning I feel I am having a cocktail with God.*

Hogweed and scabious lined the verges among long grasses where fescues and cocksfoot and wild oats were fading to pale and nearly over. I walked on. At the top of the hill I stopped to watch skylarks fluttering high over the fields, wondering at the unique identity of every bird I happened to see. Their inscape. A yellowhammer was singing from the top of a fencepost as I returned home. The notes sprinkled into the air like light rain. Yellowhammers would become regular companions on my walks until autumn.

Yellowhammer numbers are in steep decline, *a species in dire straits and still falling out of control*, wrote Chris Mead in 'State of the Nation's Birds' in 2000. Hedge-trimming at crucial times of year for nesting birds, hedgerow removal and the autumn sowing of crops depriving birds of winter stubble have all contributed to the loss of breeding pairs. The ever-increasing pressure of human populations, as predicted by the evolutionary biologist Julian Huxley as long ago as the 1960s (and not long after Rachel Carson's equally prophetic 'Silent Spring'), will do nothing to improve things for the yellowhammer.

I miss them when they go quiet in the winter.

John Clare, subject of major biographies and beloved of many, wrote some of the best nature poetry in any language. He knew the natural world intimately and at first hand, and for him there was no divide between the physical and the metaphysical. Clare was born in July 1793, a month *of sultry days and dewy nights*, seventeen days after Gilbert White, the clergyman-naturalist, had died in Selborne. A twin, his sister, died within weeks, leaving him for ever wistful for an innocence untainted by *sin and shame*. He lived in a landworkers' cottage in Northamptonshire, in *a gloomy village ... unknown to grandeur and unknown to fame*: Helpstone, now Helpston—and now more famous than it was, thanks to its native poet.

An agricultural labourer as befits his name (a *clayer* is a man who marls and manures the land), Clare was doggedly self-educated: *I always had a thirst after knowledge in every thing*. His only formal education was as a child at the church school in Glinton two miles away, but he was well versed in the family Bible, knew many of the Psalms by heart and much of the Book of Job. After chancing on James Thomson's 'The Seasons' he became an avid reader of poetry. He learned about the natural world from gypsies camped in the woods around Helpston, and exchanged botanical notes with a handful of friends at Burghley. Clare writes of *the quiet love of nature's presence* as he evolved his unique personal diction. He would dream of *islands of Solitude* as he wandered alone through the woods and fields, book in pocket, peering closely into wild flowers, watching birds and insects, and climbing trees for birds' nests: *I found the poems in the fields / And only wrote them down*. He was happiest in places untouched by human hand, where he was *left free in the rude rags of nature* where *my wild eye in rapture adores every feature*. The villagers of Helpston thought he was crazy. As a boy, truanting Sunday church with his mates, Clare found his religion in the fields: *we heard the bells chime but the fields was our church and we seemed to feel a religious feeling in our haunts*. He experienced the interconnectedness of things, and felt their beauty deeply.

Although they never met, in his time he was briefly as

famous as his contemporary Keats, who described Clare's work as *the poetry of earth*. Clare dubbed Keats *child of nature warm and wild*, but with reservations about his classical allusions which seemed superfluous to the country lad. Clare was grounded in what he saw and who he was, and his sense of wonder at the beauty and diversity of nature never left him: *the wonders of great nature's plan* coloured his view of life. It was the perspective from which he viewed humanity:

> In trifles insignificant and small,
> Puzzling the lower of that great trifle, man,
> Who finds no reason to be proud at all

But Clare's popularity didn't last: the fickleness of fame tormented him as he faded from the literary world, it exacerbated his *blue devils* and probably contributed to the insanity of his old age, considered by doctors to be caused by 'years addicted to poetical prosing'—although today he would most likely have been diagnosed as a manic depressive. He was plagued with mental illness throughout adulthood, and abject poverty also played its part in his condition which would have been alleviated by more consistent recognition (as well as a healthier income).

Birds appear everywhere in Clare's work, he wrote more than fifty poems with specific bird titles, and knew from personal observation about a hundred and forty-five. To him, as to St Francis of Assisi, the birds of the air and the creatures of the fields were his kin, the boundaries between the human and non-human worlds only nominal. He would watch for birds for hours on end: of the lesser spotted woodpecker he wrote (with characteristic lack of punctuation):

for half a day
Ive stood nor seen them till they flew away

Clare became 'the master of the startled moment' in Ronald Blythe's phrase, capturing in words the flight habits, the 'jizz' of birds: through his poetry they swing and bounce and flop, they dash and suther and sail and whirl and swee. *The crow goes flopping from wood to wood.* We *hear* birdsong as he evolves a vocabulary to describe their sounds (the holy grail of authors of bird guides). We hear the call of the heron *cranking a jarring melancholy cry*, the *sweet jug jug jug* of the nightingale, the fire-tails' *tweet tut*, the chiffchaff's *chipichap*, the quail's *wet-my-foot*, and the *whew* of the nightjar's wings.

Clare made a bird list in 1831, naming birds long since disappeared from his native Helpston: the black-necked grebe, the bittern, the red kite (now reappearing), harriers including the Montagu's, the black-tailed godwit, the ruff and the spotted crake. The wryneck was a familiar breeding bird to him, and detailed observations crowd the pages of his notebooks: what the heron feeds on, the buzzard's nesting habits, the injury-feigning and dust-bathing flourishes of the grey partridge, the mating flight of the lapwing, the intruder-display of the wryneck. Notes on the nest habitats of the skylark are a masterclass on the subject, likewise his description of the domestic habits of corvids. Through all his scribblings shines love, his love for them all, the thrushes and nightingales, the willow warblers and spotted flycatchers, the *bumbarrels* (long-tailed tits) and *little trotty wagtails* who inhabited his world.

In 'The Robin's Nest' Clare poetises his *wandering solitudes*, *soodling* (his word for sauntering) in the fields and woods around his village. The Oxford botanist Dr Druce saw him one day, *a solitary looking up at the sky*. He was a walker *faute de mieux*, he walked everywhere, his footfall inscribing the local land-scape across the seasons, a Scribble Lark making word-music, trudging for miles free as a bird *through the wild journey of the cheerless sky*, dropping down to get a closer look at a wild flower, a ground-nesting bird's eggs, an insect. He writes what he sees, directly, and about how it feels to see it, with a lack of rhetoric or artifice unknown to city writers of pastoral idylls whom he dubbed *college poets*. His attention to detail relishes the ordinary and the everyday, the tiny and the specific, down to the detail of a leaf or a feather, and in that intense focus perceives infin-ity. His was a sensibility not of the crowd.

But Clare, mild-mannered contemplative, was angry: he lived in a time of devastating changes to his countryside. The twentieth century would have appalled him further, with its unleashing of toxic chemicals on to farmland, the ripping out of hedgerows, the obliteration of swathes of ancient woodland and the ploughing up of herb-rich grasslands leading to the loss of ninety per cent of our meadows, with the resulting decline of bird and insect life and disappearance of wild flowers. In his day, the Enclosure Acts swept away the pattern of feudal England, unchanged since the thirteenth century, where narrow strips of land were cultivated by village people within open fields, beyond which lay large areas of common pasture and wild places where anyone could roam *free as the winds, that breathe upon my cheek*. This effective privatisation of the fields for larger-scale agriculture, and the coming of the railways, shattered Clare's world. He grieved painfully and angrily as he watched the countryside of his childhood destroyed before his eyes.

AUGUST

Inclosure, thou'rt a curse upon the land
And tasteless was the wretch who thy existence plann'd

The footpath up the hill into open fields behind my cottage is called The Gap, poignant reminder of a track through native woodland, now under the plough. Once a green lane through forest and undergrowth, the trees were felled during the twentieth century to make way for the mechanisation of modern farming. Before he died in the 1990s, my elderly beekeeper-neighbour Frank Bailey reminisced about a First World War childhood when small fields around the village were full of wild flowers and birds in an abundance we can only imagine, when ploughs were drawn by teams of working horses, and when the women and children helped bring in the harvest every summer. He remembered corncrakes calling, stooks in the stubble, and harvest-home celebrations up at the Manor House. The last echoes of John Clare's world.

The weather had turned unexpectedly autumnal for August. On a chilly afternoon a group of swallows colonised the aerial of Frank's cottage chimney, still named after his ancestors the Baileys: some had settled, others were darting about, navy-blue winged, copper throated. A string of them gathered on the telegraph wire that crosses the lane, neat as table-football figures. One individual achieved a seemingly impossible balancing act on a metal pole of the TV aerial, preening, tail streamers twitching as it poked its bill under its wing, head jerking at an offending pest. Periodically it fanned its tail to prevent itself toppling off, revealing long windows—the transparent oblong 'lights' on the inner tail feathers—before snapping them shut, valving and unvalving to regain balance.

Later that evening, as the air grew colder, these graceful birds were flying high above the village, distant silhouettes in the dying day, calling their shrill twittering song, wings glinting in the late light. Swirling and calling, they swooped down into the field beyond the top of the garden, circling restlessly, nose-diving and darting, zooming, wheeling low, then flashing white underbellies as they banked into the wind and floated upwards on wide wings.

I found a Gerard Manley Hopkins poem of 1866 which captures exactly the moment of the swallows on my neighbour's aerial:

> The swallow, favourite of the gate
> Will on the moulding strike and cling
> Unvalve or shut his varied tail

For Hopkins, holiness itself is grounded in *things*, not in intellectual ideas or abstract ideals. It's not a notion swilling around inside the head, it's a *being* thing. Inscape as innate, concrete. For the passionate priest, every creature speaks of itself, and by doing so of its origins in God. This revelation may be experienced serendipitously, irrelevantly even, in a moment of illumination—like Proust's madeleine, or in what Wordsworth called *spots of time*, and in that flash, an experience of timelessness, a glimpse of the unity of all creation. Birds opened up that world for Hopkins: he mentions twenty-six of them in his writings, his words revealing a close observer: pigeons go *jod-jodding* around the yard, the woodlark issues *So tiny a trickle of song-strain*, leaves on an autumn tree *Hang as still as hawk or hawkmoth*, and *The lark in wild glee races the reel round.*

On a sultry afternoon as harvest time came to an end, I wandered up into the fields, away from *the chatter that sprains the soul* (Ian Hamilton Finlay's phrase). Ever since childhood I've felt happier on my own, or with just one friend, less at ease in groups: a bit of a loner with a Garbo tendency. Whether that has anything to do with a weekday morning in Cambridge when I was ten years old and my mother took me and my sister into Holy Trinity Church, I don't know. We went in to look around, the church was empty, and all I know is that there was a moment when something changed. A timeless moment, perhaps, a glimpse. Whatever it was (and it was indescribably beautiful and has never left me), I felt the existence of what we call God for lack of words for what is ultimately unknowable and unnameable. When, many years later, I read something Wittgenstein said—*To believe in a God means to see that the facts of the world are not the end of the matter*—it took me back to that moment. What happened that day I had no idea and still don't know, although it certainly wasn't a domesticated deity, the old-man-with-the-beard-wagging-his-finger kind of God. The memory of that moment remains, completely down to earth yet suffused with light not of this world. Ever since, I've loved going into quiet churches and listening to the silence, an experience not unlike waiting for birds in quiet places.

Expanses of cornland, mostly reaped but some crops waiting for the maw of the combine, lay serene, the all but hedgeless undulations punctuated by dreaming trees. It's one of the few compensations of living in factory-farmed fields, with the unbearable loss of wildlife and flowers, that crop-planting transforms the landscape through the seasons: from the browns of ploughed earth in autumn to the spectrum of greens of early spring growth, to snowdrifts of cow parsley in the May verges, to the vivid yellow of oilseed rape and oceans of sea-blue alfalfa, to the silver-green of young wheat and green-gold of ripening barley, to the June dazzle of scarlet poppies, to the blond wheatfields of harvest, through to the sheen of stubble-fields before the land is ploughed again for winter wheat, beet or brassicas.

The ash tree by the footpath caught late sunlight, the dome of a horse-chestnut cast deep shade, and bryony clambered around thorns of tangled undergrowth by fields where horses graze. I came to an opening between two hedges and saw swallows swooping over the stubble in the field beyond. Some were flittering over a patch of mud left by night rain on the footpath, veering in and out of the tall hedgerow, squeaking and chattering to one another, soaring and sailing, stream-ers streaming (the tail of a swallow is of some importance, it appears, since the female chooses males with the most symmetrical streamers for her mate). They changed direction with a sudden flick measurable only in nanoseconds, floating, diving, calling a sharp *vit vit vit* alarm call when they spotted me. Thomas Bewick wrote of their *windings ... so interwoven, and so confused, that they hardly can be pictured by words*. Some of the birds were feeding their young in mid-air, a fleeting meeting of beaks in an exchange so swift that to blink was to miss it. Some of the young were perched along the rail of a paddock fence, awaiting their turn, resting between vigorous bouts of aerobatics. Their streamers were shorter and blunter than the adults', their faces brownish-pink. The parent birds, spotting

my dog who had wandered amiably ahead of me, issued warning *chvitts* to their offspring, shooting past me like bullets from
a gun, scythe wings swept back. Sleek, steel-blue powerhouses.
How fast do swallows fly when they feed like this? How can
that be measured?

Gradually the birds began to tolerate my enemy presence, and
continued their vital business of catching insects, incessantly on
the wing with a momentary end-of-fingertips flip as they veered
and turned. Watching them, I reflected on the extraordinary
respiratory system of birds that makes this possible, enabling
them to fly vast distances: in a body cavity without a diaphragm
to act as bellows, air sacs act as reservoirs to keep oxygen
pumped constantly through the blood. Not to mention the
hollow bones (of many birds, not all) that have cross-struts for
structural strength, and the ludicrously light skeleton of a flying
machine that needs to eat up to one-third of its body weight
every day. This fragile creature will, in the case of a swallow, fly
across Europe in late summer to Africa via western France, the
Pyrenees and eastern Spain to Morocco, then down along the
west coast of Africa or the Nile valley, avoiding the Sahara (it
may attempt the desert crossing, but at its peril). Then it will
rest awhile before continuing to South Africa to overwinter: a
total of six thousand miles, to *leave us lonely till another may*, as
John Clare put it. According to a study in kinematic ratios of
winged flight, on a twelve-thousand-mile round-trip where they
cover two hundred miles a day, they travel at an average speed
of twenty-four miles an hour, although (a staggering fact) they
can make speeds of up to thirty-five.

Many won't make it: thousands will die from starvation, or
exhaustion, or as victims of predation, or buffeted by storms.
But those who do survive arrive at the same winter roosts

every year. Site-faithful, family groups often stay together and return to Europe in the spring to the same nesting sites. Then I learned the amazing fact that some yearling birds, who make the return journey alone, never having done it before, arrive back to within a few miles of where they were born, sometimes even to exactly the same place. The 'poetry of fact'.

Swallows are birds of good omen—possibly since, being farmland birds, they are insectivores and keep pest levels down (or used to before the farming industry decided that toxic pesticides were a better idea). They are a potent force in country lore: you'll get lucky if swallows nest in your building, but unlucky if they leave or if you harm them in any way. When swallows fly high, it's a sign of good weather: when it turns humid or thundery they fly low (as does their food source, insects)—thus are they rain-bringers, foretelling a shower or a storm. They are fire-bringers too. A legend tells how the swallow got holes burned into its inner tail feathers: after all the fires on earth had been extinguished, the Promethean swallow retrieved fire but got burned as it did so. The 'windows' appeared in the tail feathers, its plumage was darkened, and its face and throat scorched to flame-red. Subsequent birdlore declared it unlucky to kill a bird so highly favoured by the Almighty (or conversely it had a drop of the Devil's blood in it).

Just as I had become aware of them, I realised with wistfulness that I was about to lose them: swallows depart in late summer, leaving our skies bereft of their presence. John Clare mourns their annual disappearance:

Emigrating Swallows now
sweep no more the green hills brow
Nor in circuits round the spring

But this is the bird that does the rounds, it is the bird of return, in Italian *Rondine*, in French *Hirondelle*. A traditional mariner's tattoo uses the swallow as an emblem of safe return. A bird of hope.

As summer passed I was learning much from James, and reading avidly, on ornithology and natural history. Barry Lopez' advice to writers is this: read what interests you, but discover your own beliefs and speak directly from them, otherwise all you are doing is passing on information. I was listening to sound recordings, trying to learn that most difficult of skills, birdsong recognition, and teaching myself how, on my long walks, to take time, to wait for birds to appear, to stand and stare in ways I'd never done before. The focus required began to create a new world from the one I stepped out of each time I wandered into theirs, helping me in quiet ways to recover from the unanticipated loss of someone I had trusted and loved deeply. Betrayal has happened before in the history of the world, but just not to me. It's a universal story, a painfully personal one and I had to deal with it. To my surprise, the stillness and silence required helped in many ways, not least because in the midst of devastation it engendered a state of contemplation whose calm I couldn't analyse—and didn't particularly want to.

All appeared new and strange at the first, inexpressibly rare and delightful and beautiful, wrote the wonderful Thomas Traherne, another priest-poet. It did, and I wanted it to stay that way. I wanted never to become blasé about birds, nor did I aspire to become a twitcher, reducing birds to a competition for the longest list. Aware of the line, of course, between ignorance and innocence, Krishnamurti's maxim appealed: *You must begin without knowing anything about it, and move from innocence to innocence.*

When I saw my first hobby I had no idea of what a hobby looked like, at all. One bright August morning James and I arranged to meet at Lakenheath Fen. A sedge warbler was chittering a squeaky treble from reeds bordering a dyke (it's a bird, I learned later, that never sings the same song twice, endlessly shuffling fifty elements to sing new songs). A whitethroat sang scratchy notes from the dead branch of a stunted tree. We were walking towards the reedbeds where a cormorant perched on a post, still as a statue. The last of the summer swifts swooped and wheeled high above us. The aquamarine heavens, streaked with pearl-mauve drifts of cloud, were suddenly severed by a hobby dashing across the reeds, sickle-shaped thunderbolt turning and twisting on powerful wingbeats, aerobatic acrobat, deadly fast, the light catching the dark blue of its back, the dappled underwing, the white throat and streaked front, even a glimpse of the rust-red trousers and staring yellow-rimmed falcon-eye lasering on to its staple diet of dragonflies and beetles. The dark streak of the hobby's flight had a remorseless grace as it went speeding through the air like a missile from a crossbow, its aerial flexibility appearing almost casual. The long pointed wings scythed over the reeds for only a few moments, then this force of nature tornadoed away towards a distant wood where it disappeared, leaving the landscape changed. Smaller than a buzzard, slimmer than a kestrel, the sudden falcon left an invisible trace on the morning.

*

Without James beside me pointing to that hobby, I might never have seen it, let alone identified it. I felt such a beginner. I was in awe at how he could identify an invisible (to me) blackcap as it hopped through a tangle of undergrowth, or tell a kestrel from a sparrowhawk as it flew across the sky high above us, or single out the song of a willow warbler among a chorus of spring birds. He knew their voices, their habitats, their silhouettes, their flight patterns, their migration habits, their mating games, their social or anti-social ways, what they fed on, and their most likely predators. Following him through the labyrinth I did sometimes wonder whether I would ever be anything but a beginner. But then I decided that might be a Good Thing.

In Zen, there's a saying that in the beginner's mind there are many possibilities, but in the expert's there are few. As Aldo Leopold wrote, *No matter how intently one studies the hundred little dramas of the woods and meadows, one can never learn all the salient facts about any one of them.* That made me feel better. Added to which, St Thomas Aquinas declared that all the efforts of the human mind could never discover the essence of a single fly.

Nor of gulls neither, not that I cared. This was the one bird that I couldn't get excited about, let alone appreciate its inscape. To my beginner's eye, it was impossible to distinguish one species of gull from another. In addition to which, their plumage changes after the breeding season, making a black-headed gull unrecognisable (to me) without its black head. Black-backed gulls (the 'black' being a very dark brown) looked bull necked, squat tailed, ugly and heavy. James spent some time trying to persuade me—unsuccessfully at the time—that gulls are interesting. I refused to be convinced, not just because of their looks, but because they are so difficult to identify. This hostility was to change over time, but in the initial stages of birding my view was coloured by memories of herring gulls in Aldeburgh: I'd been staying in a house overlooking the beach at a lonely time in my life, and associated it with the endless sound of herring gulls, their grating scream, a scream that dominated the daytime and echoed in my nighttime wakefulness. I came to think of herring gulls as thugs, as garrulous vandals. Watching them hovering over fish-and-chip picnickers on the beach was to anticipate a mugging.

Yet undoubtedly gulls have their beauty in the wider picture of things. Driving along the A14 one day the previous winter I'd glimpsed black-headed gulls standing in a field of green winter wheat silvered with frost, ash-grey backs and pure-white undersides catching the low sunlight. In 'The Peregrine', J. A. Baker describes *the white plume of gulls at the brown wake of the plough*. Emma Turner, whose books I had now begun to read, writes of the *rush of wings* as she photographed them on the Norfolk Broads, of a *battalion of gulls over water red-gold under the setting sun*. Ronald Blythe sees from his window at Wormingford black and white birds in the meadows beyond the river, and notices how they swirl together and then fly apart: *I see wheeling phalanxes of black and white birds, seagulls and rooks, cross and recross the hillside . . . and the white and black birds get all mixed up.* The Chilean poet Pablo Neruda, self-styled 'incorrigible birder', wrote:

> I celebrate the skydance
> of gulls and petrels
> attired in snow.

In the Ogilvie Collection of Taxidermy at Ipswich Museum in Suffolk there's a bird labelled 'Glaucus [sic] Gull'. Its size astonished me. It is a giant of a gull. This whopping bird is eight inches longer than a common gull, its wingspan sixteen inches wider, and it tops the herring gull's biometrics by at least four inches in all directions. Although it's similar in size to a black-backed gull, I had never been that close to either: distance diminishes them, and even the best binoculars don't give relative size unless two species happen to be in the same frame.

The 1928 catalogue of the collection says this about the glaucous gull: *It not only feeds upon carrion of all description, dead animals and refuse from whaling stations, but also murders such smaller birds as it can catch, and will swallow whole a bird as large as a golden plover.* This did nothing to endear me to gulls. But it served its purpose. I'd been lured to the museum by the possibility of having close encounters with birds. It is a special privilege to get as near to a bird as a glass case permits, because no (healthy) wild bird would allow it.

Taxidermy may have gone out of fashion or even have a bad name, but viewed in the context of its heyday, before photography when 'shooting' meant something different, it had an important place when wild birds were unimaginably more plentiful, and when experimental science was in its infancy. In its early days, ornithology was a study that took place in the museum and the laboratory: being out in the fields observing birds didn't catch on (with the exceptions of the dedicated— John Clare, Gilbert White *et al.*) until binoculars came in.

Taxidermy advanced the cause of avian taxonomy, added much to the study of endangered and extinct species, and gave to bird lovers the very special experience of being able to observe at close range the beauty of wild creatures they would only otherwise see at a distance, and with little sense of their relative size. Looking at the glaucous gull in the Ipswich Museum was to be startled by its gigantic proportions.

Sad displays of faded, moth-eaten, more-than-lifeless birds in cases exposed to too much light and the ravages of insects are common enough, but at its best taxidermy is an art form. The Ogilvie Collection is an example of this art at its best. The vision that confronted me as I exited the lift to the first floor of the museum was of an Arctic tern high in an eggshell-blue sky, hovering ice-white, tail streamers trailing, silver-grey wings elevated into a pointed V. The black-capped head and red beak of the swallow of the seas point to where a common tern perches on a stump in the grass below. On the other side of a tuft of marsh grass, a little tern stands shyly to attention: the art and technique of taxidermy at its most engaging. Even after a century of display these birds, mounted by master-taxidermist Thomas Gunn of Norwich, are pristine, partly due to the use of arsenical soap in their preparation, a technique discovered in France around 1800 (the arsenic protects the skins from bio-deterioration, but since it's toxic to humans it is no longer used).

Alongside those of lesser craftsmen, Gunn's birds stand out as life affirming in their glowing colours and naturalistic beauty. He took fresh birds in prime seasonal plumage, and since freezing techniques hadn't yet evolved, he and his colleagues had to work fast before degradation of skin tissue set in—known as 'slip' in the trade. If skin follicles deteriorate, the feathers fall out, so they had to be arranged and smoothed quickly while the skin was still supple. The number of man-hours for each bird is astounding: a golden eagle has around eight thousand feathers, and Gunn has mounted two birds, the female about to feast on prey, the male on the lookout in archetypal profile, golden-brown and bright-eyed, with proud hooked beak, feathered legs and golden claws. Somehow Gunn preserved not just the skin of this creature, but its spirit: its majesty, disdain and power.

Born in Sizewell Hall in Suffolk in 1861 into a landowning family, Fergus Ogilvie suffered injury and chronic illness as a young man, became an eminent ophthalmologist and FRCS, and cultivated orchids as a hobby. He was an expert shooter and had a particular interest in waders, whose *special beauty* as he described it drew them to him. He used his marksmanship for a purpose, and the birds who defined his life and gave it so much pleasure became his legacy: not just the taxidermy collection, but eventually part of the Sizewell Hall estate which became Suffolk's reserve at Minsmere.

Over many years Gunn and Ogilvie collaborated closely: the latter shot the birds on his estates, the former preserved and mounted them. The art-deco simplicity and naturalism of the settings are designed from drawings done by Fergus Ogilvie himself, using grasses and stones and wild plants from the habitat of each bird. According to friends who knew him well (an introvert, he had only a handful of intimates), he was self-deprecating, abnormally sensitive and very shy. Birds were an obsession into which he poured his life's artistry, his zeal and his characteristic thoroughness. Like many who prefer watching birds to sparkling in social spheres, he found he could be who he really was with them.

*

Five bearded reedlings inhabit one tall case full of reeds, as seen (or not) in reedbeds anywhere, cheeky adorable birds, mustachio-streaked and alert, flitting between the stems in the search for insects. A Montagu's harrier, rare breeder and scarce migrant to the UK, has a yellow-amber eye fixed on prey, barred secondaries and dark primaries lifted in flight, the four-foot wingspan dominating the case. A ptarmigan in winter plumage scratches in the snow of a rocky Cairngorm habitat, the finely vermiculated plumage of its wings as smart as Savile Row tweed. A peregrine's dark eye glares majestically down, hooked beak a statement of supremacy. A Pallas's sandgrouse startles with alert eye and subtle patterning of creamy-beige and chocolate plumage.

The haunting nightjar is virtually invisible in its cover of tree bark and scrub, nestling in its scrape in a pinewood clearing. A stone curlew with characteristic grin, yellow beaked with staring amber eye, conveys its shyness. A snipe, so difficult to see except in flight, is shown with the glorious geometry of its patterning, the wing plumage of gold and chestnut and dark browns. A merlin looks down inscrutably, blue-backed, perky pied wagtails perch and lift their tails just as they do in life, about to hop, and a group of fabulous choughs, blacker than soot with carrot-red legs and bill, inhabit a rocky landscape, calling anyone drawn to the natural world to experience our connection with the beautiful, the mysterious and the wild.

Beginner's mind is a mind that sees things as they are. As if for the first time, simply, directly, without reading into them and trying to turn them into something else. Like a child sees. The experience of seeing the hobby at Lakenheath had, for me, an essential purity. I imposed nothing on that falcon as it rapiered over the reedbed, because I didn't know what it was or anything about it. I just saw it. I saw its beauty, and was awestruck. It was what it was, in the sublime beingness of its being. One day in the future I might be clever enough to recognise a hobby (possibly), but that response might be over-ridden by clutter. The purity of that moment in Suffolk—it was only a moment—came from a mind that was empty, but ready. It made no discrimination, it had no knowledge or anticipation or longing attached to it, no goal, it saw the hobby with an innocent eye, just as it was.

The German artist Anselm Kiefer once remarked that *the innocent eye can see beauty in everything*.

I did a little brain research. I had no idea until then that knowing and seeing are separate neurological processes. My challenge was to keep those two parallel worlds in balance as they developed, and not let the knowing take over. *Explanation*, wrote the avant-garde playwright Eugène Ionesco, *separates us from astonishment, which is the only gateway to the incomprehensible*. I wanted to stay astonished. The second time I saw a hobby marked a degree of progress in my birdwatching learning curve, because by then I had begun to know what to look for, even to recognise it (sometimes). This tempted me to feel quite pleased with myself, but a warning light came on. I reminded myself

away into a distant wood, gathering the formidable speed that enables it to catch the swiftest of swifts. Yes, really: sprinter of the bird world, hobbies can dash at over a hundred miles an hour, sometimes picking off a swift, sometimes not, appearing to enjoy tumbling and gliding and looping the loop just for the hell of it. They will dive into a flock of swallows or martins (for which eventuality the martin has cleverly evolved a special hobby-alarm call) causing a flurry of whirling and chittering.

This phenomenal falcon, unjustly persecuted by gamekeepers in the past, was a bold and courageous favourite of beginner-falconers in the sport of what they called 'daring' or frightening larks (sometimes even quails and hoopoes), so they might be more easily caught. John Clare kept a hobby as a pet. It flew after him when he took a walk in the fields, and would come when he whistled. When Clare went away for a few days it refused to eat, perched glumly on its owner's empty chair. On his return, Clare was distraught to find the hobby had died, and felt *heartily sorry* for his *poor faithful and affectionat hawk*. I was recalling this story as I walked down a reed-lined board-walk to where, alone in the silence of a bird hide, I could sit and watch. There is a thusness about waiting for birds in a hide. What is, is. What will be will be. What happens happens, and nothing you can do will change that. It's a place to connect to things as they are, as well as to what is unknowable. I was finding it deeply refreshing, not to know, not to have to know, not to need to know. Just to look. *The whole of life lies in the verb seeing,* wrote the Jesuit Pierre Teilhard de Chardin, adding later that *nothing here below is profane for those who know how to see.* I watched a pair of cormorants standing on the edge of the mere as a handsome young marsh harrier flew past. A swallow swooped over the water with flickering wings. A moorhen grunted. There is a holiness about this time of day with the little squeakings and trillings, the rustlings and callings and chirpings from the water and the reeds. The hour of evensong at the ending of the day—*Te lucis ante terminum*—sitting quietly doing nothing but wait for birds.

SEPTEMBER

Cambridgeshire, Essex, Norfolk

migrations

The wary snipe, like the woodcock, if it hears you coming, won't move unless you tread on it. Then it explodes from underfoot. *Extremely watchful* is Bewick's observation of snipe as they fly into the wind, *turning nimbly in a zigzag direction ... sometimes soaring almost out of sight*. Their unpredictable flight is a challenge for the most competent marksman: hence the definition of a sniper as a skilled sharpshooter. Pow. Zigzag, like cartoon lines. Some birds are easy targets, but not the snipe with its starter-gun takeoff. It used to be necessary to shoot birds—not just for food, but to learn their identity and to study them. But shooting birds with a camera has largely displaced the shooting of wild birds with guns—or in enlightened parts of the world it has.

The moment in history when the camera began to replace the gun can be pinpointed to the early 1900s. One day at the turn of the century, a spinster of private means in her thirties from Tunbridge Wells, feeling *in need of an outdoor occupation*, met the pioneering wildlife photographer Richard Kearton, who with his brother Cherry had taken the first ever pictures of birds in their nests: capturing images instead of trophies. Their chance conversation changed her life. During that exchange Richard Kearton encouraged Emma Turner to embark on bird photography. Although she knew nothing about birds, and little about photography, by the time of her death in 1940 Emma

Turner had become one of the leading ornithologists of her generation, a gold medallist of the Royal Photographic Society and among the first women Fellows to be admitted to the Linnaean Society. She took the first-known pictures of a bearded tit, a Montagu's harrier, a water rail and a grasshopper warbler, and became a regular contributor to the science journal 'British Birds'. A pioneering woman in a man's world, she published several books which combine close observation with lyricism and passion, illustrated with her black-and-white photographs that capture what Henri Cartier-Bresson termed the *elusive moment*. Starting from zero, the eccentric Miss Turner became obsessed with birds.

Little is known about her life story, except that subsequently she spent several springs and summers (and two intrepid winters) on her houseboat on the Norfolk Broads, developing photographs in a thatched hut on an island in Hickling Broad. A self-confessed 'born vagabond', this fearless and determined woman built a houseboat called the 'Water Rail' on which she lived with her dogs. She came to love *the witchery of the marshes and their mystery*. She befriended local ornithologists as well as a marshman and his son, the deliciously named Alfred and Cubitt Nudd, locals who knew the ways of waterbirds. From them she learned everything she needed to know: they introduced her to the marsh birds, guided her into their hidden habitats and helped her with heavy work. She used sailing boats, punts and canoes to get about, and developed what she called the *rubbish-heap method of photography*: in all weathers she would bunker down in the reeds and get the Nudds to camouflage her beneath heaps of rotting plant material. There she would lie in hiding for hours at a time until she caught the picture that satisfied her. Or she would climb a tree in her skirts, and wait. Before the days of telephoto lenses and film, the only way to get close to a bird, or to gather details of bird behaviour, was to stay very still, for a very long time. She had to carry a bulky camera with chemically treated glass plates, and a heavy, unwieldy tripod. She was working with film that took time to register an exposure, which meant the subjects to be captured had to stay still for several seconds. In spite of all the odds, her photographs, triumphs of infinite patience and care, are ground breaking.

In her late fifties Emma Turner became the first 'watcher' of terns on Scolt Head, working as a National Trust warden to protect the colonies from, as she put it, *the acquisitive collector who must adorn his cabinet with their spoils, the stupid yokel who stamps on eggs and young for the mere pleasure of destroying them.* Small in stature but physically tough, she lived cheerfully in a shed on a remote shingle spit, with several dogs (she kept terriers and trained them to flush birds so she could count them). The press of the day hounded her, drawing unwanted attention to her sojourn on Scolt Head and dubbing her *the loneliest woman in Britain.* To which her riposte was, *I was never lonely and seldom alone. Ten days was the longest consecutive period of solitude.* That wasn't long enough for Miss Emma Turner.

Born in 1866, two years after John Clare died, like him she was known in her lifetime and then largely forgotten. Her prose, her field observations and the black-and-white photographs that remain (most were lost after her death in 1940) stand as memorials to an individualist and loner whose life changed when the birds flew in. Hers was the kind of nature writing whose response to the natural world, and particularly to birds, retains a sense of wonder without sentimentality. She never indulged in the narcissistic nature writing so despised by John Clare, of the pretentious literati of his time who had little familiarity with nature and adored the idea that its sole purpose was to put up a mirror to their reflections so others could gaze in wonder at their refined souls. Emma Turner the clergyman's daughter saw things differently: nature was not to be reduced to a self-reflective commodity, it was a gift, and you didn't have to be anyone special to appreciate it. *Glimpses of pure beauty are part of our entail,* she wrote, *they are vouchsafed to anyone who will stand and stare.*

Once, under her camouflage, hidden beneath a heap of reeds photographing a reeve, Miss Turner felt a snipe's bill prodding her cheek gently and caressing her ear. She described how one would regularly descend with almost motionless wings like a pipit, creaking loudly and dropping on to a fencepost on her island. She wrote how *newly-hatched snipe are the prettiest of all young birds (except, perhaps, tiny dunlin) in their seal-brown nestling down speckled with black, and tipped with red and white.* During the breeding season she would watch male snipe perform their territorial 'drumming', flying high at sixty degrees to the horizon, the 'bleating' display so called since the sound is exactly like a sheep or goat bleating. The two outer tail feathers splay out beyond the others, taut as the strings of a harp, and as the wind whistles through them they vibrate with the precision of a musical instrument, producing the bleat. To Emma Turner, the sound *seems a fitting herald of the dawn,* and on warm evenings this performance could last for as long as an hour. She would watch snipe loop the loop a hundred and fifty feet above the nest in a dizzying display of zigzagging and switchbacking, dropping into kamikaze descents and flying up again like a yoyo just before they reached the ground. Snipe's Old English name was *Haeferblaete,* or Goat Bleater, after the extraordinary sound made by those outer tail feathers. There's a local name of Heather Bleater, and Robert Burns called snipe *the Blitter frae the boggie*. Richard Jefferies, in his journal of 1886, describes the *low cooing plaintive notes of summer snipes love-making, racing after each other on the white salt surface of sun-dried sea pools*.

Waterfowlers used to shoot snipe regularly, in huge numbers. Some still do, although habitat loss has led to the snipe's decline. Even so, twenty or thirty million migrate to winter in Britain, but they are shy and rarely seen. *Nought gazed on but the sky*, as John Clare observed of them on the *washy flag-worn marshes* around Whittlesey Mere, a two-thousand-acre lake drained in the 1850s to create the farmland that so upset him. The camouflage of the snipe enables them to vanish as if by sorcery, rather like a bittern melts into the chiaroscuro of the reedbeds. They may be glimpsed in reeds after cutting—cropped for thatch in Clare's day—but even so, setting out to watch snipe is a mug's game. I certainly never expected to see one: 'going on a snipe hunt' means a practical joke played by the experienced on the credulous, a fool's errand where as often as not you draw a blank. But waiting for birds is a pastime that guarantees nothing.

A moorhen floated among reeds under waterfed trees at Fowlmere, dabbling for weed with orange-red beak. Its amber eye pierced the dark surface of the water before making an S-shape plunge, smooth and muscular. Upended, a flash of white tail patch. Then calmly drifted on, soot-smudge plumage merging with the murky water. From the deep cover of reedbeds came the sound of murder, a water rail screaming. A streak of electric blue seared the water as a kingfisher dashed from willow to willow.

The great silences of a bird hide.

Along the water's edge the reeds had been cut, leaving stubble. Gazing long at the shoreline, the shapes of two birds emerged, camouflaged by straw-coloured stalks and umber mud: standing motionless, a pair of snipe lit by the low light of late-afternoon sunshine. The brindled plumage glowed rich browns, golden and tawny with shades of chocolate, the darkest feathers trimmed with white, a complexity of patterned wing feathers as rich as an Isfahan carpet. The dramatic head stripes melted into the rushes, elongated by slanting rays of light. Why is it that every bird, however small and however common, is so exquisite in close-up? Why did God bother with such detail? Just for fun? Could it be that beauty is an element of successful evolution? I have no idea. The diversity of birds is baffling to me, but watching those snipe made me think their beauty would turn anyone into a believer. Turned towards one another in half-profile, the two waterfowl showed plump dappled chests and white underbelly, the wing feathers glowing cream-white and rust, rufous and burnished yellow. A pencilling of dark and light umbers defined the forewing, a dramatic zigzag of reddish-brown and black, edged with white, merging with the broken shadows of the reeds. The dark beady eye, the bill reaching vertically to the ground, absurdly long and heavy looking, all out of proportion to the dumpy body—of *rude unseemly length* as John Clare has it. Originally *snite* in Old English, the name relates to sniff, snuffle and snout, appropriate for a bird which searches the mud for invertebrates with a sewing-machine action. There's something primitive about the line of the forehead continuous with the bill, something profoundly ancestral.

The two birds shifted occasionally, one turning its head away and then back again, the other sliding the long bill under a wing for forty winks. This couple were going nowhere, they were settling to roost. At the ending of a September afternoon two small snipe rested, sleepy in their quiet glory, while the lowering sun sank in the west.

One definition of migration, according to the 'Shorter Oxford English Dictionary', is *a loop in space and time, involving an outward journey and return*. Looping space. Birds have flown the skies around Planet Earth for millions of years, making the same annual journeys like blizzards in the flow of time. Globally, eight billion birds take part in return migrations every year, inscribing flyways high above the clouds, as invisible to earthbound eyes as the electromagnetic forces that guide them. If you traced all the streams of bird migrations around the globe, and laid them out on a drawing board, the lines would look like the arteries of a body, vehicles of lifeblood, streams of life, branches of a world-tree. Migrations, invisible currents, birds flying hundreds even thousands of feet above us in the Tree of Life, beyond our sight.

From early March through to late May, about sixteen million birds arrive in the UK, having travelled thousands of miles through sandstorms, crosswinds and cloudbursts, surviving windfarms and gunfire and the best efforts of their predators. Brave little creatures, travelling uncountable miles to unseen destinations, against all weathers, risking their relatively short lives in the simple business of being alive, each one unique. Yet *there is a special Providence in the fall of a sparrow.* The Arctic tern, which stops over in Britain on its way, flies from the Antarctic where it winters, to the Arctic where it breeds, twice a year for up to thirty-four years. Which means this little bird may cover one and a half million miles in its lifetime. The bar-tailed godwit, a bird half the weight of a curlew, flies in a single hop of eight thousand miles, without rest or food for a week, on its migration from Alaska to New Zealand. An albatross can fly three thousand miles in ten days (albeit with stopovers), white storks fly similar distances to their breeding grounds, the snow goose two thousand five hundred miles. Even the spectacularly unaerodynamic rock-hopper penguin manages six hundred and twenty. Pacific golden plovers fly the three-thousand-mile journey from Alaska to Hawaii using, as all birds do, seemingly supernatural powers of navigation guided by the sun or the moon, the stars, earth's electromagnetic field and some as-yet-unidentified low radiation. An internal clock in an unknown location in the brain, and a built-in compass triggered by light, steer them to wintering grounds they've occupied for thousands of years (vagrant birds are birds blown off course by serious weather rather than failure of navigation systems). Deviating just one degree off trajectory would create an error of one mile in every sixty. They don't deviate.

I discovered that birds show migratory restlessness before they leave, but if you put migrating warblers on a plane and take them to their destination to see if the restiveness stops, it doesn't. In caged birds, this restlessness is directional: however much you turn the cage, or black it out, the birds will face the direction of their migratory destination. From the second year onwards, an imprinting facility is awakened in the bird's brain to remember the way there and back. The northern wheatear, I learned, makes one of the longest round-trip migratory journeys of any bird in the world in proportion to its body size: thirty-seven thousand miles at a rate of just under two hundred miles a day, flying to Africa from circumpolar breeding grounds that stretch from the Canadian Arctic to Greenland, through Eurasia and into Alaska. The Alaskan population flies nine thousand miles each way, crossing Siberia and the Arabian desert, averaging a hundred and eighty miles per day, following corridors of migration established millions of years before man evolved on the planet.

Weighing in at less than an ounce, the wheatear is one of nature's miracles. That mileage is astonishing: some populations of this little bird, which is only six inches long and weighs a scant ounce, cross from the New World to the Old and back again every year, flying over the Atlantic where it measures one thousand eight hundred miles.

A windy September day. Flurries of wind scurried the clouds and swept the fields. Autumn migrations were in train: swifts had departed, swallows were gathering to leave. Blackberries hung ripe, glossy on the bramble, but elder bushes were bare, the berries already stripped by the birds. Did this bode a severe winter? I turned into a wooded lane and walked up the hill through to open fields.

A pale bird landed on the edge of the track ahead of me, clear against a dark clod of newly ploughed earth. This slim, sharp, delicate creature was too far away to identify, added to which the wind was buffeting my binoculars. I walked slowly, carefully forward. The lone bird, long legged for its diminutive size, was motionless for a while, then started picking at invertebrates in the grass. Once near enough, I saw to my surprise that it was a wheatear: I had never expected to see one so close to home, here in arable East Anglia—James had told me of seeing them on trips to southern and eastern Europe, but even then, mainly black-eared wheatears. This one was the glamorous northern wheatear, *Oenanthe oenanthe*, the poetry of the name reflecting its luminous beauty. *Oenanthe* after the wine-scented water-dropwort of the Greeks, a bird which returns to Greece in the spring as the grapevine comes into blossom, this one blown off course by gales (my guess) on its journey south to winter in Africa.

Observing them on the Sussex Downs, W. H. Hudson describes in 'Nature in Downland' seeing masses of wheatears, how *on rapidly beating wings, they had the appearance of great black-winged butterflies flitting across the green sward*. The staggering statistics of their migrations reflect in the name 'wheatear' nature's prodigality, how an ear of wheat multiplies a hundred-fold the single grain from which it grows. The stray bird landed in front of me was an adult male in autumn plumage, with buff-brown back, ash-grey head and perky upright stance. Distinct the white eyebrow, the black grain-of-wheat eyemask, the white rump. Sleek and elegant, with apricot blush on the chest feathers merging into whitish underparts, and dark wings edged with white, this bird was in the realm of the classically handsome. *Oenanthe oenanthe*, fragile creature with bones of air at the mercy of the elements, yet historically (prehistorically even) one of evolution's success stories, resting on a farmland track by a ploughed field in Essex, looking around for several minutes, feeding a little, resting before finally flying off like a dart across the bare land and skittering into a distant hedge.

Oinanthe, coined by Aristotle, means 'wine flower', flower of the vine, but English rustics named the bird White-arse, from the Old English *hwit*, white, and *aers*: 'wheatear' with a white rump. This small bird of immense character, with its squeaky warbling song and a chacking that sounds like falling pebbles, answers to numerous vernacular names, now largely forgotten, including Chick-Chack and Stone-Chacker (in County Kerry the wheatear's local name meant 'the cunning old man under a stone' and toads were believed to hatch out of the eggs). John Clare knew it as Clodhopper, here observing the female: *A bird which the common people call a clodhopper appears to be of the lark tribe it is a brown slender bird and hops from clod to clod wagging its tail at the same time like a wagtail* . . .

In the past, wheatears were eaten, equivalent delicacy to the ortolan in France. *At the time of Wheat harvest they wax very fat,* wrote the seventeenth-century ornithologist Francis Willughby in his 'Ornithology', and to Gilbert White they were *esteemed as an elegant dish . . . at the tables of the gentry.* From July to September thousands of wheatears used to be massacred on the South Downs as they flew south, caught in nets placed at the entrances to shallow pits dug to trap them. Thomas Bewick, in 'British Birds', describes how *In some parts of England great numbers are taken in snares made of horse hair, placed beneath a turf; near two thousand dozen are said to have been taken annually in that way, in one district only, and are generally sold at sixpence per dozen.*

Pointing to the folly of human ways, the Book of Isaiah has a famous passage about the ruins of Babylon: *But the cormorant and the bittern shall possess it; the owl also and the raven shall dwell in it: and he shall stretch out upon it the line of confusion, and the stones of emptiness.* Thus the King James version. God works in mysterious ways, like a wise old owl. The proverbial wisdom of owls.

The grief of unexpected loss was slowly, gently, being assuaged by exploring the world of birds, reading about them, learning about them, watching them: *The most important thing is never lose a holy curiosity,* said Einstein. The attention and stillness involved in birdwatching immersed me totally, and the pleasure the creatures gave me was a powerful antidote to sadness. By now I was in the habit of taking notes, jotting down the species I saw and keeping an informal record for myself so I could look up the birds when I got home and learn more about them. Those scrappy lists (very far from being a twitcher's records) served as memory prompts for writing about them later, recalling the landscapes and weathers and flora of the places the birds inhabited.

James and I went walking at Snettisham where, at the edge of East Anglia, at the breathing of tides under the Norfolk sky, waterbirds winter on the flat stretches of the Wash. He'd heard that short-eared owls were arriving from Scandinavia to winter: traditionally they arrive at the first full moon of November—so these were early birds. That day, gusts of knot swept over the mudflats at low tide, silvery underwings gleaming, tight-knit groups of shimmering birds sailing fast and low over the shoreline of England. The plaintive, wistful, bubbling trill of a curlew floated along the beach. A pair stood half facing one another with long downcurved bills, the gentle browns of their plumage merging with the wet sand.

On the marshes behind a shingle bank, a gull made a sudden dive into scrub. There, motionless, camouflaged in a rough tangle of decaying plant life, was a ghost. Only as it turned its head did the pale face give it away: a short-eared owl. Within moments it started flying around, low over the ground, a vision of beauty, the fanned tail brown-barred gold, the wide wide wings of golden feathers mixed with ivory and rich browns, the streaking and barring of the plumage, the round disc of the owl face, the enormous yellow eyes. The soft flight—softer even than a moth's—seemingly weightless, lighter than the wind yet powerful, intentional.

If pressed to choose my favourite bird, it has to be the short-eared owl. Otherworldly creature of ineffable grace, smooth and silent in flight, it's a bird of special beauty that sets it apart. The large round eyes, *when the pupil is contracted*, writes Thomas Bewick, *shine like gold*. This bewitching creature is called by some the Woodcock Owl, since both birds arrive as winter visitors at the same time. Others call it the Pilot Owl after a legend that migrating goldcrests hitch a lift in its wide wings to ferry them over the North Sea. Migrant short-eared owls will themselves sometimes catch a lift on ships, and rest on oil rigs out at sea. Barn owls hunt mainly at dusk and after dark, but short-eared owls are the least nocturnal of the owl family, often seen quartering treeless terrains over rough grassland, tundra, moor and saltmarsh, especially visible in winter in the UK as visiting migrants arrive. The wingspan is, at forty inches, considerably wider than the average front door, certainly mine—which is a pity since I would very much like one to fly through it and move in with me.

One evening at the in-between time known as owl-light, I was driving down a narrow road leading out of the village. I stopped to give way to an oncoming car. As I drove slowly onwards, a large bird flew up out of the verge, whitish, wide winged. It veered towards me, zigzagged across the lane and plunged into the bank. I braked, stopped the car and for a few moments had a full view of an almond-white bird with heavily streaked front, an owl with a round face—not a barn owl then—and distinctly golden tinge to its plumage. As I watched, it flew out in slow motion on long, rounded wings, up into a tree on the opposite side of the road where it sat looking at me, intently, with huge eyes of flame: the fierce stare of the short-eared owl. The full moon of its face, the compact body, the feathered legs. The stillness. In the mottled light its plumage was muted to salt and pepper, biscuit smudged with shadow. Then it opened wide wings in an expanse of creamy feathers, and flew towards the car with languid wingbeats like an oarsman, weightless snow-soft swimmer, gazing into my face through the windscreen. Buoyant bird of noiseless flight, giant ghost-moth gliding effortlessly towards the car, piercing my gaze with gold eyes. Then it swooped over my head, flew on behind me and disappeared into the trees. In that look, those eyes, unblinking and depthless, an encounter with eternity. Henry Vaughan's lines floated into my head:

> I saw Eternity the other night,
> Like a great ring of pure and endless light,
> All calm, as it was bright...

Short-eared owl, in French *Hibou des Marais*, owl of the marshes. The lady of the marshes, Emma Turner, rescued orphaned short-eared owlets, and as she raised them found them *far more intelligent than any birds I have ever kept, not excepting members of the Crow family*. They have the softest voice of all the owls, a lovely *who who who who who* as they sing. Yet 'short-eared' is misleading since the so-called 'ears' have nothing to do with hearing: they are tufts of elongated feathers on the crown of the head which can be raised and depressed at will rather like eyebrows, probably playing a role in owl-communication of which we know next to nothing. They are classified as *Asio flammeus*, flame-birds (*Asio* is the Latin name used by Pliny for a horned owl, and *flamma* the flame of the golden-tinted plumage—or maybe it's those eyes). Locals called them Fern Owl, Moor Owl, Marsh Owl, or Cat Owl and Cataface, nicknames from the cat-like look of the raised ear tufts. There is comedy in the looks of an owl as well as wisdom (surely a wise combination): President F. D. Roosevelt said he felt like a boiled owl after the Teheran Summit of 1943.

Their migration paths, as those of all birds, appear to be a form of ancestral memory. The developing science around migration tells us it seems to be triggered by a chemical mechanism in the eye, providing a compass. Magnetite receptors in the beak appear to be sensitive to the earth's electromagnetic field, providing a map. Satellite transmitters now bring in streams of information: forty per cent of the world's ten thousand birds—four thousand species—are migratory, and one and a half billion of them fly the Africa–Eurasia flyways annually. The poetry of the fact world: sedge warblers increase their body weight by eighty per cent before they set out, heart rates can increase by four hundred per cent and baby puffins can't even fly: they start the journey by swimming. Certain female waders leave the males behind to look after the chicks before they follow on later. Some Manx shearwaters, most unaerodynamic-looking of birds, fly from South America to Bardsey Island off the west coast of Wales, clocking up a total of five million miles in an average lifetime, using their sense of smell to navigate. Some birds fly at mind-boggling altitudes:

Eurasian and demoiselle cranes fly more than three miles above sea level as they pass over the Himalayas from Siberia to India. Airline pilots have seen bar-headed geese flying over the Himalayas at over thirty thousand feet—five and a half miles, a height at which we humans would be unconscious within two minutes, requiring the pressurising of an aircraft cabin to survive at such altitudes. These and other astounding bird facts (whether it was learning that birds are the longest living of all warm-blooded animals relative to body size, or that pelicans can ingest a gallon of fish in one gulp, or that jackdaws have blue eyes) had me enthralled.

This much facts can tell us. The rest is a matter for wonder. The poets for their part create metaphors, as did R. S. Thomas:

> Escape from your mortal cage
>   in thought.
> Your migrations will never
> Be over...

Given their astounding life histories, it's no surprise that birds have long been thought of as celestial beings, linking our world to the realms of the supernatural. Mediators of the human and the divine, metaphors for our inner world, omens for what we cannot explain (I discovered that the Greek word for bird, *ornis* or *oionos*, also means omen). They appear as messengers of the gods—and not just to our primitive forebears: the first radar observations of bird migrations in the Second World War, projecting a kind of cloud on to the screen, were referred to as 'angels' until the true cause was discerned in 1969. Yes, really. Perhaps they are. There are innumerable stories about birds and the supernatural. As I drove home from Snettisham that day I was reminded of a true story told me by a friend, prompted by the sight of a white barn owl drifting over a verge. It had flown ghost-like out of the hedge, scattering the dusk in the winding lane, floating on silent wings away from me. No wonder some call the barn owl Silver Owl, Ghost Owl, Church Owl—the French call it *Effraie des Clochers* from its habit of haunting bell-towers. As it flew over the hedge into the darkening field, my mind drifted to Michael's story.

The funeral was over. It was November. Tall trees along the verges were bare branched, skeletal against a grey sky. Smoke-puffs of travellers' joy drifted in dank undergrowth. The afternoon was cold, numb with the death of a woman before her time, my friend's beloved wife, his companion, their children's mother. The undertaker's car drove the family back up the wooded lane from the village church to the empty, locked house. Michael's son walked along the passageway to the sitting room and opened the door.

On the back of an armchair was a bird. Biscuit-pale, perching motionless, looking at him with dark, unblinking eyes. A little barn owl, a juvenile, impassive. As they gazed at each other, the bird showed no sign of fear or distress. The young man looked around: how had this bird made its way into the locked house? All the windows were closed, the fireplace undisturbed, and all the interior doors had been closed too. The bird was untouched by trauma or damage of any sort.

As he walked towards the young barn owl, it remained completely calm, staring at him with fathomless eyes. Gently he picked it up with both hands. It didn't struggle. It wasn't much longer than the length of his fingers, light, soft and downy, fragile. Its feathery legs and long-taloned toes hung softly down between his wrists. It looked at him thoughtfully and he gazed back at it, wondering how this little bird had got there, and then what to do with it. The proverbial wise stare of the owl. The white mask of its heart-shaped face was disproportionately large compared to the immature body with delicate torso, long tail and small beak—and concealed ears that can hear a mouse's heartbeat from thirty yards away.

The dead woman's son went over to the window and unlatched it, holding the bird carefully. He opened his hands. Watching him intently, the owl made no move. The young bird was in no hurry to leave. After a while, it flapped slowly across the garden with the eerie silent flight of the barn owl, and settled in a tree. There it stayed on a branch during the funeral tea, until the light failed and night came.

The spirit of a woman hovers over Hickling Broad. Her houseboat has vanished, the jetty gone. Our silent boat skimmed over the water, drifting towards swans and Egyptian geese feeding contentedly in the shallows. Early evening light. As we paused at the tiny, deserted islet known as 'Miss Turner's Island', a tern dashed overhead like a white paper plane, calling its thin throaty call. Ripples slapped against the hull as we came to a standstill. The reeds whispering above our heads were outlined against a skim of cloud. A lone apple tree struggled among reeds where Emma Turner's hut has fallen into ruin. Satin water gurgled under the boat, reflecting milky patterns of sky.

We rustled through a channel of Norfolk reeds, *Phragmites australis*, past bulrushes and a clump of milkweed where swallowtails flutter in summer, to a bird hide. A wood sand-piper flew past, a pair of black-tailed godwits sailed overhead, a lapwing fed on mudflats next to a snipe, long bill poking down into yellow butterknot weed. They lingered for a while, unusual companions, the snipe surprisingly (to me) small and compact beside the lapwing, as barnacle geese and greylags moved around behind them. Teal flew in like a gust of rain, gulls swirled and screeched, a pair of ruff floated in to land. A single herring gull fed in the shallows, mirrored in detail in the shiny pewter water. Black-backed gulls had claimed marker-posts to perch on: a line of sentries preparing to roost, assured of a safe night beyond the reach of predators. A pair of marsh harriers circled over the flat fields behind as pink cirrus threads streaked the blues and greys of the evening sky. A spit of land was doubled in the mirroring water as clouds drifted past, pale grey edged with white and rose, smudging the surface of the lagoon with their colours.

Suddenly a bird came towards us out of the sky like an avian aircraft. Too large to be a gull, a huge owl-like bird flew over the reeds, feet trailing. With head retracted and great wide wings, a bittern, the clear light catching the dappled colour-ing, the spangled nutmeg and fawn of its feathers, the long beak elongating the head, the keel-shaped breastbone. Sailing low with slow wingflaps, bright brown radiating light and dark gold, barred pinions on rounded wings, it was bulky and bulbous chested. Visible for less than a minute, the image of one of our most secretive waterbirds burned into my memory. It sailed down, landed feet first and disappeared from sight in the reeds where once a middle-aged lady hid for hours on end with a vintage camera waiting for a close-up before the days of zoom lenses: Emma Turner, whose photograph of a live bittern in 1911, the first ever, was developed by her in the now-disappeared hut on her island.

Their flight is low and stately, noiseless like that of an owl, she writes, *its bright brown plumage tinged with cinnamon.* She describes the light and dark markings of *this strange elusive creature, much of whose life history is enveloped in mystery... What goes on in the reed jungle is hidden from sight.* On one occasion she picked up a half-grown bittern which disgorged a nine-inch eel and seven inches of a second one. She describes how the gullet of the young bittern swells *to the size of a fowl's egg on such occasions* (in the early nineteenth century a bittern was recorded as eating a fourteen-inch pike). In 'Broadland Birds' she describes the ongoing competition between bittern and marsh harrier—*the dark and sinister shadow of the marsh harrier hanging over the bittern's nest*—and witnessed a battle between them: *I suppose no living ornithologist has hitherto seen such a thrilling sight in the British Isles.* She describes how, when startled, a bittern will stop motionless and point its bill upwards, becoming one with the reeds and virtually invisible, turning the head on a vertical axis to locate the source of danger. And how reed cutters can accidentally kill them thus camouflaged. She records seeing one bittern eat a water rail whole, and writes of the dread aroused in locals' hearts on hearing the bittern boom across the weird silences of windswept places, superstitious fen folk driven to make their wills if a 'Bittourn' flew over their heads at night. *Botaurus*, the bittern's Linnaean name, means 'to roar like a bull', a foghorn sound audible up to three miles away and taking one-fifth of its bodyweight in muscles to produce. It was a sound Emma Turner came to love: *the loneliness of the reedbeds seems incomplete without it.* The first time I ever heard a bittern boom, in the cold mists of Lakenheath Fen one March day sitting in a hide with James, I thought it was the sound of some weird industrial process coming from a distant factory.

Bittern, emblem of desolation in John Wycliffe's translation of the Bible—*And bitourns schulen anwere there*—and in the King James version—*the cormorant and the bittern shall possess it* (not according to ornithologists however, who think there were unlikely to be bitterns in that part of the world). During the fourteenth century, bitterns in the Isle of Ely—Island of Eels—were under special protection: a poem of 1430 extols *The Bootoore that etith the grete eel*, and it was a criminal offence to take eggs out of the district. In the sixteenth century William Turner wrote that *The Bittour is a bird like other herons in its state of body generally, living by hunting fishes on the banks of swamps and rivers, very sluggish and most stupid, so that it can very easily be driven into nets by the use of a stalking horse* (Emma Turner protests: *it can behave with unsurpassed dignity and condescension*, she states firmly). Continues her namesake William, *So far as I can remember, it is nearly of the colour of a pheasant, and the beak is smeared with mud; it utters brayings like those of an ass. Of all birds it aims at men's eyes most readily.*

Bitterns were common in John Clare's day, inhabiting the now drained Whittlesey Mere: he knew the bird as Butter Bump and was familiar with its haunting boom.

I often wanderd in the fen with the boys a bird nesting and when I enquird what this strange noise was they describd it as coming from a bird larger then an ox that coud kill all the cattle in the fen if it choose and destroy the villager likewise but that it was very harmless and all the harm it did was drinking so much water as to nearly empty the dykes in summer and spoil the rest so that the stock coud scarcely drink what it left...

Then the bittern disappeared, victim of wetland drainage and human predation.

After the rapid improvement of firearms during the eighteenth century, bitterns were shot to extinction in the British Isles. Up until the 1850s, fen shooters regularly killed up to thirty a day. The birds were victims of egg collectors as well, and the last known bittern's nest of the nineteenth century was recorded in 1868. On Hickling Broad in Norfolk that evening, we were watching a descendant of the bird Emma Turner photographed forty-odd years later, only a couple of generations after John Clare's death, using a double-extension reflex camera designed for the naturalist. Through this unwieldy instrument with focal plane shutter and revolving back, after waiting for hours lying flat in the marshes, she caught unprecedented stills. Her photograph of a sky-pointing bittern, taken in 1911, marks not only the watershed between shooting with guns and shooting with cameras, but the return of the breeding bittern to Britain.

It makes a great story. While out one afternoon with Jim Vincent, a local estate keeper and respected ornithologist, Emma Turner caught sight of a young bittern. They watched a parent bird fly between two areas of reedbed, and moved closer as Vincent searched, initially unsuccessfully, for the nest. After pausing for the essential ritual of tea and Madeira cake, they waded into the reeds, knee-deep in water, and flushed out the adult bittern. Emma then stood still while Vincent waded through the reeds in circles around her until they found the nest. There, according to Vincent, was a young bittern 'two-thirds grown' with its head pointed skywards, the alarm posture of the species. But it had grown too dark for photography: it was past eight o'clock, *so I carried the wild, beautiful thing to dry land*, wrote Emma, and *After stowing the bird safely away for the night ... we returned home.*

At three o'clock the next morning she and Jim Vincent set off again, collected the bittern and released it where they had found it, Emma describing how the bird—assessed by her as being four to five weeks old—*stalked off in a solemn, and what was intended to be a very dignified, manner*. Her pictures taken then and over subsequent weeks show the first bitterns known in Britain for many decades, and the sky-pointing bittern picture was awarded the Gold Medal of the Royal Photographic Society.

A century on from when the species was rediscovered, the number of booming bitterns in England topped the one hundred mark.

The great silences of waterscapes. That evening, decades after Emma Turner's death, a single tree on the shore of Hickling Broad was reflected between low-lying strands of land. Reeds made squiggly lines in the water, masts and rigging of sleeping boats impaled an orange sky splashed with magenta and lavender and blue. The orb of the sun turned to gold. A family of great crested grebe floated in silhouette on water ablaze in a final fling of tomato-red and violet. Sunset in the water, Ruskin's *opening into eternity*, fading into darkness as the flames of day melted into the blue dark.

OCTOBER

Suffolk, Norfolk, the Essex woods

ornitheology

St Francis of Assisi would have applauded whoever came up with the epithet 'ornitheology'—not that it's particularly original, he had already kind of invented it. Famously, he conversed with the birds, was charmed by their variety, preached to them, read to them and called them his sisters. A contemporary biographer tells *how St Francis went among them and even touched them with his garments, and how none of them moved*. Francis, patron saint of ecology who saw no distinction between the physical and the metaphysical, took it as read that the material world is sacred.

It's an old idea, that the first book of scripture is nature. The Psalms are studded with jewels of the natural world reflecting the glory of—as they name the unnameable—God. Medieval cathedrals all over western Europe glorify, in the stonecutter's art and the craft of the glazier, the beauty of flowers and foliage, birds and animals. The fourteenth-century German Dominican Meister Eckhart declared that *Anyone who truly knows creatures may be excused from listening to sermons, for every creature is full of God, and is a book* (whereupon the establishment accused him of heresy. *Great spirits have always encountered violent opposition from mediocre minds*, muttered Eckhart). But the Bible tells us so: the author of Sirach cries out, *How dull are all people who, from the things-that-are, have not been able to discover God-who-is, or by studying the good works have failed to recognise the Artist* . . .

Through the grandeur and beauty of the creatures, we may, by analogy, contemplate their Author.

Many of the 'ornitheologists' I came across during my novitiate as a birdwatcher—writers and artists, philosophers and poets, as well as new friends—aren't or weren't religious in the institutional sense, but they shared a sense of the inherent mystery of nature. They meet on the ground of things-that-can't-be-explained, things beyond notions of secular and religious, non-binary things. This is the ground of the mystical, an unfashionable concept but which is only a word for something that eludes definition and awakens intuition, provoking fundamental (usually unanswerable) questions. The kind of questions children ask.

There are, indeed, things that cannot be put into words. They make themselves manifest. They are what is mystical. Wittgenstein, the man who couldn't subscribe to any established church, said that although he was not a religious man, he saw everything from a religious point of view. It was enough for him to acknowledge the mystery of things, while having his feet firmly on the earth: *the mystical is not how the world is, but* that *it is*. As the Chinese sage Chuang Tzu said, *Nature makes everything as it should be; and nothing needs to understand why it is as it is.*

The Jesuit Teilhard de Chardin posited a *mysticism of action*, bringing the 'mystic' right down to earth as someone who has moved from mere belief systems or belonging to organisations, to actual everyday experience. It's what the Zen Masters teach: in plain words, total attention to what is right under your nose, the awareness of what is, stripped of symbols, ideas or words. As Kathleen Jamie, a nature writer who connects everything with everything (and notably with birds), writes in 'Findings', describing her response to the sudden and dangerous illness of her husband: *...I had not prayed? But I had noticed, more than noticed, the cobwebs, the shoaling light, the way the doctor listened, and the flecked tweed of her skirt, and the speckled bird and the sickle-cell man's slim feet. Isn't that a kind of prayer?*

Other saints, as well as Francis, got 'ornitheology'. In the seventh century St Cuthbert had a special affinity with wildlife: living in his hermitage on the Farne Islands, he came to love the seabirds there, and especially eider ducks, forever after known as Cuddy's Ducks. By introducing laws to protect them, he set a precedent which has had him dubbed the world's first conservationist. Another seventh-century saint, Columban, retreated with some companions to the forests of Burgundy where they lived on wild herbs and berries. Columban went off on his own for long periods to commune with the creatures of the woods. They came to obey his voice. The birds landed on his shoulders and allowed themselves to be handled by him. It's a special thing, to hold a live bird: ringers have shown me how to do it, and the moment of being handed a lesser redpoll to let it fly free after it was ringed, is an experience I'll never forget: the fragility, the beauty, the life force, the all-seeing eye. The isness of that bird.

It was a damp, still day. An autumn afternoon, muted. The wild-flower year was almost over, just a few yellow hawkbits, an occasional knapweed in the damp grass. A solitary oak loomed bronze in thin fog. As I followed the footpath along the edge of a field into a spinney, sunbeams streamed through mist into splinters of light. Late-turning leaves hung motionless in the damp, splashed with yellow, glowing amber, stained with crimson between faded greens. Cloudlets of traveller's joy drifted over brambles. A wood pigeon purred, fieldfares flew chakking out of an ash tree into the fields. Rustling came from an overgrown hedge: the rushing of little wings as a pair of bluetits bounced out and away. More rustling: two very small birds darted around inside the thicket, hovering and shifting in the tangled stems. An incredibly thin, reedy high-pitched call, almost a whistle. I kept very still. Was I hearing *the smallest of small songs*, as W. H. Hudson put it? One of them disappeared from sight, but as it darted away, the other perched on a twig and what I saw was so tiny I could hardly believe it. A wren? No, wrong shape, anyway it was tinier even than a wren, a roundish bird with a short neck, olive-ish in colouring above and whitish below, a big dark eye with quizzical expression, vivid white wingbars—and the trademark John Clare described as *a narrow line of a bright yellow rising on its crown*.

I realised I was looking at one of the smallest birds in Europe: the goldcrest, a female this one, eponymous saffron dash on the top of the head. By now I knew that goldcrests were nicknamed Woodcock Pilot, after a wildfowlers' myth that goldcrests hitch a ride across the North Sea on woodcock wings (they make the crossing at about the same time, along with the short-eared owls). And Herring Sprint too, because migrating goldcrests throng fishing grounds on the east coast when they arrive from northern Europe in early autumn to overwinter in Britain. The tiny bird close to me had a gentle presence; she was quite relaxed. She wasn't particularly shy, unlike the bluetits which had flitted away nervily as soon as they'd sensed me. Perhaps she was exhausted after completing her epic autumn migration. A minuscule creation, she looked around without apparent anxiety, making tiny head movements as if to work out what I was, then hopped off after her mate. I continued on my way past laden hedgerows, inhaling the smell of fermenting crab apples. Hawthorn berries were ripening to blood-red, blackthorn scrub heavy with dark-as-night sloes.

I walked home past the lone oak tree. The mist hung over darkening fields as a sinking sun lit up the stars.

On a similar autumn day, James told me, he'd seen up to a thousand goldcrests on the north Norfolk coast, some lined up on branches of windblown pines, others hopping around on the beach, swarming over the sand dunes and perching in every available bush, a landfall of birds resting after a long sea crossing from Scandinavia. Goldcrests pour in during the autumn and are often seen through the winter in the company of tits, he told me, restlessly hovering and moving among the branches.

Although today it's a very common bird—now I know goldcrests are there I hear them in the yew tree at the top of my garden—the goldcrest was described by Gilbert White in 'The Natural History of Selborne' as *almost as rare as any bird we know*, which tells us something about the natural fluctuations of bird populations. It has a thin high-pitched call, sibilant and reedy, a *zree-zree-zree* beyond the range of some elderly ears. Living mostly in coniferous or deciduous woods, goldcrests prefer spruce and fir (and are particularly—incongruously—fond of the Giant Sequoia). The goldcrest is the smallest of the passerines (the tiniest bird in the world is Cuba's bee hummingbird at a mere two inches and weighing in at just over half an ounce, hardly more than a bee). To Thomas Bewick *this most pleasing fairy bird* was a *gold-crested Wren* which builds a nest suspended like a hammock from a branch. John Clare, who called it Golden-Crested Wren, observed that it *builds a very curious nest on the pine trees in Milton Park hanging it from the branches and hanging it together with the glutinous substance or raisin that oozes from the grains and were this not to be had it fastens its moss and other substances to gether like a basket ... laying 7 or 8 eggs of a dull colour spotted with brown ...* It can take the bird up to twenty days to construct this nest, usually on the opposite side of the tree from prevailing winds. The outer layer is made with moss, lichen and tiny twigs, secured by cobwebs and lined with small downy feathers and hair. The rim of the entrance is fitted with larger feathers facing inwards to screen the entrance from the cold. The nest is suspended close to the end of a branch by a basket handle made of cobweb filaments. So clever.

Goldcrests are fearless little birds, agile and vocal, confiding and easy to approach, bold around humans and even known to land on a shoulder to investigate the fabric of a coat—prospecting for nest material perhaps. But being so tiny, the goldcrest is susceptible to minus temperatures and, as an insect-eater, can be a victim of hard winters. The head marking that crowns the 'little king', the *regulus* of its denomination, is not always visible, as the seventeenth-century naturalist John Ray reported: *This crest or crown (if you desire so to call it), it can when it lifts, by corrugating its forehead, and drawing the sides of the spot together, wholly conceal and render invisible.* A bird that can frown. Its little face has a large, dark peppercorn eye set in a pale eye-ring, and a black gape line which looks like a downturned mouth, giving the bird a comical look. Our Kinglet, our Wood Titmouse, our Golden Wren.

Worldwide, birds have been thought of as mediators of the sublime, winged messengers of the deities linking the human world to the supernatural and the divine. Myths relating to birds have embellished literature with symbols and stories: the Venerable Bede compared life to the flight of a sparrow through a banqueting hall, flying out of the darkness of a winter's storm and disappearing through a door at the other end, never to reappear. Coleridge's albatross floating on thermals with motionless wings ten feet wide becomes an angel, nemesis of the Ancient Mariner, symbol of the Holy Ghost he destroys in his own heart by murdering the great white bird, spirit of the seas. The phoenix, universal symbol of rebirth, rises from the ashes of its destruction, pertinent symbol of human pain and suffering. Metaphors of any life, one way or the other. Myths link birds to the arrival of life—as in, famously, the stork. Owls are ambivalent, sometimes ominous or even stupid, but often wise. The Ancient Egyptians depicted their god of wisdom with the head of an ibis, a bird revered and sacred. The heron was their symbol of sun and rebirth, the falcon a bird with special protective powers. Vultures represented eternal protection, and in Mongolian culture they still do: it's believed that, scavengers of the dead, they consume the soul of the departed and carry it to heaven. Many birds are associated with the journey of the soul after death, as guides through the afterlife: in Arctic burial chambers the skulls of great auks were placed alongside the dead to guide them to the next world. And a Japanese legend tells how departing spirits of the dead assume the form of a bird. Which bird, I wondered? A wraithlike bird of the dusk? The mysterious stone curlew perhaps?

Ever since hearing them calling in Thetford Forest that July evening as James and I waited for nightjars, I'd longed to set eyes on a stone curlew. I'd learned that its life is spent secretively, that it's a shy bird struggling to retain a foothold as habitats diminish under human population pressure. With a three-foot wingspan and about eighteen inches long, stone curlews look something like mini-bustards, but are classified as waders. They have lumpy tibio-tarsal joints or 'heels' (which is where the knee would be on a human leg: their unflattering binomial *Burhinus oedicnemus* means 'ox-nosed thick-knee'). They have traces of webs between their front toes, and—as with most running birds—no hind toe. Rapid runners, these birds of steppe and open heathland scuttle with a suspicious run-stop-look, run-stop-look gait: roadrunners, neck outstretched and bobbing the head, lanky and knobbly kneed.

A protected species in the UK, stone curlews mate for life, are site faithful and can live for as long as seventeen years. Breckland farmers protect nesting sites of their Norfolk Plover, not spraying near by and delaying harvest until the chicks are fledged (a species of bird challenging our accountancy culture!). Some landowners even get grants to do this, an enlightened example of a subsidy tuned to a specific ecology issue. Carrion crows and stoats are the stone curlew's main predators, but man isn't far behind: the onslaught of modern farming practices means that nesting stone curlews fall victim to chemical sprays and machinery. The lucky ones who avoid egg-smashing or -stealing, or nest-destruction, risk colliding with overhead wires as they migrate, or being shot and either killed or maimed.

This inscrutable, cryptic bird with malevolent glare arrives in the UK—the northerly edge of its range—in March. Hatching two broods of two eggs over the summer, these secretive spirits of stony heathland seek quiet and isolation, just as monastics do in our world. After laying their eggs they sit immobile during daylight hours on a nest-scrape lined with white stones (and often rabbit droppings), among sandy hillocks between gorse, heather and brambles. They thrive on cropped grassland alongside rabbits and sheep, and as far from human habitation as possible (although a Norfolk friend had them nesting in his—admittedly very large—garden). They feed on insects, on snails and slugs and lizards, and on mice and frogs. Gregarious with their own kind, they call with the wailing trill that gives them their curlew name, forming flocks in late September and October for the return journey to sub-Saharan Africa.

This time I went birdwatching on my own, feeling brave (looking back it makes me smile, how much courage it took at first to attempt identification alone, without my mentor, how damaged my self-confidence was) to Cavenham Heath where stone curlews are known to spend the summer and early autumn. I had little faith I'd spot one without James to guide me, but by now I was hooked on being out with binoculars, camera and dog, walking for miles in new places and seeing what turned up. Every walk brought a different sighting, as often as not unanticipated. The addiction had taken hold. Sometimes I was frustrated at not knowing the name of what I was looking at, and wishing James was there to tell me. At other times I was content not to know, simply to absorb the beauty and not to mind too much. To accept the mystery of it all. Mystery, declared Einstein, is not a challenge to intelligence (he even went so far as to say that imagination is more important than intelligence, adding, *The most beautiful thing we can experience is the mysterious*). Thomas Merton, twentieth-century Trappist monk, wrote: *Actually our whole life is a mystery of which very little comes to our conscious understanding.*

Seeing with the freshness of a beginner's eyes, as I was determined to do, had its difficulties but also meant, if I could let go of needing to become an expert (impossible anyway), I could appreciate birds without a driving need for identification every time. It would help retain my sense of wonder—as Teilhard de Chardin puts it so memorably: *We imagined [the divine] as distant and inaccessible, when in fact we live steeped in its burning layers.*

I set out in late afternoon in early October, after learning that the largely nocturnal stone curlew feeds between dusk and dawn. Cavenham Heath lay quiet under a moonstone sky. Copper-topped fungi gleamed in the nettles at my feet. Sheep grazed among the rabbit warrens. Rooks and jackdaws, blacker than black against the fading sky, cawed and chacked over the treetops, the sound a reminder like the evening Angelus bell that day is done. Tattered strands of cloud drifted past a rising moon. A green sandpiper called, flying past as I scanned the sandy gravel stretching over ridges and hillocks between occasional scrub and mauve-mist drifts of late-flowering heather.

I heard the wailing call long before I saw them. There's something otherworldly about the eerie piping, the mournful trill, the haunting minor key. Something metaphysical about a transparent ghost-bird blending so completely with its native heathland. As afternoon faded into evening, five stone curlews emerged into being from their camouflage, bathed in low light through a muted veil of stunted hawthorn and grass. One was standing on a single leg, with the other poised in mid-air, staring with enormous eyes. The lemon iris with reptilian rim of gold beading appeared to belong to a disembodied creature: the eye of an alien, the fixed stare of the Gorgon. It stood motionless, bird-statue with plumage the colours of shingle stones, ivory-cream belly, white wing-stripe edged with black, meditating in evening light. The stillness of this bird. Only the golden legs, illumined in the last rays of the sun, betrayed the streaked sepia camouflage. A severe white eyebrow and white jowl gave it a quizzical, thoughtful expression.

The others remained rapt in contemplation. Then a couple of them started stabbing for invertebrates with yellow, black-tipped bills. From time to time they changed position, imperceptibly, as in slow motion. An autumn chill rising from the ground settled into my boots. Were these birds preparing to fly south for the winter? Conditions were ideal—windless and clear, a gauzy lantern moon hanging over the treeline. As darkness fell, the whirring treble of their night-lament would float over the heath as these all-too-few nesting pairs preened black and white wingbars in preparation for the annual autumn migration across sea and mountain, city and plain, to warmer winters.

A swirl of lapwings gusted over a distant wood like scraps of wind-blown paper, white fronts flicking in the evening light, rollicking the air with loose wingflaps. Are stone curlews more active at full moon, as lapwings are thought to be? Who knows? Is there any bird so still, so strange as the stone curlew? That evening, undisturbed by rabbits cavorting and bouncing in the heather-scrub, these mystical birds took absolutely no notice, rapt in their stillness. Their Zen-like poise was cocooned in privacy, imperturbable. For half an hour I stood in silence, watching. I was lucky to see them: stone curlews are vulnerable, and one day we may lose them. Their wistful lament haunts the heath.

The sun had dropped low in the sky. Rooks were returning to the wood to roost, accompanied by their chacking jackdaw mates. One of the stone curlews shuffled a bit, another turned to look the other way. One shifted gracefully to the other leg, another preened itself. A youngster, paler and plumper than the others, ran in from stage left hunched and horizontal, seeming hardly to touch the ground. A rabbit poked head and ears above the grass close to them. Another pair danced and chased and cuffed each other. Still the stone curlews took no notice, continuing their meditations as they merged with the darkening evening, until they faded from sight.

I was increasingly drawn to the life stories of people who loved birds, knew about birds, were fascinated or consoled by birds. I wanted to find out how those lives had been changed when the birds flew in, just as mine was being. These people became my virtual companions, along with the mostly silent birders I shared bird hides with when I went out on my own, or passed on remote footpaths—the presences of the writers whose work and biographies engrossed me: John Clare and Emma Turner, Henry David Thoreau and Gerard Manley Hopkins, R. S. Thomas, Fergus Ogilvie, even the so-called Birdman of Alcatraz among many others including, unexpectedly, Henry Williamson.

Tawny owls hooted through the night. The intervening silences were intense. I'd come to the north Norfolk coast to house-sit for a friend of a friend. Insulated from the village by tall trees surrounding the valley, the place felt remote: wouldn't I be frightened to be alone there, people asked, or bored being away from 'civilisation'? Never, the immediate and emphatic response to both. Here, away from all sounds except those of nature, I had found myself on a miniature reserve half a mile from the sea, green refuge in a world of crowded cities and white noise—*over grown prisons that shut out the world and all its beautys*, mutters John Clare.

Nighttime silences were broken only by occasional quacking of mallard. Alone with three dogs on the old farm, with chickens and doves to feed, and sheep to keep watered and watched over, my days began at the window looking down over the lawn to a freshwater scrape where wild ducks fly in at first light. With the beauty of a wilderness around me, birds and animals for company, and silence being a language my spirit understands, this was paradise to me. Richard Jefferies' autobiography was open on the windowsill: *The sun and the deep sky, the limitless ether, were only the continuation. There is no break, no chasm, between here and there ... I have never felt so much myself, an individual, as a part of this whole ... in the same stream of space.*

In the middle of the lake lay a reedy island where tussocks of sedge encircled a green mound. Beyond stretched open water where seagulls drifted and rushes grew thick along a bank in a tangle of reed-mace and Himalayan balsam. Mature trees cloaked the hills behind. Two fat coots were feeding contentedly on the lawn, a couple of moorhen pottered in and out of the reeds. I watched the effortless landing of inflying wild duck as they slid on to the water. Gadwall, teal, mallard, shovellers and tufted ducks floated around tranquilly, unaware of my distant presence. A heron stood sentinel on the island shore, tall and kingly, shaggy white beard wafting in a light wind. Between intervals of standing completely still he preened, or turned his striped head to look out over the water, or down into it, or across the lake. After an hour or so he flew away, flapping large, languid, blue-grey wings. Bird identification was easy here: ducks and waders swimming around or feeding on mudflats give ample opportunity to work out which is which: bird guide by my side, I had a chance to learn much about wild waterbirds that week.

An autumn sun was struggling to break through, leaves hung damp off the trees, listless. Glimpses of sunshine lit up the water, brightening the days. It was turning daily colder as jackdaws circled and chacked over the woods surrounding the scrape. A string of geese flew overhead every morning like clockwork, making inland to their feeding fields from Stiffkey Fen where they'd roosted, underwings shining in the sun, pink legs and feet lit up by the low light. Flying in over the hill, they made their steady way in symmetrical formation with a chorus of cackling, that evocative cry of wild geese calling to each other, a few strays fluttering untidily inside a ruler-straight V before the leaders billowed into airborne curves.

I crossed the farmyard to the deserted cart-shed, past a seventeenth-century granary built with massive timbers rescued from ships wrecked on nearby dunes in centuries past. On the flagstones a stock dove, river-pearl grey with iridescent collar and blush-red front, had joined the flock of white doves fluttered down from the dovecote to feed on their morning grain. Beyond the five-bar gate, beech and sycamore, sweet chestnut and oak grew tall up the sides of the valley. The autumn trees were just beginning to turn, hints of bronze and copper glinting among dark-green and yellowing leaves. Dogwood was in vibrant leaf, dusky pink and faded green, the stems reddening to bright crimson. Branches of guelder rose, heavy with berries, made a splash of scarlet. With a whirr of wings the crystal-white doves took off as one, scattering startled from their feeding.

The land used to belong to Henry Williamson. As a child I'd lost myself in 'Tarka the Otter', described by Ted Hughes as *a holy book, a soul book.* Williamson's raw sensibility and radiant prose had awakened something in me, pointing me to the possibility of other realities. Brought up in cities in a family of atheists and with a lapsed Catholic mother, I'd craved the countryside. *There is always one moment in childhood when the door opens and lets the future in,* wrote Graham Greene in 'The Power and the Glory'. For me, that moment came while lying under a stand of apple trees at the bottom of the garden, a place where I spent as much time as possible, looking up through long grasses at the shifting leaves, smelling the damp smell of earth. I fell in love with nature. Another favourite place was an ageing quince tree leaning over a bank at the edge of the lawn: I would climb into it and lie in the crook of a thick branch with a book, daydreaming, escaping from the world of humans, not knowing that my grandfather, an exact contemporary of Henry Williamson and whom I got to know for only a few years after my father died (an odious family story there), and who by then was nearly a hundred years old, had been an ardent naturalist all his life and knew all there was to know about birds and wild flowers. The grandfather I never had (almost). Now, staying alone in the place that had been Henry Williamson's farm, and loving his writing for so long, was like a dream.

There was an oil painting of Williamson in one of the rooms, a brooding portrait with a self-tortured look, the look of a man haunted by the trenches of the First World War and psychologically maimed by the sights of the Somme. A prolific author of novels, he became his truest self in his nature writing, *a secret self of longing and emotion and possibly imbalance,* as he himself admitted. His identification with and passion for the natural world, and for its care, shine out from a wounded but untamed personality with a beast on its back: the memories of war that became the powerhouse of his prose. Beauty was his solace: it pulses through his nature writing. *I do not think*, wrote Williamson, *I could write outside the belief that the purpose of life is to create beauty.*

Henry Williamson farmed this land below Stiffkey Church during the Second World War, and by some flick of fate's wrist I had found myself there, with time to absorb its quiet beauty and to read his 'A Peregrine's Saga and Other Wild Tales' which transports the reader into a world both imaginative and closely observed of what it must be like to be a bird (as do C. F. Tunnicliffe's illustrations). A quotation on the title page, *Ad astra per aspera*, hints at the wider context of human pain, an epithet chosen by Williamson to signal his personal destiny along with countless others who through adversity learn to reach for the stars. Venerable wisdom: as Aeschylus put it two and a half thousand years ago:

> Even in our sleep, pain that cannot forget
> falls drop by drop upon the heart,
> and in our own despite, against our will
> comes wisdom to us by the awful grace of God.

Blackbirds were *tchinking* in the woods. My feet squelched into a sodden blanket of leaf litter, pheasants taking fright grated and clattered into the undergrowth, and the thin *zree-zree* of goldcrests filled the canopy above my head as I walked through an avenue of fir trees. Bluetits and great tits were flitting and calling, a robin investigated as I passed with the dogs, and a wren gave them a loud ticking off. I had entered a universe in miniature, a world of interdependent plants and birds and mammals and insects and invertebrates, nature's supreme ecology. This one was, mercifully, managed with a light hand and left largely to its own devices. I stopped to examine a smooth fungus on a moss-covered log, velvet to the touch, and thought of Richard Jefferies, he who recognised that we all live in two worlds, the material world and the world as we interpret it, the world of the imagination. He loved solitude and allowed his soul to yield *to the green earth, the wind among the trees, the songs of birds*. Those two worlds were not separate for him because he experienced transcendence in immanence. *It is*, he wrote, *very curious to touch anything: it is as if the soul thereby ascertained the existence of matter.*

I followed the sound of water rushing over boulders to where kingfishers lance the reedy river. Here otters live under one of the wooden bridges, one diving into hiding with a heavy, extended splosh as I crossed. A buzzard mewed from high above the sheep field. Through a screen of reeds I could observe wildfowl on the lake without being seen: they are so shy, these wild birds. I found that the least disturbance spooked them and they would fly off to Stiffkey Fen over the other side of the rise, leaving the place empty. From the house across the lawn I felt forlorn without them in their temporary absence: they had become my unknowing companions over the days. A mountain of cloud banked over the treeline where the evening sun lit up bronzing leaves. Three little egrets flew in, standing bright white on the jade-green grasses of the island, heron-like. A pair of female shovellers were shovelling for food below the surface, not far from their male counterparts in handsome livery of rust-red flank, dark head, striped black and white body with wingtips crisscrossing over a sharp tail and white bottom.

A pair of gadwall sailed past, the male so smart in his tweed front, dark tail and flash of white on the wing. Low afternoon light illuminated little teal standing on the bank, the chestnut heads with the eponymous teal-green teardrop, short beaks and grey underbelly with straw patch glowing under the tail. And the blue-grey bill of the black and white tufted duck. Low sunshine glinted on the water, breaking into silver rags of light as a breeze ruffled the surface. Moorhens were running around nibbling at the lawn, mallard floated in the tranquil quiet of mid-afternoon. The innocent beauty of the lake refreshed my inner world, healed it of the vulgarities of the world, of the crude trivialities that dominate mass culture.

Was it just me? I don't think so. Disenchantment with the ways of 'the world' and of cultures grown coarse has fired scribes ever since they began to express themselves, right back to the divine discontent of Isaiah in the eighth century BC, of the men who wrote the Psalms, of the Upanishads and the Bhagavad Gita in the first, and so on up to today. There's a lot of *plus ça change* in the literature of the world, and myriad stories provided to console us with a symbolic universe to live in: an *imaginarium* to bridge the outer world with the inner. To connect, to find *the thread that runs through the pearls, as in a necklace*, as the Bhagavad Gita has it. The power of metaphor, 'that which carries you across', like birds flying into our lives from their world into ours, awakening us to the reaches of our psyches.

As daylight faded over Stiffkey Fen, the blueness above paled into bleached brightness, and land merged into sea and sky. A lone whooper swan curled its long neck to preen under a wing with yellow black-tipped bill. A small bird struck an evening song from a tangle of bramble alongside the ditch, a young hare bounded across the field. Waterbirds swirled over the marshes, unaffected by the tragic follies acted out in human lives below, answering only to each other and to the windy sky. As the sheen of evening glided over the water, I watched the rounded black and white wings of lapwings flapping, circling, settling on a mud spit for the night. A fling of dunlin scattered silver from pale undersides as they gusted up and over the mudflats, undulating specks of light. The silence was punctuated with the whistle of redshank, the cackle of geese, the *peeeuwing* and piping and fluttering of wild waterbirds. The immensity of the sea beyond the sea wall, the infinite sea and the sky, instilled an ache, knowing that all too soon I would have to leave, and that being engrossed by this natural beauty with its great silences was more real and more deeply experienced than 'the real world' to which I must return.

The woods slept, the earth slumbered. I fell asleep to the hooting of owls, and the quacking of ducks on the scrape in the inky black of night.

Man must awaken to wonder, said Wittgenstein. To see a goshawk in the wild is to awaken to wonder.

Goshawks have a high literary profile, what with T. H. White's 'The Goshawk' and Helen Macdonald's 'H is for Hawk'. It's an old story: fossil evidence of the goshawk dates from a hundred and twenty thousand years ago, and the hunting with hawks which started in Babylon three thousand years ago arrived in England in Saxon times, in the eighth and ninth centuries, and is still widely practised from the Middle East to Mongolia to the Far East. To clarify some confusing ornithological taxonomy: a 'hawk' is an accipiter—the falconry term for all true hawks including the goshawk—as opposed to the longer-winged, dark-eyed falcons, *Falco*. *Accipiter* means hawk, from *accipere* to grasp: its prey (maybe the falconer's glove too?). On the shorter-winged accipiters like the goshawk and sparrowhawk, the fourth primary is the longest. The broadwings, the *Buteos*, Harris hawks, buzzards, vultures, eagles and owls are specified by the first primary being the longest of the wing feathers. The longwings comprise the *Falco* species—merlin, kestrel, peregrine, gyrfalcon, lanner and saker *et al.*

In spite of its specific name *gentilis* meaning noble, the goshawk was the yeoman's falconry hawk, and was also Cook's Bird because it could catch edible prey for the pot: fast food (literally) for dinner. The peregrine was the nobleman's hunting bird, the gyrfalcon the hawk of kings, the merlin of the queen. In strict order, according to the 'Boke of St Albans' written in 1486, the emperor flew an eagle or a vulture, the knight a saker, the squire a lanner, the young man a hobby, the priest a sparrowhawk and the knave or servant a kestrel. The goshawk was widely thought to be the fastest of its group: an early falconry primer declares that, in the company of a first-class goshawk, the austringer (wonderful word for a keeper of goshawks) is likely to find that hawking with other broadwings pales by comparison.

Attila the Hun bore the emblem of a goshawk crowned on his armorial badge and helmet. Shah Jehan kept thirty goshawks in his royal falconry collection (the collective is 'a flight of goshawks'). In Japan, goshawks were traditionally flown to catch geese, even cranes. Hawks and falconry have spawned some terrific vocabulary besides the all-but-obsolete austringer: the falconry term *yarak*, originating in the Far East, means to be sharp set, keen and ready to be flown. *Yarak*. The French call short-winged hawks *Rameurs* because of their rowing action as they fly, and their name for the goshawk *Autour des Palombes* conjures the scattering in panic of a flock of pigeons in the path of their predator (a local English name for the goshawk is Pigeon Hawk). Falconry has left tangential traces on the language in other ways too: the word 'mews' comes from the French *muer*, to moult, originally the name for a side-building used to keep birds for the annual moult of feathers when they can't fly. The Royal Mews in London was built to house the monarch's hunting birds, and stretched from Charing Cross where the National Gallery now stands, across Trafalgar Square to Whitehall.

With rounded wings and relatively short tail, the medium-size goshawk is mostly resident, although birds from colder regions migrate south for the winter, and they thrive in mature, old-growth woods where human activity is relatively low. If you're lucky enough to see it hunting, wingtips drawn back in falcon-like profile, you'll get a glimpse of a missile shooting between trees and through thickets at up to thirty-eight miles an hour. This is a hawk that can successfully chase prey on foot through undergrowth, too. Fastest and potentially most lethal of the *Accipiters*, goshawks hunt a variety of creatures: opportunists, they select from nature's *à la carte* squirrels, voles and rats, pigeons and doves, waders and gulls, corvids and waterfowl, even buzzards, owls and kestrels. The larger females sometimes take rabbits and even hares. Geese too, hence goshawk, goose-hawk. Staggeringly fast, a goshawk can take a pheasant mid-air with scimitar claws, unlike any other predator: a peregrine will down one on a stoop, but not catch them flying horizontally as the goshawk can. The eyesight of both these birds of prey is prodigious: one much loved (by me) bird fact is that if our eyes were the same proportion to bodymass as the peregrine's, they would weigh four pounds and measure three inches across—by ratio the size of grapefruit in our human faces. This is where imagination falters at the poetry of fact, except for a being like Hildegard of Bingen who was in the habit of awe and wonder, and saw beyond what she saw: *I am that living and fiery essence of the divine substance that glows in the beauty of the fields. I shine in the water, I burn in the sun and the moon and the stars.*

Hawks are beautiful objects when on the wing, wrote John Clare, describing a goshawk which *haunts the heaths about holy well and appears to hide among the furze.* At the time the Domesday Book was written, it's estimated that around a hundred thousand pairs flew in Britain's forests, yet by the end of the nineteenth century these great birds were eliminated from the British countryside by egg collectors, specimen collectors and game-keepers. Thankfully their numbers are being restored by birds reintroduced from the Continent, and by deliberate releases by falconers into the wild.

I would never have seen them, those two goshawks, had not a friend of a local gamekeeper told me that a pair of juvenile males had been seen down in Debden woods on an estate a few miles from my village. Public footpaths cross the land, so I set off with the high hopes of the innocent. Considering what happened that day, my resolution to retain beginner's mind was an advantage: had I been more hardened and experienced I would have weighed up the likelihood of a sighting and dismissed it. It had been raining heavily that morning, and birds of all kinds would be taking shelter from the deluge. But by the time I got there, an autumn sun was shining from a clear sky, casting long shadows over glistening fields. Late blackberries gleamed on a bramble by the gate. Under the blueness of the wide East Anglian sky, grassland and arable fields sloped down to a lake in parkland where the footpath led to mixed woods of oak, ash and spreading sycamores. An oil painting, a haven for birds.

Nobody was about. The cornfield alongside the footpath had been ploughed and harrowed into crumbly umber soil. In a dense cluster of trees a cedar of Lebanon towered over mature beech and willow. I walked down to the bridge crossing the river that feeds into the lake, its water mirroring the sky between patches of bright green algae. Then, a flurry of activity in the bird world as a flush of corvids and wood pigeons scattered out of the trees. A sudden kestrel streamed across the bright sky, making me catch my breath, salmon-backed shrapnel shooting past me, silver underwing catching the light, flapping and floating across the field in flight.

It was the cry that gave them away, more of a yelp, quite different from now more familiar birds of prey like the kestrel or the sparrowhawk. I recognised at once that this was no buzzard mewing or red kite calling. Over the distant treetops I saw a pair of large hawks, not buzzards in outline and definitely bigger than a sparrowhawk. With relaxed wingbeats, sinuous, the two raptors flapped and glided, narrow tails acting as rudders as they banked towards the cedar of Lebanon. Goshawks.

I watched, incredulous at my luck, for goshawks are secretive birds and sightings are rare even in East Anglia, one of their strongholds. I followed them through glasses as they wheeled and chased, floating down occasionally behind the treeline before reappearing. I was enthralled by their bulk, by the power of these birds as they reconnoitred. I was gradually able to make out colouring and detail: dark backed, mainly brown, with streaked plumage on chest and belly. These were the juveniles I had been told about: evidently a pair of young birds had found an ideal winter habitat, with all the food and water they needed in the protection of dense woodland. Plenty of pheasants and partridges had recently been released from breeding pens into the woods to their alternative demise— being shot for fun by humans—so the goshawk larder was teeming.

Hawk of the age-old practice of falconry, nobility of the air, descendant of Babylon, winged bull of Assyria, Egyptian hieroglyph with mythic provenance. I watched until they disappeared. I continued walking through the park, down a lime avenue and out again on to pastureland where horses were grazing, and back towards the wood. I'd heard that goshawks will stand in a tree for hours on end, and was imagining them poised, inscrutable, on a great branch high up in the trees. But to my joy the two of them appeared again, flying out over the treetops. They soared, apparently enjoying the bright October sunshine, chieftains of the air prospecting for prey, lit by the lowering sun against a clear sky. The dark mantle, the chevron-streaked chest and striped underbelly, sailing on the wind, circling and calling. Turning in tandem, in silhouette against the light, the barring of the underwing gleamed silvery below the chestnut tinge on the shoulder. What struck me was the presence of these birds. The glaring eye and strong beak, and the intense stare that T. H. White describes in 'The Goshawk': the *mad marigold or dandelion eye . . . an alert, concentrated, piercing look. Hawks are sensitive to the eye and do not like to be regarded. It is their prerogative to regard.*

Chinese yellow at the nares (fabulous word for the nostrils of a hawk), the black-tipped upper mandible is downcurved into a razor-sharp hook for tearing flesh: T. H. White aptly calls the goshawk *exquisite assassin of the woods*. Not many creatures will mess with *Accipiter gentilis*, even humans. The uncompromising downturn of the beak adds to the goshawk's fierce expression, borne out by its behaviour as a top predator. Accumulating immense speed on impact, this bird can inflict dire flesh wounds with beak and claws, savage meat cleavers (for a few minutes I was more than concerned for my dog). They flew close enough, and the afternoon light was good enough, to see the strong yellow legs which make a sparrowhawk's look puny, the enormous yellow claws which make a sparrowhawk's look dainty. The yellow eye of the juvenile, that in adulthood will mellow to amber, gave rise to the goshawk—according to the Italian naturalist Aldrovandi in the seventeenth century—being known as the Bird of Apollo: sacred to the sun, bird with a flaming eye, with ferocious strength, the power and glory of our woodlands, refuge from and antidote to (Aldo Leopold's phrase) *too much modernity*.

NOVEMBER

Essex, Cambridgeshire, a refuge on the Suffolk coast

freedom

My bird obsession was doing a good job of distracting me. It stopped me dwelling on what I'd lost. Rerunning the past would trap me there, like Lot's wife. She who disregarded the angel's warning to flee Sodom and looked back over her shoulder, ended up as a pillar of salt. I was all too often in danger of ignoring the angel's warning, but luckily for me winged creatures (alias birds) were helping in the most gentle way. Becoming immersed in their world made me realise I had a choice: to huddle in self-pity, or to accept the throw of life's dice and surrender to what was. In any case, in the bigger scheme of things, in the wider perspective of history, what was my little trauma, however painful? The story of love and betrayal and loss is well known to the tides of humanity. Aeschylus's *pain that cannot forget*. Nothing unique in the eternal cycles.

My impetus to solitude was a double-edged sword. Introspection could be self-indulgence, or it could provide the space I needed to rebuild my life. I thought of the difference between escapism and confrontation that has always challenged monastics: the balance between engagement with the world, and the need to feed a hunger for the absolute. People who choose to flee the Sodom of the modern world—what Thomas Merton called *the murderous din of our materialism* (and that was back in the 1950s; what would he think now?)—are regarded with deep suspicion as eccentrics, tramps or weirdos. But the great solitaries of history, removing themselves from the busyness of a noisy and corrupt world, had the courage to jettison the padding of inessentials insulating them from eternal things. Discarding the straitjacket of conformity, they found the freedom that costs not less than everything. Many have been profoundly cultured, literate, educated people, embracing holy austerity with courage and intelligence. But only a true vocation, tempered by the strictest discipline and training, could qualify the hermit: even with the best will in the world, many found they couldn't make it, unable to deal with practical challenges of aloneness and self-sufficiency, or the terrors of solitude and silence. I certainly couldn't do it, I am far too impractical: but my loss of self-belief and fear of being left alone in the world had left me with a need to rebalance. To access an independent strength, not by totally withdrawing, but somehow by integrating and unifying my life.

Based on simplicity and purity of life, work and prayer—and in its extreme form, complete silence, the Cistercian order has survived for a thousand years (who would imagine that the number of Trappist monasteries throughout the world more than doubled by the end of the twentieth century?). Its founder, St Bernard, wrote, *Everything I know of the divine sciences I learned in the woods and fields. I have had no other Masters than the beeches and the oaks. Listen to a man of experience: thou wilt learn more in the woods than in books. Trees and stones will teach you more than you can acquire from the mouth of a Teacher.*

Earlier that summer, preoccupied as I was with looking over my shoulder, those words had inspired me to visit a Trappist monastery in the Midlands. I needed to clear my head. Which way should I go? I was facing a choice, to remain a prisoner of the past, of my lost expectations, or to accept what had happened, learn from it and open up to new directions. If I couldn't have what I wanted, I could try wanting what I had. Now was the chance to find a freedom I'd always longed for beyond the constrictions of conformity. I've long been inspired by the writings of Thomas Merton, Cistercian monk with a vocation for solitude. Towards the end of his life he lived in a hermitage in the monastery woods in Kentucky, like his spiritual father St Bernard finding communion in nature: *to deliver oneself up, to hand oneself over, entrust oneself completely to the silence of a wide landscape of woods and hills, or sea, or desert; to sit still while the sun comes up over the land and fills its silences with light.*

I was hoping that an injection of silence within a monastic community would bring clarity. It did. The plainchant, the peaceful gardens and the diurnal routine of regular Office refreshed and replenished me. It was with a lighter heart that I left the monastery after daybreak a couple of days later, and drove home across England on minor roads. It was July. I took my time meandering past pasture and farmland, winding through tree-lined lanes, out into straw-coloured wheatfields punctuated by hedgerows. A windy sky raced over acres of barley burnished by the midsummer sun. Coming to the motorway, I stopped for breakfast at a service station—forlorn places where I cannot begin to fathom the mind of God—where a stainless-steel pot of tea and inedible pastry prompted me to ponder on the emptiness of an accountancy culture predicated on the value of money, of cost and profit. To cheer myself up, I made a plan to stop at a medieval church I'd visited briefly once before but without my camera. I would make the most of the mid-morning light and take photographs of this deserted building.

I entered into the cool of stone, into the ageless silence. St John's Duxford, built over a millennium ago, is a church stripped of ornament. Hardly used today, and spared over-restoration, it seems serenely content to be left alone away from the world's cacophony. Inhabited by the spirits of those who once worshipped there, it proclaims Einstein's conviction that *the distinction between past, present and future is only an illusion*, however persistent. It is simplicity in stone, architecture of the spirit with an ethereal Lady Chapel in the north aisle, and no furniture except for a few worn pews and a tiny pulpit. From Saxon times a church has stood in this place. Plain, light, with clear glass windows, flooring of clay pavers and pamments, fragments of medieval wallpaintings.

Within moments the stillness was disturbed. Somehow a swallow had found its way into the building. How long it had been up in the roof timbers I could only guess. It became frantic, dive-bombing through the aisles and across the nave, zooming past me within touching distance, aggressive and hostile in its misery. There was nothing I could do to help except fling open all the doors. For twenty minutes the captive bird stormed through the church, darting hither and thither, hectic, veering high and low on flickering wings, unresting in its efforts to find a way out, imprisoned, confined, uncomprehending, desperately seeking freedom.

Close to, the swallow seemed larger than I'd imagined: its energy turned it into a giant. I was stunned by the muscularity, the velocity, the streamlined speed, the steel-blue back, the dark-orange head and throat, the ivory underparts, the deeply forked tail and elongated tail streamers (the word 'swallow', I later discovered, comes from Old Teutonic for a 'cleft stick'). This imprisoned bird evoked its Promethean myth, a raging furnace of speed darkened by the smoke of its own fire as it torpedoed through a thousand years of silence.

As I walked around taking photographs, beguiled by the beauty of the timeworn stones, the distressed bird continued its rampaging. I sat down to write some notes, and became lost in my thoughts. After a while I realised all was quiet. Afternoon light streamed through the windows. The swallow had discovered its freedom at last through the open doors, skimming away into the silver sky, leaving the church in stillness.

In 1920 a captive man, imprisoned for life in solitary confinement for two murders (he had served eleven years by this time, and would serve a further forty-three) was taken by a guard to the bull-pen for his daily exercise. A storm broke, a violent wind snapped a branch of the only visible tree, and it fell into a corner of the high-walled yard. With it came a nest containing four baby sparrows. After a moment's hesitation he picked them up, wrapped them in his handkerchief and took them back to his cell. It proved a momentous decision. He kept the fledglings warm, gave them water, fed them on scraps of bread soaked in prison soup, crushed the resident cockroaches for them and reared them to adulthood. His name was Robert Stroud, and this was the beginning of the so-called Birdman of Alcatraz legend (although what follows actually took place at Leavenworth Penitentiary in Kansas).

The prison warden had the foresight to allow him supplies of birdseed, and a lightbulb strong enough to provide warmth. When one of his birds died, Stroud was permitted a replacement canary, a fashionable caged bird at the time. In due course another was allowed in to keep it company. They started to breed, and soon his cell was filled with singing birds perched in makeshift cages. Stroud himself wrote, *The Isolation Department which for years had been the hottest trouble spot in the prison, was transformed into the least troublesome.* Stroud talked to his birds, fed them, cleaned them out and taught them tricks: they gave him something to do and something to love. The birds changed his life. They became his family. They softened relationships between the guards and their prisoner. His six-foot-wide cell became lined with cages and equipment, the prison wing full of birdsong, with canaries flying free in his cell in the daytime, perching on his shoulders and happy to be handled.

In 1925 Stroud raised fifty-three canaries. His mother started selling them to the public, and what had begun as a hobby grew into a business breeding and selling birds. Stroud studied books from the prison library on bird behaviour and biology, on bacteriology and dietetics, on physical sciences and pathology. He even learned how to dissect dead birds with his bare hands. As numbers increased (he soon had a hundred and twenty-five) he acquired antiseptics and hospital bowls. Some birds became ill with septic fever, for which (before the days of anti-biotics) there was no practical remedy. Working up to eighteen hours a day, Stroud was on a mission. After a lengthy series of experiments and autopsies he discovered the long-sought grail: an internal avian antiseptic. By the late 1920s he was marketing, through his mother, 'Stroud's Specific', a cure for septicaemic disease, psittacosis and a host of minor ailments. He started to write articles for bird journals on canary care and treatment, and in 1941 discovered an absolute specific for 'fowl paralysis' in canaries which cured the infection with a single dose. In 1943 his five-hundred-page 'Digest of Bird Diseases' was published with his own drawings, a comprehensive study of the diseases, ailments and conditions of birds. It became a bestseller, was found in every public library and is still in print and used by bird-keepers today.

In 1942, with ten minutes' notice, Stroud was transferred from Leavenworth to Alcatraz, *Isla de Los Alcatraces*, 'Island of Pelicans' known once as Bird Island—the ultimate irony, as it turned out: Stroud's birds did not go with him, and for the next two decades he was forbidden to keep any. The film that immortalised his story, 'The Birdman of Alcatraz' starring Burt Lancaster, came out in 1962. He was not allowed to see it.

Before they were taken away from him, Stroud's birds gave him a future in a futureless existence, a life within a life sentence. They enriched his life and taught him life-lessons. Just before his death he wrote a letter which ends with the words, *the only thing that can ever defeat you is yourself.*

One bitterly cold November afternoon I lit the wood-burner and picked up Bernd Heinrich's book 'Ravens in Winter', the riveting diary of a man in his sixties who devoted several North American winters to observing ravens in the wild, deep inside the forests of Maine. After five years of watching he wrote, *To me, the raven is now not just a bird, it is a being masquerading as a crow, as it has been to almost all humans who have had extended contact with it.*

During the lengthening darknesses of those wintry evenings, Heinrich's book by my side, I fell in love with ravens.

*

Native Amerindians talked to ravens in the woods in the same way man prays to God. Providing anecdotes and legends across cultures, this special bird has attracted centuries of lore: Odin, lord of the gods, sent a pair of ravens out all over the world to collect information: one Thought, the other Memory, the ravens perched on his shoulders on their return to tell Odin all they had learned. Many have considered ravens the ultimate creative spirit, creating the moon and even the sun, and the Inuit have a legend that they created light by flinging mica across the heavens, making the glittering trail that became the Milky Way. With brains among the largest of any bird species, these intelligent creatures appear to have insight and even precognition: the Irish expression 'ravens' knowledge' means the ability to know all and see all. Ravens can problem-solve, they have a capacity for language second only to *Homo sapiens* according to Heinrich, producing a greater variety of calls than any other living creature apart from us, and an ability to mimic all kinds of other sounds including human speech. It's been shown that the brain-to-bodymass ratio in corvids is equal to that of the great apes, and only marginally less than that of the human species.

The story of St Meinrad illustrates the alleged supernatural powers of ravens. Longing for solitude, the ninth-century monk built for himself a hermitage on Mount Etzel in the mountains near Lake Zurich. Here he stayed for seven years, living the demanding life of the solitary. But people, hearing of his great holiness and wisdom, arrived in such flocks that he was forced to build another hermitage further away in the Dark Forest. For the next twenty-six years he lived in a simple hut with adjoining chapel, during which time he fed and befriended two ravens.

Assuming such a venerated and holy man to have acquired many treasures, two thieves decided to rob the hermit. Meinrad opened the door to them, calmly offered them refreshment and when the robbers found nothing of value he offered them his clothing, insisting it was all he possessed. Not believing him, the robbers turned violent. Realising he was about to be murdered, Meinrad asked one thing of them: that after the death-blow they should light one candle above his head and another at his feet.

After beating and strangling the hermit and robbing him of his clothes the thieves, awed by his serene courage, went into the chapel to find a taper. On their return they found a candle already blazing. They fled, terrified, but Meinrad's two ravens followed them, croaking and striking at their heads. When they came to the nearest houses the ravens accelerated their attacks, making the villagers understand that something terrible had happened. They seized the thieves, found the murdered monk and arrested the intruders.

Ravens are big and they are beautiful, their glossy plumage iridescent with shiny blues and purples. This is how Thomas Bewick describes them in 'British Birds': *the length is above two feet: breadth four [with] fine glossy back, reflecting a blue tint in particular lights; the under parts are duller, and of a dusky hue ... a bird of ill omen, announcing by its croaking, impending calamities ... It is a very long lived bird, and is supposed sometimes to live a century or more ...* A delightful thought and a measure of their legendary status, but in actual fact although ravens can live to a great old age (some of the Tower of London birds for over forty years), the average lifespan is half that. *It is*, continues Bewick, *a crafty bird ... it may be rendered very tame and familiar, and has often been taught to pronounce a variety of words ... The natives of Greenland eat the flesh, and make a covering for themselves with the skins of these birds, which they wear next their bodies.* The mature raven measures up to two and a half feet long with a wingspan of up to four and a half and can weigh as much as four and a half pounds. Opportunistic omnivores, they scavenge on carrion for their main source of protein, dissecting it with the largest beak of all perching birds—just a glance at it conveys a bird not to be messed with, although they have a playful side: juveniles have been observed sliding down snowbanks for the hell of it, and playing catch-me-if-you-can with wolves, otters and dogs.

Fossil evidence proves the existence of ravens on the planet a hundred and fifty thousand years ago, inhabitants of the age of tree-ferns, long before we turned up. The Anglo-Saxon for raven, *Hrafn*, is the name still used in Iceland, and ravens are one of the few birds to call the Arctic home, although their range also stretches as far south as Central America. They are the largest and most widely distributed of all the corvids— with which, however, they do not associate much: John Clare remarks how *Birds that have a kindred resemblance to each other are always the most inveterate enemys the Raven and the carrion crow never associate nay they are never seen sitting on the same tree together ...* They have few natural predators, although owls and martens take their eggs, and occasionally ravens will be attacked by a golden eagle: but generally, ravens appear to have the respect of the entire natural world.

Including us: they are a powerful presence in our cultural history, ominous as well as sublime. In the Book of Isaiah the raven is a symbol of the desolation of Zion: *the owl also and the raven shall dwell in it.* In Leviticus it's a bird of uncleanliness. There are traditional taboos against killing ravens: a soothsayer advised King Charles II that if he removed all the ravens from the Tower of London, disaster would befall England, and the royal palaces would crumble to dust. The king decreed that six should remain there in perpetuity, and to this day at least this number, usually more, remain at the Tower as protectors of the kingdom. To Shakespeare, this most intelligent of all the corvids was a scavenger of bad omen, a dark presence and slaughter-greedy, a creature that plunders battlefield corpses, a bird of death. But largely the lore acknowledges its magic: a raven's head appears on Native American totem poles (the one in the British Museum is over five feet tall). In the Bible, hermits are fed by ravens, and they bring food to Elijah in the desert. The Inuit believe that rain will fall when someone kills a raven: the heavens weeping. Some stories tell how the souls of the unbaptised go into ravens, and there is a legend that King Arthur will return in the form of a raven.

The (surely unfair) collective noun for ravens is an 'unkind-ness' or a 'conspiracy', indicative of the fear humans have always felt for the supreme corvid. Ravens, like eagles, hawks and doves, are creatures of mythology and fable, with intim-ations of a transhuman perspective, creatures of flight sailing away from the earthbound towards the heavens. In the religious imagination, these dynamic birds of antiquity and mythology who have coexisted with us for thousands of years link us to the interconnectedness of things. The twelfth-century poet and theologian Alain de Lille wrote, *Every creature in the world is for us like a book, a picture and a mirror,* birds reflecting back to us aspects of our psyches. The clever raven, the far-seeing eagle, the vain peacock, the kleptomaniac magpie, the purity of the swan. Realising its power, the medieval world used metaphor to illuminate life's puzzles and to enrich the imagination, providing for the symbolic universe that bridges the inner and outer worlds. A doctor of the great age of faith, Duns Scotus, maintained we have two kinds of cognition, rational and spiritual. In the West, the latter took a beating at the Reformation and hasn't properly recovered in a culture that developed the idea of 'enlightenment' based on the primacy of the intellect and reason. Enlightenment, in the East, has always meant something more nuanced and inclusive, and some modern thinkers have chosen to embrace the less binary model. For Teilhard de Chardin, palaeontologist and priest, there's no division between scientific knowledge (facts) and religion (in the sense of transcendent truths): science is a story, a construction based on ideas and hypotheses, and it too provides metaphors. Construed intelligently, science enhances the stories of the *imaginarium*. The theoretical physicist Richard Feynman, who celebrates metaphor, said *it is surprising that people do not believe that there is imagination in science. It is a very interesting kind of imagination, unlike that of the artist. The great difficulty is to imagine something that you have never seen, and that is different from what has been thought of.*

Clare captures, in his unique voice, the essence of our mightiest of corvids:

The sooty Raven in the winter warm
That plays and tumbles in the pelting storm

The Birdman of Alcatraz (or more accurately Leavenworth) was not the only prisoner to be rescued by birds. One day in 1940 an English scholar and poet, a prisoner of war in Bavaria called John Buxton, half starved and suffering the boredom of indefinite captivity, wrote to his wife that he had seen *a family of redstarts, unconcerned in the affairs of our skeletal multitude, going about their ways in cherry and chestnut trees.* Buxton started to study this pretty, long-tailed bird that bobs about in deciduous woodland through the summer. The male has a burnt-orange front and tail, white brow, slate-grey crown and mantle, and black face (the female, as so often in birds, is duller, dun and beige and cream, but blessed with a firetail too). Buxton was enchanted. He began to regain his zest for life. The birdwatching group he formed with other prisoners alleviated the daily hideousness of incarceration. Many wrote afterwards about how, during the time they were concentrating on watching the redstarts and assisting Buxton in his observations, they found freedom from confinement, temporary release from prison, parole inside their heads.

Buxton started to keep daily records in the camp at Laufen Castle. Throughout the following spring and summer, he observed the redstarts' behaviour, watching their courtship dances in and out of the barbed wire that held him captive, jotting down every detail on any scrap of paper he could find: *The only chick known to have died after leaving the nest met with a somewhat unnatural accident,* he wrote, *since aprons of barbed wire are not an integral part of the redstart's environment.* The prisoners' liberty to birdwatch was restricted to hours prescribed by the guards, but Buxton managed to engage some of them in helping to obtain equipment and books, papers and even bird rings. This unlikely brotherhood of ornithologists dedicated themselves to serious study: during the spring, standing on a rubbish heap at the corner of the camp, they watched their birds—without binoculars, of course—observing the spring and autumn migrations of thousands of them overhead. Immersing themselves in the natural world beyond the barbed wire, they could momentarily forget their prisoner status and return refreshed to what they had to endure. Buxton wrote to his wife, *One of the chief joys of watching them in prison was that they inhabited another world than I.*

On his release, Buxton had amassed enough material to write an acclaimed monograph, and went on to publish the definitive volume on the redstart in the 'New Naturalist' series. One of his fellow prisoners, also liberated by working with birds while in captivity, Peter Conder, became director of the RSPB. Another, George Waterston, established the Fair Isle observatory and Loch Garten's osprey nestwatch.

The November evenings grew longer and darker. Maple leaves, floating bird-like to earth, brightened grey days with yellow pools of light on the wet ground. I scuffed fallen leaves as I walked, catching the honey-scent of ivy in flower, kicking through the bronze and gold of beech, glory of the autumn woods. But I was still prisoner of my memories however hard I tried not to dwell on the past or yearn for the future I'd lost. Consolation came in watching and writing about the birds I was coming to love so much. The solitude it required, with the absorption in the present, with what *is*, began to open up (as Clare put it) *A feeling that the world knows nothing on . . . After the hustling world is broken off.*

My lifeline drew me eastwards. From a westerly corner of East Anglia I sought, and found, a bolt-hole on the east coast on the shores of the North Sea. It was to become a refuge, hidden in woods around Dunwich on the Suffolk coast, not far from the reedbeds and marshes of Minsmere: a cottage in the woods on the edge of cliffs eroded for centuries by the sea. A place to walk and write, hidden down a track in the middle of nowhere. A place to retreat, to heal, to be alone with my dog and the birds of woodland and seashore and heath. Where the silence was thick. Where I saw nobody for days at a time. *My solitude shall be my company,* wrote the Japanese master of haiku Matsuo Basho, who like John Clare had one foot in this world and the other foot in the other. The latter also understood:

> the sacredness of mind
> in such deep solitudes
> we seek—and find.

The woods surrounding the house were permeated by ghosts of a forgotten past, the traces of medieval monks, Benedictines whose priory ruins stand not far away through snowdrop-carpeted woods where the firecrest winters among goldcrests in the conifers. From the cottage I could hear the wind moaning in the pines to the sound of surf pounding the shingle beach half a mile away. Pulse of oceans, thud of waves rolling relentlessly on sea-smoothed stones, swish of white foam sucked back under oncoming waves, inexorable music of the North Sea shingle.

I was reminded of a painting by Caspar David Friedrich painted around 1809, of a monk by the sea. The monk is a tiny, black, windswept creature, the sea and sky limitless, dark, elemental, speaking of the enigma of human existence in the immensities of nature. Beyond the frame, the trappings of modern life (in any era) convey *the snare of the fowler* of the Psalmist, the diversions of mankind that blot out poetry and beauty from human life. With plenty of time to read, I picked up Hesse, a longtime favourite dubbed *poet of the interior journey* by Timothy Leary. Hermann Hesse's writing merges narratives of individuals who struggle with darkness, with realms of the transpersonal and the transtemporal. He of all writers unifies the two worlds of imagination and reality, of before and after, of inner and outer, of heaven and earth, seeing them as a continuum, managing to merge the duality of the West with the unitive consciousness of the Eastern thought. In his 'Journey to the East' he describes how his character joins a pilgrimage: *but in reality, in its broadest sense, this expedition to the East was not only mine and now, this procession of believers and disciples had always and incessantly been moving towards . . . light and wonder . . . a wave in the eternal stream of human beings, of the eternal strivings of the human spirit towards the East, towards Home.*

In 'Steppenwolf' the musician Pablo tells the eponymous hero, *You know, of course, where this other world lies hidden. It is the world of your own soul that you seek.*

The tiny village of Dunwich, surrounded by oak and pine forests, looks out to the North Sea across sandlings where gorse and harebell, tormentil and ling scramble over heathland. A rare wild rose can be found here, smaller than the field rose of England's hedgerows, a single marble-white rose in summer and bearing a black hip in autumn. It was propagated in medieval gardens by Benedictine monks and grows nowhere else in Britain. Beyond the forest, nightjars haunt midsummer twilights on Dunwich Heath, the Dartford warbler flits through the gorse, and stone curlews breed in scrapes in the sandy soil. Hedgehogs scamper for cover, the white admiral butterfly breeds in woodland clearings where woodlarks and stonechats can be seen, and bitterns stalk the nearby marshes. The monks who grew that briar and named it 'holy flower' would call to mind in their prayers how, early in the seventh century, a Burgundian priest named Felix (after whom Felixstowe is named) sailed into Dunwich harbour, his mission to bring the Christian message to the East Angles. He succeeded: Dunwich became the original seat of the Anglo-Saxon bishops of East Anglia, and later antiquarians called what is now a scattering of houses the 'former capital of East Anglia'.

Obsidian nights merged into frost-smoked early mornings, a weak sun struggled through branches emerging from darkness, casting thin shadows but no warmth over the ground. Gradually I became familiar with the many tracks leading through Dunwich Forest, its mature oaks and tall pines where goldcrests lisp their thin whistle, great tits call and winter flocks of siskin flit yellow-black through branches of alder, eager for the seed-rich cones. One walk took me along the banks of a stream where silver birches had dropped drifts of leaves making a damp carpet of washed-out greens and dun and soft yellows. The deserted path meandered through the trees to Walberswick marshes. Over a woodland floor of dead bracken, cinnamon and copper-coloured, hung the last beech leaves radiating burnished gold. Further on, through subdued, gnarled oak trees in grey and bronze garb, came a glimpse of reedbeds where a flat line of shingle divides them from the sea. Bleached-to-bone branches of a dead tree reached into a cirrus sky, stark, weathered by wind, outstretched arms sculpted against the light, sea-blown. In a sky bigger than the land and wider than the horizon, the evening sun was sinking into the reedbeds.

The wistful piping of redshank echoed over this wild place, mingling with the trill of the oystercatcher. A trio of snipe flew out edgily from a gully, displaying their sharp beauty briefly before disappearing into the reeds. Two mute swans floated in a rill by the wintering reeds, bright white against monochrome reeds and water.

Protected only by the shingle bank, expanses of water stretched out under the sky where wild birds inhabit marsh pools only a wave-storm away from repossession by the sea. *Land of wide windswept spaces and far-flung horizons, of mystic nights and great silences*, wrote Emma Turner of marshland she knew intimately from living on the Norfolk Broads. A water rail emerged shyly from the reeds, poking around for food. The handsome smoke-blue breast, the blood-orange bill, the perky uplift of white tail: a squat bird wandering in and out of cover feeding, seldom seen but often heard caterwauling like a tortured demon from the reedbeds. Beyond him in open water floated a group of gadwall, males with smart pepper-speckled breast, chestnut and ash-grey plumage, black tails and bright white speculum, females resplendent in bright brown and beige patterning.

A throaty, shrill call on rising intervals broke through the still air, a creaky *peeweep*, the plaintive cry of the lapwing. On a mud spit in the middle of open water, a line of lapwings stood facing into the wind like notes on a stave, spiky crests in silhouette, fat teardrop shapes with feathers puffed in an attitude of defiance against the cold. Some were roosting with head under wing, crest flattened by the wind, others stood curled-crested, or with head pulled back into shoulders against the bleak marshland winter. The ploverness of this bird. One preened, another fed, most were just static, daydreaming. Emma Turner described their evening meditations, how they stand *on one leg most of the time, calling to each other at intervals... There was something curiously solemn about it... in and out taking up respective positions... like some solemn ritual... Nothing ever happened.*

A sudden sun broke through intermittent cloud. The water reflected an aquamarine sky, reeds glowed red-gold, colours of orpiment. Lit, my lapwing changed colour too, from velvet-black to deep green with iridescent purple sheen. Clear the touch of rust-red on shoulder and rump, the brilliant white of the breast, the black tip to the tail, the long sweep of the thin, wispy crest.

Suddenly, as one, with a rush of wings, the lapwings took off into the bright sky over the sea, scattering white bellied and black backed, piebald rags tossed into the blue beyond the shingle. Sky-dancing over the sea with rounded wings, they lapped the air with strong, deliberate flaps, tumbling and rolling in the late light. Called Flopwings for good reason, the *hleapewince* of Old English, this 'leaper-winker' winnows the wind with dancing flight. 'Lapwing', from the lapping sound of the rounded wings in flight, the sound of fanning, giving it the Latin name *Vanellus*, little fan. Names. What's in a name... *It is enough for me that birds are,* wrote Emma Turner in her vein of how birds bridge the metaphysical world, angelic links between earth and heaven.

Stillness again. Reflections of a silver sun in the dark water mirrored a sky impaled on black spikes of reflected reeds, reeds that don't give up their secrets readily, where in a forest of stems the drama of life and death is played out among wetland creatures. Chirpings and chickerings rose from the reedbed pools, the quacking of mallard, a *whooosh* of wings. More twittering and squealings. A splash, a splosh. A blackbird *tchinking* from nearby trees, a wren tut-tutting.

As I walked back through the forest, the bubbling cry of a lone curlew echoed from the reedbeds. The honking of geese, flying in over the marshes for the night, floated through the fading light. A bitter wind numbed my face as I returned to the cottage in the woods.

Lapwings are born precocial, relatively mature with eyes open and covered with downy feathers, keen to get on with life: Shakespeare provides the image, *The lapwing runs away with the shell on his head,* words spoken by Horatio in 'Hamlet'. Parent lapwings guard their eggs and hatchlings by guile, feigning injury. On the approach of a predator they will, a little distance from the nest-scrape, act up with a broken wing, becoming a decoy. They then see off the enemy with all their force, having tricked it into false belief, earning the collective nomination of a 'deceit' of lapwings. The Greeks have a saying, 'more beseeching than a lapwing', after these stylish drama-queens of the bird world.

Lapwing eggs used to be sold as 'plover's eggs', a luxury of Victorian cuisine and a delicacy of the British aristocracy. The practice so diminished their numbers that in 1926 the Lapwing Act was passed prohibiting egging, and numbers recovered. But another onslaught awaited them. Lapwings are farmland birds, known as 'the farmers' friend' since they rid crops of invertebrate pests—those snails, slugs, worms, beetles and insect larvae now victims of intensive agriculture. Pesticides and herbicides based on the chemistry of poison gases used in the Second World War, sprayed on food crops since the 1960s, have *war-like names*—thus Ronald Blythe who adds, *I always add suicide and homicide to herbicide to keep a perspective.* (Some of these agrochemicals are documented as suspected carcinogens, including the world's most commonly used herbicide glyphosate.) The consequence was to leave the birds with so little to eat that they have deserted our fields. *Britain's wildlife which inhabits the farmed countryside has, for the past sixty years, been subject to one big, crazy chemical experiment, the costs, benefits and impacts of which on society, economy and the environment, have never been fully and objectively assessed,* wrote the ecologist Sue Everett in 'British Wildlife' in 2014. I fear for the ever more silent arable fields of my home patch: future generations may wait for them, but the birds may not come. Or maybe it will be the other way round: that mankind will topple off his evolutionary twig first, leaving the birds to recover their poisoned habitats.

For the dark places of the earth are full of the habitations of cruelty, sang the Psalmist three thousand years ago. Legend has it that our 'Hornpie', horned bird, the lapwing crowned with a crest, is the keeper of King Solomon's secrets—but disappearing along with his wisdom, it seems. What is happening to the birds who have so dramatically declined in numbers may be telling us something about what is happening to us as ours increase. *A bird is at its fiercest when it thinks its living space is threatened. Is it too much to hope that man might learn something from this?* asked Eric Hosking in 'An Eye for a Bird' in 1970.

The poetry is all being efficiently removed, excised, from our land, wrote Roger Deakin in the early years of the twenty-first century. His was one of many voices warning that ignoring our interdependence with nature not only threatens eco-systems we rely on for life itself, but inflicts damage on ourselves: in choosing to reduce the priceless to the valueless, we disconnect from what it is to be fully human. *The earth lurches like a drunkard and sways like a watchman's shelter,* prophesied Isaiah, a warning that mankind is capable of creating a version of hell in the Garden of Eden. The Greek word *aornos* means 'birdless', and it's no coincidence that Virgil called the entrance to hell *Avernus*, a place without birds, after a lake in a volcanic crater near Naples where birds flying overhead were asphyxiated by sulphuric fumes rising from magma beneath the water. An infernal world where birds fall out of the sky, a world without the presence and beauty of birds.

Who cannot be aghast at today's treatment of the natural world as a dustbin? Einstein considered a moral environment which separates humanity from nature, deluded: *Our task must be to free ourselves from this prison by widening our compassion to embrace all living creatures and the whole of nature in its beauty.* St Thomas Aquinas went so far as to declare that any mistake we make about creation is a mistake about God. To him, the natural world is our Bible: starved of it, we are deprived of connection with the numinous. In his time they called it the *sensus divinitatis*, an intuition that the beauty of nature exists because God is in every leaf and creature, every herb and stone. *Deus est ens,* said Aquinas: simply, God is Being. God is what is, *I am what I am,* the nameless one, omnipresent. Denying our part in the creation we evolved from and into, results in crucial privation, leaving us to starve in a desert for the soul.

When all the beasts have gone, man will die from a great loneliness of spirit, said Chief Seattle of the Nez Percé in 1884. Fossil evidence of the northern lapwing goes back a hundred and twenty thousand years, the sadly misnamed *Homo sapiens* only ten thousand. Time alone will witness who outlives who.

But Nature is wise: I cannot remain pessimistic, despite the gloom pervading the environmentalist discourse. Temperamentally I prefer hope to despair, and wonder to cynicism. There is a place for the positive force of optimism. *Yea, the stork in the heaven knoweth her appointed times, and the turtle [dove] and the crane and the swallow observe the time of their coming,* proclaims the Prophet Jeremiah. Nature is too extraordinary, too mysterious and too powerful to be vanquished by the greed and stupidity of a single species. Nature is full of miracles. After all, ninety-nine per cent of earth's biomass is plant life, which like the birds was around for hundreds of millions of years before humans evolved. Some life-forms outlive the worst attempts at destruction. The gingko tree can live for two thousand five hundred years: a species with no close living relatives, and similar to fossils dating back two hundred and seventy million years, the gingko survives everything thrown at it including the atomic bomb at Hiroshima. Although charred, six gingkos survived where all other plants and animals were destroyed, and are alive to this day. If the human race does not survive, magnificent and inexplicable creations will continue.

John Clare, resident in Northampton General Lunatic Asylum for the last two decades of his life, adapted to incarceration by revisiting his past and restoring it to the present (I like to picture him with a friendly raven on his shoulder, helping him out: Odin's raven of Memory). He found a kind of freedom in reimagining the village of his childhood, dredging up from the recesses of his mind places he had known and loved long ago, places where he had experienced an intensity he could not forget, where his senses had been heightened, finding wistful consolation in memories of birds, and wild flowers, and first love and innocence, recreating in his old age the beauty of small things. In one fragment of his writings, he listed among memories of 'Pleasant sounds' *the crumping of cat-ice and snow down wood rides*—the sound of his footprints as he walked, boots inscribing his local landscape with his steps and his thoughts.

As I crunched through the frosty woods of the Suffolk coast, the spirit of this lover of the natural world, unknowing prophet of environmentalism with a consciousness of deep ecology, never seemed far away. His story is haunting. In the asylum, mentally unstable and frequently deluded, the moments of clarity in which he struggled to write poetry produced some of his greatest work. He reached out to what was truest in himself, obscured as it was behind a curtain of debilitating illness. He likened himself to a caged starling: *I would try like the Birds a few Songs i' the Spring but they have shut me up.* The workings of his mind were as much a prison as the asylum that had necessarily divorced him from his life in the fields and woods. In his illness, the difference between reality and the life of the mind, present and past, became blurred, the latter a refuge in times of lucidity, memory and imagination becoming liminal locations between actuality and dream, places of temporary freedom. Places are our story, our habitats, and Clare, like a bird divorced from its habitat and struggling to survive a fractured story, mined memories of his childhood home, his native Helpston: *I felt that joy was dwelling there.* When he had not much hope, Clare chose joy. He held on to joy, to the end. You get a sense of it in the only photograph of him, beaming genially, taken not long before his death.

The poems of Clare's madness return again and again to the past, but instead of incarcerating him there, they released in him a rediscovery of the unspoiled places where birds and wild flowers had been his close companions and where, as he put it, *I kept my spirit with the free.* In his late poems he integrates past with present in an attempt to unify his broken life. Among his final works, written in 1860 within the walls of the asylum, is a poem on early spring, evoking a saunter down a green lane beside a brook, along a hedge, seeing a robin, a beetle and his beloved wild flowers. His very last poem, written at the age of seventy a few months before his death in 1864, 'Birds Nests', is a memory-poem as immediate as if it were composed on the spot:

> Tis Spring, warm glows the South
> Chaffinchs carry the moss in his mouth
> To filbert hedges all day long
> And charms the poet with his beautifull song
> The wind blows blea oer the sedgey fen
> But warm the sunshines by the little wood
> Where the old Cow at her leisure chews her cud

DECEMBER

Dunwich Forest, the Suffolk coast,
the Ouse Washes, Essex

solitude

There is a charm in solitude, wrote John Clare. He and Bernard Moitessier, lone round-the-world yachtsman of the 1960s, would have understood each other: *What you call isolation,* wrote Moitessier, *I call communion.* I can only imagine what it must be like to sail around the world's oceans alone: as I am no sailor, the reality would be way beyond me, but it appeals as an idea. I absolutely get how, for Moitessier, he saw his gruelling adventure as an encounter with natural forces, with himself and with his God. The experience of solitude with its difficulties and challenges left him changed. He liked it so much that instead of heading for the finishing line to win the race, he turned back and made the return journey alone. Moitessier called his book 'The Long Way', its subtitle 'Between the Seas and the Skies'. Like a bird.

After a few hours walking along the cliffs one afternoon, I returned across Dingle marshes and paused at the edge of the woods near the cottage. I leaned against the wrinkled bark of an ash-tree trunk, balancing on the curved roots that spread like giant fingers into the ground. I looked up into the leaden sky as it began to drizzle. Subdued twitterings started up. Space, stillness. *Sweet solitude, thou partner of my life,* Clare exclaimed once. To him, it was a scarce commodity. His daily round was crowded with people: out in the fields Clare was just one of many labourers working the land: at leisure he relaxed with his drinking mates, or visited his educated friends at Burghley with whom he discussed botany and birds. Home was a crowded cottage with an ever-increasing family. For him, aloneness was a rarity, and he developed what he called *a passionate fondness for Solitude*, confessing to loving *Nature, with a boundless love... My heart burnt over the pleasures of solitude... seeking the religion of the fields.*

Mocked by fellow villagers, mistrusted for his love of learning, jeered at for his scribbling, laughed at for his reading and for his 'mutterings' as he walked behind the plough versifying, Clare was feared as a freak. He would dream of *islands of Solitude* where he could commune with *the quiet love of Nature's presence*. His disappearances into the woods and meadows to *drop down* and observe nature were his refuge, where *disdaining bonds of place and time* he could become who he was, *a soul unshackled like eternity.*

Clare was by no means the only artistic soul to hanker after what he termed *lone seclusion and a hermit joy*, that aloneness generally so feared by the crowd. Erik Bruhn, legendary Danish ballet dancer of the 1950s and 1960s, found his need for solitary renewal largely misunderstood by those close to him. *My desire to be alone is more often than not a time when I am in the process of replenishing myself as a human being.* He had an imperative need to be himself, by himself, a withdrawal which offended or confused them. *But what I was doing was trying to keep myself sane.* The twentieth-century hermit Charles de Foucauld wrote about living alone in the desert: *It is so pleasant and so healthy to set oneself down in solitude, face to face with the eternal things ... I find it hard to leave this silence.* Emma Turner felt the same way: living among marsh birds in the Norfolk reedbeds was heaven to a woman drawn to solitude: *something I love, and my ultimate refuge from the strife of tongues.* The psychologist Anthony Storr saw this impulse as a sign of maturity: *Human beings easily become alienated from their own deepest needs and feelings. Learning, thinking, innovation, and maintaining contact with one's own inner world are all facilitated by solitude.*

At first, I thought that being alone would make me feel even lonelier. I feared emptiness and loneliness after losing the love and companionship I'd believed—and been assured—was for life. But gradually I discovered that the elements of aloneness in those weeks in the cottage in the woods, the silence, the stillness and the solitude, provided the habitat I needed. I found solace in the space the isolation provided, even though the cowardly part of me was afraid of being alone in such a remote place. I dreaded being lonely and missing people. Yet as time went on, I found it a perfect place to put down temporary roots. Being there made it possible for another part of me to flourish, and I soon realised that being alone was nothing to be scared of. What I had feared would be missing, wasn't. Solitude began to feel like relief. It became a source of revitalisation. It was not only painless, but productive. Much to my surprise, I wasn't lonely.

Walking back to the cottage along the shingle beach each day was a time to dream, to imagine the skeleton town beneath the waves. Beyond the cliffs where the cottage stood, marine archaeologists had discovered the largest underwater medieval site in Europe. Using sonar to map the seafloor, divers recovered stones with medieval lime mortar stuck to them, they found the ruined blocks and carved stones of monasteries and churches. Stretching for more than a mile were traces of streets and hospitals, a guildhall and gates, and a shipyard. A drowned city.

I often wandered through tracks in Dunwich Forest down

to Westwood marshes, where an overgrown path leads to a sanctuary, a birch grove. A low sun flared off a frozen pond where birds drink. Ice-covered trees glittered in the bone-cold afternoon. The ivory skin of a fungus peeped through leaf litter. High above, naked branches opened to an empty sky, stripped of the leaf-curtain that screens the secret life of a wood during the rest of the year. Metaphor of life, death and continuity, winter trees filtered thin light on to a damp carpet of leaves, of tawny and rust, gold and bronze—or palest green and yellows where sap clung to life. The very last maple leaves hung bright yellow over the track. A sudden blaze of copper: fallen beech leaves. Brambles scrambled untidily over a mossy stump and tumbled into a ditch. Smooth beech bark lit up in sudden sunshine. Stopping in the stillness, I absorbed silence.

The hibernal tapestry glowed with bryophytes and fungi. Under my magnifying glass, mosses metamorphosed into an evergreen forest of tiny fronds and deep shade, feathery and springy to the touch. Lichens had come into their own in winter's nudity, encrusting a rotten tree stump hollow with age, its girth wide enough to stand up in, one of John Clare's *ancient pulpit trees*. Near by, a moss-covered fallen branch made a bench to sit on that December afternoon, looking upwards through cathedral arches of bare trees. Salve to the soul. Here by the marshes in years gone by some old boy had laid a hedge alongside the path, his winter task to splice strong growth to the base, then layer branches horizontally to renew the hedge from the bottom. Neglected, gnarled and overgrown, still sprouting withies, memories of his cleaver lay buried inside mossed and lichened timber.

Deep inside a wood there's a special kind of quiet. A quiet with substance. If you sit for long enough, tiny rustlings and shufflings emerge from the half-light. The sound of wind pours softly through branches. A scattering of fieldfares, the *chook-chook-chook* of a blackbird, the flap of a wood pigeon. Silence. The cawing of rooks and crows. Pause. A jay screeching. Kestrels and buzzards float above the treeline, hunting. Corvid hammocks balance in the branches above deserted nests of migrant birds which had sought the shelter of the forest in spring and summer. Maybe a woodcock even, the slow-flying, most furtive and cryptic of woodland birds with plumage the colour of dead leaves, had made his scrape in the leaf litter. The bell-like music of a robin spilled into the wood momentarily. A wren tisked and tutted loudly from the undergrowth, big voice in a tiny body.

Sitting alone in a wood is to join a ghost species, defined by writer and academic Robert Macfarlane as one who belongs to a disappearing culture, a race threatened by an alien world. The Nobel Prize-winning ethologist Konrad Lorenz (one of the greatest of this species) wrote in his acceptance speech in 1974: *Surprisingly late, I got involved with the danger of man's destruction of his natural environment and of the devastating vicious circle of commercial competition and economical growth. Regarding culture as a living system and considering its disturbances in the light of illnesses led me to the opinion that the main threat to humanity's further existence lies in that which may well be called mass neurosis.* Lorenz considered that so-called civilised mankind's alienation from nature, and the vandalism it inflicts on the natural world with which it is interdependent, will ensure its own destruction.

Simply observing the minuscule detail of a winter wood I felt the timeless beauty of the forest and wondered at its mystery and power. Paul Valéry describes trees as *strange prayer of the universal warp*. The silence and stillness of trees are balm. To be alone with them is not to be lonely, but to be whole. It's as if the little 'I' becomes permeable, translucent as a ghost, as time disappears and immensity becomes apparent: *Doth the hawk fly by thy wisdom*, God challenges Job, *and stretch her wings toward the south?* My little dog, waiting patiently and vaguely perplexed at the interrupted walk, stirred me to my feet.

Life in the cottage in the woods was monastic and I came to love it. I saw few people, ate simply, wandered for miles with my dog, watched birds, followed a routine of walking and writing and reading and watching films, of sleeping deeply and rising early in the stillness of the dark mornings. *Some development of the capacity to be alone is necessary if the brain is to function at its best, and if the individual is to fulfil his highest potential*, wrote Anthony Storr. Montaigne, with his sense of separation from the crowd and disdain of the stupidity of society, called solitude a *cavern of clarity*. In the 1950s William Golding prophesied that in a hundred years the ambition of every sensitive man may turn out to be the tranquillity of the hermit's cell.

In 1286 a great storm silted up Dunwich harbour, blocking the entrance. The shipbuilders and fishermen moved away, and within a decade commerce in the town was all but dead. A witness described the drama of that tempest, how claps of thunder shook the shore as the storm approached, uprooting trees and prompting thousands of small birds to take wing in confusion. Dogs howled and goats kicked their pails in panic. Chickens flew up into the trees, and fish leaped from the waves when a

flash of lightning struck a ship in harbour, incinerating everyone in the vessel. Two hundred merchant-ships at anchor were
smashed to matchsticks against the boats and barges of the
fishing fleet. A curtain-wall of rain deluged the town and the
violent wind caused the waters to rise, engulfing the city. Furious waves tore into the limestone cliffs and mounted the city's
churches, St Leonard, St Martin, St Michael, St Nicholas, St
Mark, lifting tombstones, tossing them around like dead birds.
Stone coffins were shattered, salt-water poured through broken
skulls. The stones of the Dominican friary thundered down the
cliff. The wind whirled the heart out of hundreds of houses,
and sheepcotes and livestock were swept away. Windmills were
blown on their backs as water surged through Maison Dieu
Lane, swamping everything and everyone in the surrounding
streets. The sea's jaws opened and Dunwich, wrenched from the
cliffs, was engulfed in a winding sheet of water.

The titanic opposition of land and sea over, terns wheeled
under a blood-red sun. Shingle higher than the tallest man
blocked the harbour under a pall of rain. The few inhabitants
who remained saw the soaked corn, the storm-wracked fields,
the torn branches of ancient oaks rolling in the rumbling flood,
the ripped-up harbour, the silted estuary. They saw how the
boiling sea had flattened houses and swallowed a slice of the
town. Ships at anchor were smashed to flotsam, aqueducts to
fragments of lead piping. Debris from churches and cemeteries
scattered over the shingle beneath the cliff was sucked down the
sea's throat. Human bones once decently buried were exposed
to view sticking out of the broken limestone. A stone coffin,
split in two, lay on the beach until the bones, bleached by sun
and salt, were swept away to a second burial by drowning.

The surge left the harbour inaccessible, the pastures flooded.

The Franciscan monastery with its infirmary garden of wild thyme and medicinal herbs, although it survived with some damage and no casualties, was now perilously near the cliff's edge. Its place of sepulture was washed away with its bones, and nothing remained of it under the foaming mud. The most easterly streets of the town lay ten feet under the waters, slowly choked with sand and shingle, left to ghostly marine inhabitants, crabs and starfish, eels and sponges.

A day later the milk-blue sea lay under a cloudless sky, hardly ruffled, gentle waves crumpling its sheen. At certain tides, goes the local legend, the ringing of church bells can be heard beneath the waves.

Grey days loomed out of darkness before sliding back into night. Increasingly, I enjoyed the aloneness. Walking, watching birds, learning and thinking about birds, preoccupied me with something other than my personal orbit. This was more than a distraction, it nourished and balanced me in ways nothing else could. Returning to the cottage after long rambles felt like coming back to my cell. *I laud a safe and humble condition,* wrote Montaigne in his essay on solitude, *content with little ... content with myself and the condition wherein I am ... silently meditating in the sanity of the woods.* St Antony, returning to his desert cave after travelling, said: *Just as fish die if they stay out of water, so the monks who loiter outside their cells or pass their time with people of the world, lose the intensity of inner peace, so, like a fish going towards the sea, we must hurry to reach our cell, for fear that if we delay outside we will lose our interior watchfulness.*

DECEMBER

Sudden mild weather brought scattered hours of blue skies and blinding sunshine. Heavy rainfall filled empty ditches and swelled the streams. Mud was thick and omnipresent, a walk through the woods involving a lot of slithering and slipping. I frequently stopped to watch winter flocks of birds in flight, stark against sepia skies. Small groups of goldfinches erupted out of alders by the reedbeds, darting among undergrowth to peck at the ground, metallic flashes of red and gold. Flocks of fieldfares fed on the heath in the bleak winter landscape. Bevies of wood pigeons rustled off the field, startled. Murmurations of starlings wafted over the marshes at evening, shoals of birds curling and unfolding into myriad shapes to the rhythms of a divine choreography. Radiant yellowhammers caught the late-afternoon sun, all tan and yellow and sleek. Large flocks of corvids flew in to roost as the light failed, swirling in untidy swarms, turning the late sun dark. Watching a crow alighting on a post in the reeds, glossy, shiny, perfect in its blue-blackness, was to notice how this 'ordinary' bird has a special beauty. Winter gives them time to mess about: one day I watched a pair of them playing in the wind, a yoyo game where one flew up as the other flew down, up, down, up, down, dancing, just for fun. Rooks took off from the ploughed fields into grey clouds, paradoxically their blackness making them the most visible of winter birds. These crows and rooks and jackdaws of the English countryside punctuated heath and stubble alike with their dark gleam, scattering from treetrops with raucous voices when disturbed by a foraging raptor, or emerging funereal through dawn fogs.

Dormancy prevailed in this quiet place, a world away from lives fed on valueless values. Nobody was about. Lovely aloneness. I had been reading Eckhart earlier that day: *God would sooner be in a solitary heart than any other,* he wrote in a sermon on detachment. *Keep yourself detached from all mankind.*

My voluntary solitary confinement was proving to be the best medicine.

Many of the saints and doctors of the Catholic Church yearned to be hermits but were refused the option by their superiors who considered their talents should be put to use in the community as teachers, bishops or pastoral carers. Thomas Merton, Cistercian monk whose longing to be a hermit was not indulged by his Abbot for more than a few weeks at a time until late in his life, wrote about what he regarded as a vocation to solitude: *to deliver oneself up, to hand oneself over, entrust oneself completely to the silence of a wide landscape of woods and hills, or sea, or desert; to sit still while the sun comes up over the land and fills its silences with light . . .*

That was his true calling: *I am a solitary and that is that,* he wrote. *I love people OK, but I belong to solitude.*

I decided to go down to Havergate Island, a few minutes' boat ride from the quay at Orford where the river meanders away into the North Sea. Waterlands stretched out under pewter skies on the wide estuary of the Ore. The boat dropped me off at a small wooden pier. I walked into flat vistas of marsh grasses reflected dimly in tidal pools, inhospitable land where brown hares run freely. A little egret, hunched, brilliant white and black billed, stood on a spit looking down into the murky water, stabbing violently into the mud. It shook the drops off its head vigorously and stalked on, deliberately, through the water, periodically elongating its S-shape neck to full stretch. By now I knew that the black legs and vivid yellow feet distinguished it from its bigger cousin the great white egret (all-black legs and feet, yellow bill). Redshank were feeding in the shallows, poking into the mud. Shining bright through the faint light a pair of shelduck and some black-backed gulls populated a landscape of greys and browns tinged with khaki. I looked across to the deserted shingle spit of land that is Orfordness, where abandoned facilities for atomic-weapons testing loom pagoda-shaped, indistinct in the distance against leaden skies, sinister. Like needles, radio transmitter masts pierced the gloom above the horizon, smudged by low visibility. Codenamed Cobra Mist in the 1960s when it housed an experimental radar tracking device, the building was home to the BBC World Service until it was abandoned in 2011.

A weak sun made an attempt to shine through the murk. I watched a pair of avocets feeding on the mere, birds of grace and light, the momentarily silver water almost covering their legs. The vivid black and white of this balletic bird, the hallmark retroussé bill with elegant upcurved scoop which gives it its designation *recurvirostra*, designed to sweep from side to side below the water in the search for invertebrates in the mud. The tapering body ending in a black blob of a tail, wings covering the back as dark as night, on white as white as snow. The neat white breast, the onyx headband running down the long white neck. Dazzlingly and impossibly elegant, the avocet is my prima ballerina of the waterbirds. The Venetians call it *Avosetta*, bird with the advocate's cap once worn by lawyers—or, less poetically, Scooper and Crooked-Bill. I was to discover that, for all their beguiling beauty, they are extremely belligerent birds—but then, they have every right to defend themselves and their territory and their young.

Avocets, extinguished from our shores during the nine-teenth century by hunting, egg collecting, taxidermy and human pressure, returned to Havergate after the Second World War: a shell from a nearby firing range blew a hole in the seawall around the island, creating marshpools. Down at Minsmere, the grazing marshes had been flooded to prevent a landing by enemy troops, and when after the war the water drained away, shallow pools invited the avocets' return there too. Avocets came to represent a return to the natural order of things, they assumed iconic status and became the symbol of the RSPB.

Part of the fascination of the east Suffolk coastline is its fra-gility, about which mankind can do nothing. Its mortality is evident. It's as ephemeral and ever changing as it has been for centuries, well before and ever since the massive storms of the mid-fourteenth century which continued the destruction of Dunwich. The Black Death added to the decline. The circular twelfth-century Knights Templars' church was washed away in the reign of Charles I, just before St Peter's fell into the sea in the late seventeenth century. The last of the medieval churches to succumb to the grip of the North Sea fell off the crumbling cliffs in 1904, recorded in an indistinct black and white photo-graph of the ghostly tower ruins I found in a local village shop and which sits on my desk (Turner painted it too, in 1830, the nave roofless under a stormy sky). In the photograph, you can just make out a single gravestone lying on the beach. Over the centuries, coastal erosion has done the rest, erosion that continues to this day. Within a few generations, is the guess, the last vestiges of this village, once a medieval stronghold and major port, will be washed away, the cottage in the woods with them.

It was time to leave, and face the world again in its Christmas madness. Back home in the industrial farmlands of Essex, starved of birds, it didn't take long for me to decide on a trip to the Ouse Washes. The day I went, it was hard to imagine that the birds weren't as numbed as I was, unsheltered from the unremitting cold all day long. By now I was in need of regular doses of the natural world: wildness and simplicity had become necessities. Purifying, clarifying, refreshing, inducing wonder. John Clare's *sweet solitude* continued to draw me like a magnet away from chatter and trivia and screens, and rush, and noise, and cars, and tarmac, and concrete, and the violence and stupidity of human nature. *I will lead the noble soul into a wilderness and there I will speak unto her heart,* said God to the prophet Hosea.

The dual carriageway was busy with lorries trundling west. Turning right past a 'Welcome to the Fens' sign, there was a sense of arriving on another planet. A flat moonscape was punctuated by an occasional harrow with the dimensions of a dinosaur, or a farm vehicle piled high with mangel-wurzels. Here, on land reclaimed from the sea, under a sky that dwarfs the endless land, windblown trees and dull houses punctuate monotone fields. Spread out at sea level, this is a strange country where excess water is pumped up into dykes, earthbound walls of water forming two twenty-mile-long channels that cross from Earith to Denver Sluice: the Old Bedford River and the New, also known as the Hundred Foot Drain. Susceptibility to flooding has necessitated a web of smaller dykes across the fields, with numerous pumping stations and sluices to channel water up off the rich soil. Such is the landscape of the Great Levels, draining into the River Nene and the Great Ouse, in the heart of East Anglia's fenland that provides around half of Britain's top-grade agricultural land.

But excavate layers of time and you find that this was once the Holy Land of the English. Here in the Middle Ages monastic communities dominated and contributed other dimensions to life: Peterborough, Ramsey, Thorney, Crowland—and Ely, on the Isle of Eels. Towering (from less than a hundred and thirty feet above sea level) over surrounding waterlands once teeming with eels and bitterns is one of the great cathedrals of the medieval world, visible for a thousand years through waterland mists, floating like a great vessel. The Ship of the Fens, presiding over a past where once God prevailed, largely, over Mammon, and when the bread of life had a different significance.

It was a few days before Christmas. I made my escape from the shopping hoopla of the cities and malls. *They have abandoned me, the fountain of living water, only to dig cisterns for themselves, leaky cisterns that hold no water.* Words from Jeremiah suited my grumpy mood. I had an urgent need to escape the digital world with its me-ness and where the word twitter has become synonymous with vacuous soundbites—the ultimate insult to birds. The so, so straight road at Manea (pronounced maynee) led to a vanishing point on an ever-receding horizon. I drove through mud and potholes on an untarmacked track where, just visible over a dyke, poked the eaves of abandoned houses built unaccountably below sea level, ghosts of frequent

flooding, left to decay. Past a peopleless pub. A pumping station. A desolate car chassis.

Tree sparrows were hopping around feeders at the deserted
visitor centre, vivacious and showy with wine-red heads and
white collars. A small flock had gathered in brambles near
the bridge, and as I crossed the dyke the cheerful music of a
sparrow chorus came from the thicket. Walking towards the
hides I saw a woodpecker perched on a rail up the embankment to a hide, dark olive-green against the light, blood-red
streaked the head, the powerful beak in profile. Its mate,
hidden in wintering grasses on the bank, flew out with a shrill
warning call and flash of peridot, and the pair swooped away
to perch on a distant five-bar gate.

That day twenty thousand lapwings were on the reserve,
according to the board in the deserted visitor centre. My soul
was refreshed by this uninhabitable place, inimical to human
comfort and alien to secular-materialist preoccupations. A
welcome antidote to the frenzy of consumerism going on in
the cities, the life of nature continued uninterrupted in its
abundance and untamed prodigality. Sitting alone in a hide to
the sounds of redshank piping, oystercatchers peeping, and the
chitterings and trillings of waders and waterbirds, I saw the
elegant pintail, the well-dressed gadwall, wigeon and a pair
of goldeneye—the male ultra-smart with emerald sheen on
his dark head, the eponymous gold eye, the proud, high brow
and the black and white stripes of the folded wing. A pair of
whooper swans drifted over the water towards me, talking to
each other with a faint, slightly croaky *whoop whoop*, bobbing
heads and feeding, distinctive the long necks and yellow beaks,
black tipped. They were followed by a juvenile in dusky plumage dashed with white. Sitting in that deserted hide on the

Ouse Washes I could see Ely Cathedral sailing like a sea-liner on the horizon, the ethereal wooden octagon piercing the sky, the turrets of the West Tower at the stern. Made by the hands of believers. A reminder of what we have forgotten and what we have lost by forgetting. How near these stonemasons were to working out not only the architecture and physics of beauty (a science in its infancy according to Aldo Leopold), but its metaphysics.

The spaciousness of the Fens around Ely, pancake flatness lying under dramatic skies not far from where I spent my childhood in Cambridge, always evokes in me a sense of an empty space disappearing into nothing. I have a memory of climbing to the roof of the cathedral tower with my uncle when I was ten years old, and writing later in a school composition that I could see for a thousand miles. I remember the adults laughing at me. But what's in a zero or two? The child knew something without being told. She later discovered that there are eighteen words for zero in Sanskrit, including space, point, hole, complete, immensity and void. It was the Indians who first came up with a symbol for zero—and, remarkably, not until the seventh century AD, the concept having evaded even the Greeks. The Indian astronomer Brahmagupta defined zero as the result of subtracting any number from itself, and went on to define infinity as the number that results from dividing any other number by zero. The Indian mind immediately connected this mathematical formula with meanings for nothingness and the void, fitting neatly into a philosophical spectrum of something born of nothing and to which it returns, endlessly. Nought, zero, nothing, representing emptiness or absence, but also everything. Zero equalling infinity and infinity zero. Zero, a circle that can shrink to its centre to a single point, a circle and a single point containing emptiness and nothingness that is also fullness and being. Mathematicians had stumbled on the mystic truth of the Nothing from which everything arises.

Montaigne's collection of 'Essays' is one of the world's great bedside books. I had it by my side through the dark evenings and long nights of that winter. This goldmine of wisdom, humour and level-headedness was written by an independent spirit who abhorred the rigidity of dogmas and ideologies. Forever exploring human nature and using his own as template, Montaigne found, and fostered, inner solitude even in company. Rattling the chains of convention while staunchly maintaining tolerance for others, he stood up for what was natural in himself. We should free ourselves from the bonds that trap us, he said, disentangle ourselves from the knots that imprison our true selves. And he posited all this with a radical humility: *Que sais-je?*, What do I know?

Counsellor to kings, mayor and family man, from his mid-thirties Seigneur Michel de Montaigne, who lived from 1533 to 1592, retired daily to his tower at the edge of the family estates near Bordeaux to think, read and write, away from the hubbub of the crowd and the distractions of domestic life. There he could keep a corner of himself to himself and learn how to be himself, learning to live without needing the approval of others. *Living to oneself*, as Hazlitt put it two hundred years later. But for Montaigne this did not involve judging others; he learned to be always ready to examine every side of an argument with an attention and humanity that shine through the thousand or so pages of his essays. To know himself, and remain true to himself, he sought inward liberation with such sincerity that the Vatican dubbed him posthumously *the French Socrates*.

It was not an easy path. Montaigne, after Seneca and Marcus Aurelius, defines solitude as a sense of separation from the crowd, tempered with a disdain for ambition. But as he discovered, solitude is not necessarily the answer to the world's ills: dogged by melancholy, and latterly by excruciating kidney stones, Montaigne excavated the difference between escapism and the experience of solitude, discovering that *It is our own self we have to isolate and take back into possession . . . We take our fetters with us*. What Montaigne eventually learned was inner detachment from his attachments, without jettisoning the latter. This gave him the freedom to live his own life rather than the life expected of him by others and by society, while remaining rooted in family and professional life. *The greatest thing in the world is to know how to live to yourself.* How to live properly according to your gifts, and not allow yourself to be disturbed, to plough your own furrow. *Restez à soi-même:* to remain oneself. He who thinks freely for himself honours all freedom on earth. Such was the wisdom he imparted to kings.

The week after Christmas is the quietest time of the year in my village. It's as if the world is stunned into silence (whether by excessive indulgence, or ecstasy at the birth of their Saviour can only be guessed at, but the effect is wonderful). The local lanes are empty of cars and vans, the footpaths deserted, the commuter rat-run to the station two miles hence halted, leaving the early mornings profoundly quiet. Silence reigns over the rooftops. I relished the solitary walks, proving to myself the truth of the Hippocratic dictum that walking is the best medicine, providing thinking time—as well as the even more important *not*-thinking time. *No man ever will unfold the capacities of his own intellect who does not at least chequer his life with solitude,* wrote Anthony Storr.

It had snowed heavily all night. Thin fog smothered all sound, muffling the white world. It was bitterly cold, the temperature well below zero. Hibernal quiet. Bitter air. Silent at noon. Flora and fauna were sleeping. Stray snowflakes drifted from a ghost-white sky. The only marks on the night covering of snow were four-pronged hieroglyphs where a lone blackbird had hopped across the path. Fields of sparkling white awaited the dent of a fallen berry, a slip of snow sliding off a dying leaf. In a sudden flash of gold a goldfinch, feeding on skeletal burdock, intent on excavating life-giving seeds from the deadheads: thistle-tweakers to the Anglo-Saxons, *thisteltuige*. Another flew in, bright jewel of scarlet, black and gold. Two brilliant gems against the white.

The fields were hibernating, the trees bare, birds hiding from the cold, so a sighting of even one was enough to brighten the deserted lanes as daily I walked my little dog. Often, it was a kestrel: there was one who regularly surveyed a patch at the edge of the village, perched on a telegraph wire, or sometimes in the top of a bare-branched tree in the middle of a field. It was as if my kestrel was waiting for me. He became 'mine' because every time I walked up the hill towards the wood during those snowbound days, he was perched on the wire, or had flown across the field to a tree ahead of me.

There he was, my Kes, stocky and strong and streamlined,

handsome with salmon back and speckled breast and slate-blue head. The slim dark-rimmed tail, the russet wings tipped with black. The fierce head, the strong shoulders, the aloof demeanour of the raptor. The all-seeing dark eye looked down at me uncompromisingly. He would grant me a quick look with that yellow-rimmed eye before taking off with the unique grace of his species, offering a view of the fanned, black-banded tail, the quivering wings as he hung high above me in the air over his prey. Or a glimpse of folded arrow-wings on his descent before he opened them to float back down to earth, all cinnamon feathered and grey-blue. The collective for kestrels is a 'hover', a 'flight' or a 'soar', as described in 'The Hawk in the Rain' *by* Ted Hughes:

> Effortlessly at height hangs his still eye.
> His wings hold all creation in a weightless quiet,
> Steady as a hallucination in the streaming air.

My kestrels had colonised an abandoned corvid nest in the copse beyond the field (sometimes they will nest in cavities in buildings—including the House of Lords, where they feel appropriately at home). His nest, up in a row of tall trees behind low-lying grassland too damp to be cultivated, made a convenient hunting hide for the small rodents he relied on for food, using eyesight adapted to seeing UV light and so tracing urine trails to their source. He would need to eat four to eight voles a day, or the equivalent in mice, rats, frogs, even earthworms and lizards. Sometimes small birds, too, such as sparrows. For years on end (the maximum recorded age for kestrels is sixteen years, although a typical lifespan is more likely to be nearer four).

*

I've always loved dictionaries. The derivation of words intrigues me, how they migrate from one language to another, from one era to another, accumulating connotations and meanings. I love the consonances and music of words whether discordant or harmonious, rural idioms delight me, and the bird world is rich in them. An exploration of the name 'kestrel' reveals treasures to the word-detectorist: it comes from Old French *cresserele*, suggesting the *kee-kee-kee* of its call and relating to *tinnunculus*, its specific name, Latin for 'ringing' or 'bell-like'. There is further poetry in the modern French for kestrel, *Crécerelle des Clochers*, bird of the belltowers. *Falco* comes from *falcis*, a sickle, from the cutting blade of the bird's hooked talons (or even the tooth inside the beak which distinguishes falcons from hawks). The Gaelic for kestrel *golan gaoithe* means 'a windsweeper', bird of the wind—even in remote rural Macedonia where the (smaller) lesser kestrel is known as *vietrushk*a: *vietra*, 'wind': wind-bird. Common names for kestrels include Wind-Hoverer, Fan-Hawk, Fan-Winged Hawk, Hover-Hawk, Wind-Cuffer, Willie-Whip-the-Wind, Stone Falcon (where 'stone' comes from the roots of 'stand', i.e. the hawk that stands still), Stand-Gale, Stannel, Keelie-Hawk (keel from the Gaelic *ciol* meaning 'red-ochre'), Mouse-Falcon, Furze-Kite, Field-Hawk and Rock Kestrel.

With the wise words of the Renaissance sage Montaigne echoing in my head, I walked the quiet winter lanes. For many who read him, Montaigne becomes a friend, a one-off, a force of nature whose passionate love of life is infectious, who is as witty as he is trenchant, a man courageous enough to stand alone, utterly original. *The wise person will flee the crowd, endure it if necessary, but given the choice, choose solitude. We are not sufficiently rid of vices to have to be contending with those of others.* But then, he says, *It is not enough to have gotten away from the crowd . . . we must get away from the gregarious instincts that are within us.* But how? He quotes Lucretius: *We must take the soul back and withdraw it into itself: that is the real solitude, which may be enjoyed in the midst of cities and courts of kings; but it is best enjoyed alone . . .* But even if he achieves aloneness in a crowd, there's more: the hardest thing of all is not to be enslaved by convention and conditioning. *A man must free himself from the popular conditions that have taken possession of his soul.* Montaigne tells the story of when someone complained to Socrates that 'getting away from it all' hadn't helped him in the slightest, Socrates' reply was, *I can very well believe it, for he took himself along with him.*

With Socrates, Montaigne found that to truly 'know thyself', both physically and metaphysically, means to know, somewhere deep in the darkness, what mankind calls God.

Returning down the hill through ghost trees in the fog, I could see my kestrel perched on top of his telegraph post, a shadow in white mist. He took off over the treetops, flying high, wings raised in a shallow V, and hovered into a headwind over a field of set-aside, cruciform with soft grey barred underwings, black-tipped tail feathers fanning, piercing his gaze through the rough grass on to an unwitting shrew below whose moments were numbered. *Daylight's dauphin*, Gerard Manley Hopkins' 'Windhover', first recorded in the eighth century, now on amber alert in the UK: *dapple-dawn-drawn falcon*, bird of our woods and fields, affirming presence in a place and time starved of the sacred by our loss of connection to the natural world.

JANUARY

Cambridgeshire, the north Norfolk coast,
the Ouse Washes, Essex

stillness

Most years January, greyest and grimmest of months, feels longer than any other. But this one was different. I was so hooked into the world of birds that I didn't notice. Walking the lanes and woods of East Anglia, keeping eyes and ears open and noticing things I'd never noticed before, made me increasingly aware not just of the birds themselves, but of the scope of their world, how it has affected ours, of their relationship to us, of ours to them, of what it is to be human in the world of nature. And, always, of how beautiful they are.

The rains came again. For days, mountains of clouds drum-rolled over the fields, pelting the land with water. Swollen streams gurgled under hedgerows and filled the ditches. Then the weather lifted. Clear skies brought bitter cold to the dark evenings. I took myself off to the reserve at Fowlmere not far from Cambridge, small bird-oasis in prevailing monoculture where strands of thin cloud stretched across the sky, bringing serene stillness to the afternoon as a slight breeze came and went. Water lay like silk under a clear blue sky, reflecting a couple of male teal in bright plumage. Like a Japanese scroll painting, sharp spears of sedge sliced into the mirror sheen of the chalk stream that meanders through the reserve. Looking down into the still water was to gaze into the heart of silence. The afternoon grew colder as the sun sank over the reedbeds, branches of willow, poplar and alder sketching dark lines against the still sky. A wren tutted from the undergrowth and hopped into a hiding place inside a fallen ivy-covered tree.

On the mere, ducks drifted and dabbled, upending and feeding, some in pairs and some in groups: mallard, teal, greylags and a pair of white ducks with orange beaks—escapees presumably—radiating against the glossy emerald of the mallard drakes they mingled with. Hunched against the edge of the reeds on the far side of the water, a heron stood sentinel with his back to the hide, all but invisible until he turned his head to show the long yellow beak, the mean head, the cold eye. A reed bunting dived into the rushes just below the hide giving its *tseeep tseeep* call, chunky little bird, flash of reddish-chestnut wings and pale belly. Then silence. I was reminded of T. S. Eliot's *At the still point of the turning world*. There's something quasi-religious about the quiet of a bird hide. Hours can pass with no sound and very little movement. Sitting still on pew-hard benches, watching and waiting, looking at a marsh, a sky, a wetland, a wood, scanning for birds to see what might happen, even if it's nothing much.

A pair of teal swam slowly around the water, the male smart in elegant livery. The ash-grey body is actually white, speckled with dense charcoal vermiculations like posh worsted. A white streak along the wing, the triangle under the tail gleaming yellowish-buff like straw in evening sunshine, edged in black. The little breast speckled buff and brown, the slightly retroussé charcoal-grey beak. The head, masterpiece of artistry with a dark-green teardrop—teal of course—surrounding the eye, running down into the neck and outlined with a white line. The chestnut cope, the dark bead of the eye. For all his small size, he is a jewel in the world of ducks. His female offers no competition: she is dull and brown and could be mistaken for a small female mallard but for a shot of emerald under the pinions. They floated around, he leading, before finally disappearing into the reeds.

Two greylags stood together on a mudflat at the water's edge, serene, solid presences. Greylags have a kind of anchored gravity. The larger, the male, started to preen, effortlessly rotating his neck, spiralling all the way down his back to get at the furthest feathers. He spent some time poking under the wing. Emerging, he shook his head vigorously and proceeded to stand on one leg, in perfect balance without a hint of a wobble, poised on a wide-webbed foot, spindle-pink. The couple remained where they were, looking around in the winter sunlight. Not even waiting, just standing. Close up, I could make out the line where the orangey-pink beak closes: it was curved, as if into a gentle smile. They have a benign expression, these wild geese. The rim of the eye is chrome yellow, the pupil dark. The folded wings, at first sight uniform light brown, are the colour of milky coffee, white fringed. Dove-grey head and neck are partly streaked, the tail barred and alabaster-white underparts. Common as they are, greylags are as beautiful as they are exceptional, pair-bonding for life, a life based on apparent love and fidelity within a cooperative community as they rear their young year after year. The Nobel Prize-winner Konrad Lorenz, who followed them in the wild researching their life cycle, bred them, fell in love with them, and to him the trilling call of greylag goslings as they fell asleep became a sacred sound. Lorenz came to the conclusion—and this was in the 1970s—that

Far too much of civilised mankind today is alienated from nature. Most people seldom encounter anything but lifeless, manmade things in their daily life and have lost the capacity to understand living things or to interact with them. That loss helps explain why mankind as a whole exhibits such vandalism toward the living world of nature that surrounds us and makes our way of life possible. It is an important and worthy undertaking to try to restore the lost contact between human beings and the other living organisms on our planet. In the final analysis, the success or failure of such a venture will determine whether or not mankind destroys itself along with all the other living beings on earth.

As the light failed, the ducks continued serenely to do nothing much, well fed and content just to be, drifting quietly all afternoon, doing nothing, until the time came to sleep. Wrote a Zen poet,

> A water bird comes and goes
> leaving no traces at all
> Yet it knows
> How to go its own way.

On my return home those January days my resident robin, perched high in his favourite tree, declared ownership of the winter garden with melancholy cadence as I walked through the gate.

James and I decided to brighten a grey winter weekday with a trip to the north Norfolk coast. As I drove at sunrise towards the coast to meet him at Titchwell, a pinkish-orange globe hung over the cold land, haloed in haze behind bare trees, fiery star of our galaxy, speck in a multitude of universes. Up on the coast, skeleton weeds of winter were silhouetted against a sleepy sky. A steel sea glinted at low tide, the shallows crumpled by ruffling waves. The winding strand was deserted, earthline meeting sealine in a haze of violet shadows.

Silver-green sea holly misted the leeward dunes, dagger leaf-edges outlined in white. Carline thistles punctuated gravel spits between tidal pools, sepia-tonsured. A single clump of sea purslane was flowering late, sea buckthorn berries the colour of rusty iron dotted the plant's spiky blue-green leaves. A nodding harebell, palest azure, had somehow made it through the winter protected by dune grasses, leaning under a breeze that fluffed the rushes. A skein of pink-footed geese flew across the sky, snaking and twisting on shimmering wings, an unfolding momentum of wildfowl sliding and veering into the distance.

There was a sudden flurry below the dune where we were standing: eight birds had fluttered down on to the damp sand to grub for insects and seeds on the wrack-line of the tide, stabbing among stranded seaweeds and shoreline plants. Striking white panels striped the dark wings, ermine-white underparts showing up bright against the dun beachscape. Snow buntings, 'White-Winged Larks' of the frozen north. Flying in from Iceland, Greenland, the Arctic even, they make landfall from September onwards, some to feed and rest on passage during their epic migration south for the winter, others like these to winter along our shores. To the Inuits these enchanting birds are 'Arctic Sparrows', ubiquitous and semi-tame. John Clare writes how *the Snow Bunting has all the domestic virtues of our English Red breast it has always been considered by [the Esquemaux] as the Robin of these dreary wilds and its lively chirp and fearless confidence have renderd it respected by the most hungry sports men.*

As they hopped around busying themselves, a female flew up into the dune next to us, and started feeding intently among the stunted windward grasses. We had a close-up of the sandy shoulders and crown, the hint of rusty yellow under the wing, the upper parts streaked with brown and buff and black. The white wingstripe, yellow-orange beak with dark tip—and the snowy breast and belly. She had a perky demeanour, this sturdy bird, the muted tans and creamy whites of her colouring deliciously elegant. Oblivious to watching eyes, our plump snow bunting continued feeding for several minutes before flying off to join her companions on the sand below.

We continued sitting there, just watching, hardly talking for a while, sheltered by the dune looking out to sea, wrapped up against the cold. *Most of the world's ills spring from the human inability to sit quietly in silence,* wrote the seventeenth-century philosopher Blaise Pascal. He could have added, *to sit still and watch birds.*

A self-confident black-headed gull approached and hung around, hopeful for food. The shoreline was peppered with sanderlings. That day, according to my notes, we saw grey and ringed plover, oystercatchers and knot among the many waders and gulls. Teal and goldeneye pottered along the gullies inside the sea wall behind us, a marsh harrier flew over to fields beyond where brent and pink-footed geese were grazing on marshland. Black-tailed godwits mingled with a pair of avocets, unusual in Norfolk in winter, and a crowd of lapwing and curlews.

Watching our black-headed gull (without a black head of course, being in winter plumage), enjoying the scraps of bread we were throwing to him, got me going on about gulls again. Determined to reform me of my Gull Prejudice, James pointed to where some common gulls were hanging out further along the beach. They were his favourite gull, he told me, pointing out their sleek grey wings and black and white wingtips, delicate and dainty in comparison to the bulky seabird befriending us. I could kind of see his point. But I was not enraptured. I was more taken by Barry Lopez' description in 'Arctic Dreams' of the film-star of the family, the ivory gull who winters on pack ice in the Arctic (genus *Pagophila*, 'Ice Lover'). This ravishing bird has adapted to polar temperatures by having shorter legs (black, so smart with the white plumage), and feet less webbed than other gulls, to preserve heat. The longer, sharper claws have evolved so they can pick up prey without landing in water, preventing it from freezing on their legs. Amazing. To line its nest, the ivory gull uses seaweed to trap the sun's energy and help incubate eggs. Not just a dumb blonde then. I have never seen an ivory gull, nor am I likely to since it's a rare vagrant to our shores. But the bird guides persuade me of its pure-white loveliness.

I would like to think—this might do something to redeem gulls for me—that the white birds in the tree in the legend of St Brendan were ivory gulls. Sailing in a curragh with his monks in search of the Isle of the Blessed, Brendan arrived at an island off the west coast of Ireland, called in 'The Voyage of St Brendan' the Paradise of the Birds. He saw a tree *covered over with snow-white birds, so that they hid its boughs and leaves entirely.* He and his monks asked the birds who they were: *We are partakers in the great ruin of the ancient enemy resulting from the fall of Lucifer. The Almighty God, who is righteous and true, has doomed us to this place, where we suffer no pain and where we can partially see the Divine Presence, but must remain apart from the spirits who stood faithful.* After Satan was banished from heaven these pure-white birds, granted glimpses of the divine, had been sentenced to exile on earth. St Brendan realised he was in the presence of something beyond his understanding, and addressed them as angels. The snow-white birds joined the monks in Daily Office, and advised St Brendan on his ongoing journey. At the end of a voyage full of incident, he and his fellow monks returned to the Paradise of the Birds before finally finding the Promised Land of the Saints.

Birds (even gulls?) granted glimpses of the divine, present around us in our lives, giving us who care about them something of what they possess.

As we fed our fearless gull and scanned the sea beyond the foraging waders, we could make out a distant group of sea-birds bobbing on the waves. Visible through the scope were half a dozen long-tailed ducks, cavorting and playing in the sea. Harlequins, theatrically black and white, nature's Bridget Riley birds, graceful, slender and elegant, displaying and diving, dancing and flicking. They are neat birds, these sea ducks, the drake in winter plumage mostly white at first sight, with round head and dark eyes, white face and neck with a black cheek, sleek body charcoal-breasted with white flanks, white underparts, black-and-white wings folded over its back. Kind of water-wagtails, their elongated black tailfeathers sweeping upwards. Incredibly smart. They played and dived and bobbed on the luminous sea as the sun, pearl-white through a grey mist, became partially obscured by wisps of cloud, emerging momentarily to shine like a diamond as the sky drained of colour. Sea ducks dancing and flicking on rippling waves shining under the sun seemed a glimpse beyond time into the infinite: as fourteenth-century mystic Meister Eckhart puts it, *'In the heart of this moment is Eternity.'*

A murmuration of starlings drifted over the marshes as we walked back, swirling their aerial dance, twisting and writhing, bulging and shrinking, streaming into ever-changing shapes before wheeling in to roost with a rustle of wings. Surrounded by a coral glow, the sun sank lower until the horizon swallowed it up and twilight obscured it. As in Thomas Traherne's 'Centuries', *all appeared new, and strange at first, inexpressibly rare and delightful and beautiful . . . All Time was Eternity.*

February was approaching. After a series of storms, the days became windless—cloudy, neutral days when nothing very much moves. The turning axis of the year. The stillness at the hub of the wheel.

James had heard that the hen-harrier roost at Wicken Fen not far from Ely was doing well. That winter, there had been good sightings of these threatened birds. We drove through the Fens where flat fields stretch away to the horizon and where enormous skies arch over lower-than-sea-level land. Wicken Fen's mosaic of habitats—reedbeds, woodland and marsh—is connected by wide droves rich in wildlife and history, and usually busy with birdwatchers, but nobody was about that day as we sat in Tower Hide. We waited, gazing out over reedbeds to bare-branched trees and thorn scrub. I thought of Montaigne in his Tower, and wondered how much time he spent gazing out of the window watching the birds of Bordeaux. Maybe more than we will ever know. Here at Wicken Fen the flat land was steel and dun under a colourless sky except for patches of cut reeds where green shoots were peeping through. Cormorants sat sentry in an oak tree facing over a mere, black shapes somehow sinister against the late-afternoon light.

For a long time nothing much happened. As we scanned with binoculars, or sat still, waiting, time passed without seeming to. *The now that stands still*, according to Aquinas, *is said to make eternity,* as rediscovered by Richard Jefferies in 'The Story of my Heart'. As Jefferies sat on the edge of the South Downs absorbing what was around him, he experienced how *It is eternity now. I am in the midst of it ... Now is Eternity.* Time, suggests Aquinas, is no more than the flow of now in the eternal present: *Nothing exists of time except now.* Seven hundred years later Wittgenstein came to the same conclusion: *If we take eternity to mean not infinite temporal duration but timelessness, then eternal life belongs to those who live in the present.* Restless bodies and minds cannot be in *the now that stands still*: thus contemplatives have always centred their practice on physical stillness, because to exist in the moment requires stillness. The stillness humans are so bad at. *Humans are constantly on the go,* wrote a Zen Master, *we seem to have lost the ability to just be quiet, to simply be present in the stillness that is the foundation of our lives. Yet, if we never get in touch with that stillness, we never fully experience our lives ... It is a very important part of being alive and staying awake. All creatures on the earth manifest this stillness.*

All of a sudden a barn owl floated out of nowhere and sailed around the reedbeds, turned in our direction and flew across the lode beneath us. Wide-winged, ghostly the soft silent flight, the heart-shaped face, the dark penetrating eyes deep inside white feathers, the creamy scalloped fan of the open tail, barred with smoke grey. Underparts white as milk, but the upper side of the wings, seen so close, a mixture of pale gold and cinnamon, pewter and ivory. On huge moth-wings it floated silently up into a tree where it remained for a while. Later we saw it hunting along the far bank of the mere behind us. A couple of days before, I'd watched a falconer fly his barn owl and he'd told me that its brain was the size of a golf ball and that all of it, except an area the size of a raisin, was given over to hearing.

Over the next hour we got lucky. As daylight dimmed, several hen harriers came in to roost in the reeds, one after the other with longish intervals between. A female flew in first, all dazzling white rump and elegant flicking flight. The wings, held angled as she hovered and turned, displayed the patterning of flight feathers barred with chocolate brown, the rest of her plumage soft shades of chestnut and rich browns. The long tail, fanning as she banked and turned, was striped with nutmeg and edged with white like lace on a blown silk skirt. She swerved and circled, more delicately proportioned than the chunky marsh harriers we'd watched earlier, her wings more pointed, the hawk head with yellowish streak around the eye decidedly owl-like. We had clear views of the striping, the barring, the dappling of this bird's beauty as she flew around the fen before dropping into the reeds.

Then a male came in, whitish in the winter gloom, gull-like at first glimpse. On closer inspection this bird was even more owl-like than his mate, with round head and startling amber eyes. Wide wings of bluish-white were held raised in a deep V, the pointed wingtips soot black, flapping heavily. Dramatic creature, he soared and sailed over the reedbed before floating down into a distant spot and disappearing from view.

Another female drifted in like a ghost, this time flying towards us, close enough for us to see detail on the plumage, the gentle colouring of the barring and striping, the loveliness of the luscious browns. Her flight had a grace and a beauty beyond other birds of prey. There's something ethereal about the hen harrier, some quality of otherness, the *soul stirring beauty* of John Clare. Later, as we walked back along the lode in the failing light another male landed in the reeds and started to move along a bank, smoke-grey tinged with lavender: partially obscured by the phragmites he foraged, wraithlike, as another male and two females flew in, circling and drifting over the reedbed like flakes of ash, preparing to roost before darkness fell.

Hen harriers are among our rarest breeding birds in the UK, persecuted to near-extinction: in 2013 they failed completely to hatch young in England. This most persecuted of Britain's raptors is still being, as it routinely has been, shot or trapped or poisoned by gamekeepers on red-grouse moors. Easy pickings they are too, since hen harriers are ground-nesters and fiercely protective of their young. Yet in John Clare's youth hen harriers were common: he knew the bird as *a large blue [hawk] almost as big as a goose*, describing its movement in flight as *swimming*, and *not unlike the flye of the heron*. But harrier habitats declined under the plough as wetlands were drained, and by the beginning of the twentieth century numbers were further diminished by the criminal activities of egg collectors. This practice, as well as persecution at the end of a barrel, slackened during both world wars when men got busy killing each other instead. The birds slowly re-established themselves southwards, finding lowland heath and rough grassland, marshes and moorland to inhabit. Nevertheless, one in six hen harriers are still killed illegally in Scotland every year, in spite of it being a wildlife crime (all birds of prey are protected by law under the 1981 Wildlife and Countryside Act, and maximum penalties for killing them are six months in jail or a fine of £5,000).

Called 'hen harrier' from its alleged habit of harrying poultry, *it gets this name among our countrymen from butchering their fowls.* Thus William Turner in the sixteenth century: *It suddenly strikes birds when sitting in the fields upon the ground, as well as fowls in towns and villages. Baulked of its prey it steals off silently, nor does it ever make a second swoop. It flies along the ground the most of all* ... Bane of the landowner, hen harriers chase small birds including grouse (although seldom hens, in fact), and their diet is mostly nestlings, eggs, small rodents and sometimes frogs. Characteristically they fly low above the ground, with relaxed wingbeats followed by a glide with wings half raised, before grabbing their prey. During courtship and when feeding young, the male will pass his capture to the female in mid-air, either directly from foot to foot, or by a drop in the air. Hen harriers indulge in startling courtship acrobatics, flying steeply upwards to a great height, turning a somersault then plummeting downwards with closed wings (it used to be thought, so dimorphic are the sexes, that the male and the female hen harrier belonged to two different species).

On returning home that evening, the word-detectorist in me got to work. The hen harrier's generic name comes from the Greek *kirkos*, a kind of hawk, and the specific *cyaneus* from the Greek for a shade of blue, that bluish tinge of the male feathers. Females and juveniles are commonly known as Ringtails because of the white upper tail coverts. Local names for the male include Grey Buzzard, White Hawk, White Kite, Dove Hawk, Blue Sleeves, Smoukie and Marsh Hawk. In France the hen harrier is *Busard Saint-Martin*, after folklore connecting it to St Martin of Tours who, before he was converted, divided his own soldier's cloak and shared it with a beggar at the gates of Amiens. That night, Martin dreamed of Christ wearing the half-cloak he had given away, and heard Him say to the angels: 'Here is Martin, the Roman soldier who clad me.'

The snows came again. Drawn back to the Fens one afternoon, stray snowflakes were drifting down as I set out. By the time I got there, there was whiteout on the Ouse Washes. Silver birches were frozen to immobility, smooth-skinned bark gleaming in the glare of low sun, haloed by light in the whiteness. Ice-covered trees glittered in frost. A small bird struck a sudden song from a snowladen bramble. Water stretched out like a mirror under a wan sky, glinting in late-afternoon light.

I sat in a deserted hide, waiting. A sinking sun sparkled on the shining water as a pair of Bewick's emerged like ghosts from behind a dyke, swimming close to the bank, unmistakably the smallest of the swan world (*Cigno Minore* in Italian), lighter in build than the mute, more buoyant, more ethereal in line. They swam serenely beside each other, bobbing heads gracefully, turning to the other with a wistful *whooh-whooh*, occasionally dabbling, a dignity in their bearing, a fragility belying their long migrations. Slim tapering necks streamline into a poised head, more softly rounded, more satisfactory somehow, than their close cousin the whooper, more perfect, more compact. And the beaks, antimony yellow with soot-black tips—each marking unique, defining the individual just as does a human face, never the same twice since time began.

Bewick's swans fly in every year to the Ouse Washes from the Palaearctic, choosing these waterlands to overwinter, migrating two and half thousand miles past the shores of the White Sea from the northern reaches of Siberia, just as they have done since the Pleistocene, aeons before *Homo sapiens* evolved. Dazzlingly white, the 25,216 feathers (according to someone who could be bothered to count) equal the distance in miles of their migration flight, insulating this creature from the bitter cold of its Arctic habitats. Bewick's, dabbling for food in the middle of the Fens, drifting, upending, floating, bright white in the fading light.

I had been watching since mid-afternoon. I continued waiting, numb with cold as the sun set over the water, glinting on diamond ripples. Aldo Leopold commented that there are some people who can live without wildness, and some who cannot. I now knew for sure I counted myself among the latter. I looked up as, out of the silence, came bugling notes, high pitched and throaty, honking diphthongs, a conversation of birds, the language of swans. A mass of billowing snowflakes, a ghostly phalanx of Bewick's arriving to roost, dark legs trailing. Birds of snow and ice, spirits of the wild flying in from the Kara Sea bringing with them the whiteness of their snowbound lands, bodies as radiant as the snowfields they'd left. Elegant in flight, waves of white, an eddying swirl of calling swans lit by a silver sun, they swept in with a brightness that does not belong to this world. Birds beyond space and time.

Beyond Time and Space, the spirit-soul Shiva danced in a spotless sky, his long flying hair lashing the stars and flinging them throughout the universes. With each movement he scattered the stars, encompassing creation and destruction in his cosmic dance, merging all things into one.

Lit by the colossal sun, the Bewick's glided down towards the water on gently curved wings, skidding on to the surface, webbed feet fore-stretched, skimming, sploshing, running on water, sliding, still calling, settling on to the water, merging with the elements until they became glimmers of white radiating in the gathering dusk as freezing night enveloped the Fens. I knew now what Richard Jefferies meant when he wrote, *the water was more than water, the sun than sun ... Inexpressible beauty ...*

Smallest of our three swans, Bewick's swans were named by William Yarrell in 1830 after the engraver Thomas Bewick, he who wrote and illustrated 'British Birds'. *Cygnus* comes from the Greek *kuknos*, swan, and *Columbianus* after the Columbus river in the western United States, one of its breeding territories which spread around northern Eurasia to the North American Arctic. In 1964, Sir Peter Scott (another whose life was defined by birds) noticed that every Bewick's had a unique yellow patterning of the bill by which it could be identified, and subsequently launched one of the longest-running single-species studies in the bird world. Although similar in appearance to the whooper swan (*C. cygnus*), the Bewick's is smaller—it's four feet long—shorter necked, with a fuller, more rounded head shape and with more black than yellow on the bill. The wingspan of six feet is well short of that of the mute swan which is over seven. The male Bewick's can weigh a stone, the female rather less, and should one of them die, the surviving bird may not mate again for some years, or even for the rest of its life. They are gregarious birds, forming family groups of up to fifteen, the most recent fledglings sometimes joined by offspring of previous years. But Bewick's are threatened, as many birds are, by habitat loss, collision with man-made structures, and water pollution, and although legally they cannot be hunted in the UK, about a quarter of ringed birds are found to have lead shot in their bodies, received while migrating over countries that still shoot them for sport. The northern European population has declined substantially since the 1990s, so any chance to see these sublime swans is to be seized. Bewick's have few natural predators—only Arctic foxes, brown bears and the occasional grey wolf or golden eagle—but there is a significant casualty rate at the end of a gun.

In the nineteenth and early twentieth centuries, Bewick's wintered in high numbers in the Outer Hebrides and Tiree, but rarely in England and Wales. It was in the 1930s that their migration route shifted south, and by the cold winters of the mid-1950s they had established wintering grounds in England, in particular on the Nene and Ouse Washes. Today they fly in their thousands on an autumn journey of over a thousand miles, white specks high in the skies in V formation, seen by airline pilots at up to twenty-seven thousand feet, to winter on English waterlands.

> The stars shone forth
> like zero dots
> scattered in the sky

goes a sixth-century Hindu poem, from a culture innately at home with mystical concepts. Seeing those Bewick's was, for me, more than any other experience of watching birds so far, an encounter with the absolute. Emma Turner got it right when she said, *birds never seem quite to belong to this world*, which feels particularly true of the Bewick's. Somehow Paul Valéry's *God made everything out of nothing. But the nothingness shines through*, resonated with watching the Bewick's on the Ouse Washes that day, in parallel with Thomas Merton's *diamond of nothingness*. Nothingness as something, something radiant, invisibly present. Nothingness, a fundamental element of contemplative traditions, of the mysteries of non-existence from the standpoint of existence, a preoccupation of philosophy, theology and art, of human enquiry.

Infinity, enigma and paradox, all in a vision of swans.

This is what birds do to me, that is what the Bewick's did to my head that day. This is how birds brought peace to my soul and direction to my life.

FEBRUARY

Essex, the Suffolk coast, the Norfolk/Suffolk border

silence

In his novel 'Miss Smilla's Feeling for Snow' Peter Høeg observes how *It's always interesting to leave Europeans in silence. For them it's a vacuum in which the tension grows and converges towards the intolerable.* It's so true: when silence falls, people feel they have to fill it with something. Why? Is not silence a Good Thing in a culture of constant noise? For the poet R. S. Thomas the main prerequisites for writing were time and silence, creating the space for something to happen. Long walks in quiet places were essential to Gilbert White and Thomas Bewick, and many other writers too, including Edward Thomas who wrote how being out in nature made him aware of *the majestic quiet, of the destiny which binds us to infinity and eternity.* Silence stills our restless attention, slows us down, quietens the busy mind. Stopping to listen to silence can reveal it as something rather than nothing, a bodily thing, sacramental even, as can be felt in an empty church, as on a wild mountainside. Thomas Merton found that *out in the woods and under the trees, the sweep and serenity of a landscape, fields and hills, are enough to keep the quiet interior tide of his peace and his desire for hours at a time.*

John Cage, famous for his composition in which for four minutes and thirty-three seconds silence prevails in the concert hall, maintained there's no such thing as physical silence. Silence has its own resonance, he says: and if you listen intently enough, it does. *Even one silence is unlike another silence,* wrote Antoine de Saint-Exupéry in 'Letter to a Hostage', and Cage referred to 'the sound of silence'—the silence of the sea, of the hills, of the clouds, of outer space, of inner space, all different. *In fact, try as we may to make silence, we cannot ... there is always something to hear.* Being a musician Cage maintained that every silence has its own pitch. Silence isn't an absence of something, it's an actual *thing*, a presence—as the painter Robert Rauschenberg demonstrated in another medium. His White Paintings reveal dimensions, light, shadows, particles even, as you stare at them, much as listening to silence uncovers its sound. Sometimes, walking in nature, the silence sounds as if the earth is holding its breath. Wordsworth referred to *The calm / That Nature breathes*. The still small voice of calm, the silence between the in-breath and the out-breath, the silence between the waves.

A mile or two from home a tunnel of trees and undergrowth leads down a narrow lane to ploughed fields. Scarlet hips hung from the briars. A curtain of cloud cleared, an unwilling sun gleamed weak and low in the anaemic heavens, brief but welcome respite from dull days and sullen skies. The winter silence was broken by a throaty, scratchy *schack-schack* of fieldfares fluttering out of the brambles, the sound of my footsteps alerting them to danger. They flew up into a canopy of bare branches overhanging the bridlepath ahead of me. Flushed out wave by wave, flying out repeatedly to find cover as I walked on, they settled a little further along the track each time, flashes of silvery-white underwings looping in and out of the undergrowth. They became my companions that afternoon: walking with fieldfares on a quiet February day.

At a fork in the lane where hawthorn grows, a single fieldfare settled on a branch, herald of winter arriving from Scandinavia in late autumn to feed on ploughed soil or pasture, and to forage for berries in the hedgerows. Lit by limpid winter light, perched on a branch above him, a redwing kept company with its cousin. A slightly smaller bird with striking cream stripe over the eye, it had a dash of rust under the wing, and speckled breast, bird whose tiny *tseep tseep* song announces the arrival of one of our winter thrushes.

The fieldfare was big and stocky, handsome in blue-grey and chestnut livery. Red-brown wings, ochre breast spotted like a mistle thrush's, and ivory belly. His back gleamed slate-blue (a country name for fieldfare is Blue-Back). The sturdy presence, the stateliness. In his day, Chaucer's *frosty feldefare*—'traveller through the fields'—was trapped and eaten as a game bird, regarded as a delicacy, a practice that continued into the nineteenth century, and persists to this day in France. During one season alone in seventeenth-century Prussia, six hundred thousand fieldfares were trapped and sold on to shops and restaurants. It has won nicknames of Snow Bird, Frost Bird, Storm Bird, Screech Thrush, Blue Tail and Veldebird. The Spanish call the fieldfare *Zorzal Real*, 'Royal Thrush'.

With a gleam of off-white underwing my fieldfare fluttered out of the tree, uttering another harsh *schack schack schack*. A crowd of them followed, calling, and with a rustle of wings chased along the track which leads into a field bordered by high hedgerows. They flew across to a copse into the top of an ash tree where I left them behind, walking on for miles through the cold day under the silent beauty of winter trees. Later, as I returned down the path, my flock of fieldfares had settled to feed in a field of early beet, heads down, hardly visible, camouflaged against the freezing earth. Restless, busy feeders, they were hopping around purposefully, periodically taking an upright stance, heads held alert, watchful, looking around. When a group of busybody starlings joined them, they became quarrelsome and noisy, skirmishing and flurrying to establish who was boss. I watched as they fed, lost in the nowness of these birds for whom the present is the only reality. The iridescent petrol shimmer of starling feathers gleamed in the low light, and a sinking sun illumined the chestnut and grey-blue plumage of the fieldfares as they continued their search for invertebrates in the cold ground.

John Clare watched them too:

> Flocking Fieldfares, speckled like the thrush
> Picking the red haw from the sweeing bush
> That come and go on winter's chilling wing

John Ray, ornithologist-cum-natural-philosopher of the seventeenth century, stated that *birds are a worthy preoccupation for the philosophic mind*. They had certainly awakened that in me, and although this encouraged my Garbo tendencies, interest in the science and history of birds balanced and to some extent modified too much aloneness. Somebody I met at a bird gathering (yes, I was persuading myself to join in from time to time) told me that there used to be more red kites than people in Norwich in the late-medieval period. By Tudor times, red kites were one of London's commonest birds, ubiquitous scavengers living on carrion and garbage and doing a good job keeping the streets of the city clear of rotting food. So useful were they that they were a protected bird for over a century: however, kites not only attacked poultry but raided washing lines, stealing underwear and handkerchiefs hanging out to dry, using them to line their nests (even teddy bears have been found in kites' nests). *When the kite builds, look to your lesser linen,* warned Shakespeare. The sixteenth-century herbalist and ornithologist William Turner wrote that *in England [the red kite] is abundant and remarkably rapacious. This kind is wont to snatch food out of children's hands, in cities and towns.* Gradually 'kite' became a term of abuse: one who preys upon others, a term of detestation according to the 'Oxford English Dictionary' (which also tells us it's the bird that floats on the wind which gave its name to the recreational kite, and not the other way round). King Lear describes his daughter Goneril as a *detested kite*, one of Shakespeare's fifteen references to this bird.

By 1930 kites, victims of egg collectors and poisoning to which as scavengers they are highly susceptible, were all but extinct in the British Isles except for two pairs in Wales. They were successfully reintroduced to the Chilterns in 1989, and in 1999 the red kite was named 'Bird of the Century' by the British Trust for Ornithology. In 2006 a sighting of the first red kite to be seen in London for 150 years was reported in the 'Independent'. As of 2015, a pair of red kites started nesting in my village in East Anglia. Nature is resilient. Red kites have made a comeback.

Slipping anchor into silence as I walked out one morning that February, the grass was crisp with cold, dead leaves frosted. The fields and lanes were deserted. A fieldfare *schack-schacked*, a jay screeched from deep inside a wood, pigeons scattered out of the bare treetops. The fields were resting, iron-dark earth furrowed

under a bright sky. I felt the spaciousness of silence, how much
bigger it is than we are. How refreshing it was to be away from
the brouhaha of the noise-saturated world. I thought of John
Clare's *cri de coeur*:

> O take me from the busy crowd
> I cannot bear the noise
> For nature's voice is never loud
> I seek for quiet joys

A cold sun hung low over the land at mid-afternoon, bare
trees stark against the light as a ghostly half-moon rose in
the north-east. Catching low sunshine, hazel catkins glowed
greenish-gold in a spiny hedge beside the track. The raw east
wind had dropped, but it was still below freezing.

I came to the top of the hill and saw, in the distance above
a high hedgerow, a large bird being harried by a pair of crows.
Bigger than a buzzard by far, it stopped me in my tracks. I
stood still and watched. This was a red kite, forked tail torquing
as it turned. After several minutes of bullying, it flew away
from the victorious corvids and soared over the hedgerow trees,
heading towards me. It circled over the field, languid on enormous rust and black wings whose span measures the height of a
tall man (kites, it occurred to me at that moment, have much
to teach us about the art of sauntering). For several minutes
it floated in winter light, buoyant, feathered legs and talons
dropped, fierce head looking down on to the ploughed earth
like a great god, tawny-red back gleaming, yellow eye piercing the sunlight, hooked beak agape, prominent against the
blue heavens. Sunlight spotlit the plumage of the underwings,
dark and light as it banked and swerved, the russet-reds of this

magnificent bird intermittently aflame in the winter sunlight. I watched as it floated on thermals, buffeted by a sudden gust, steering with forked tail, then resting languidly on invisible air currents. Uncompromising raptor surveying the scene, ancestral ruler of the skies. I held my binoculars on him until my arms were tired, and he soared away with a thin piping call and became a dot in the distance.

Later in the year I had another encounter with a kite. It was a drizzly day in late summer. I stopped at a roadside stall one morning to buy the last dahlias of the season. Under the cold sky I walked a path cut between brambly undergrowth before emerging into fields newly ploughed for winter wheat. A large bird was winging its way towards me. A red kite. My little dog stopped as it circled overhead. It came closer and closer. And then too close, hanging only fifteen feet or so above us. I could see in the clearest detail the huge wings, the patterning of the plumage as its tail switched and torqued, the dark and cream colouring of the underwings, the buff underside of the tail, the dramatic black pinions fingering the wind. And that uncompromising stare, the unblinking glare of the yellow-irised raptor. The razor sharpness of the beak, the savagely pointed hook on the upper mandible designed to tear flesh. I feared for my terrier: this powerful bird appeared to be a little bit too interested in her. I held it in my binoculars, ready to yell and charge at any moment if it swooped too close.

After a long minute, during which time I guessed the kite was an adolescent and probably just curious, it gained height and started to fly away from us. Heart beating fast, I followed it in my binoculars over the newly ploughed clods of the adjoining field, watching as this impressive bird floated across to a high hedgerow, where it continued to circle before disappearing.

A wind was getting up, the gales forecast from the west were imminent as I continued my walk along the open ditch. I watched swallows swooping, a pair of buzzards hunting above the woodland edge where fleabane glowed cheerful and bright yellow among untidy grasses. I followed a deer path through a wood, thinking about red kites and how they are gradually making their way eastwards after near extinction in Britain. But however common they may become, watching these spirits of untamed wildness will never lose its thrill.

The draw back to the cottage in the woods was irresistible: eager for the silence of the woods again, I booked it for a further ten days and returned to Dunwich Forest, to the place that embraced me like a friend each time I returned. The house had been built during the Second World War as a lookout on the edge of the cliffs, an officer's quarters with an observation tower to spot enemy invasion from the North Sea. The tall rectangular stack still dominates the restored building, albeit now converted to a heating flue. The coincidence amused me: Montaigne and his Tower, little me in mine. How a 'cell', a tower, can be a place of renewal and refreshment, how Montaigne withdrew to his to avoid the banalities of everyday life, and how that turned itself around: how he learned eventually, through isolation, to connect to and deal with 'the world' in a different way. How 'living for himself' made it possible to live for others, and not in spite of them. And how he ended up imparting this wisdom to kings as well as to generations of his readers: how to be *in* the world but not *of* the world.

I had assumed that solitude necessitated a physical space to retreat to. But it doesn't require an offshore island or a desert or even a cottage in the Suffolk woods to connect with de Foucauld's *eternal things*: with practice, says Montaigne, peerless philosopher of the everyday and the personal, we can create that space inside ourselves. The idea of an internal fortress, taken with you into 'the world' becomes—instead of an escape—a part of you which remains unassailable, like the parable of the house built on the rocks. *We must reserve a back shop all our own, entirely free, in which to establish our real liberty and our principal retreat and solitude.* Thus Montaigne.

For now, that could only be an aspiration.

I made a plan to go down every evening to one of the hides at Minsmere to watch the birds as they prepared to roost, but I was not in luck. Too much TV coverage had brought it fame: its high profile had attracted the general public, and to my dismay the hide was full of people chattering. No heed was taken of notices inside and outside the hide about keeping silent, about how birds are wild creatures and sensitive to the slightest sounds, even to whispers. The tension so commonly engendered by silence prevailed: these were people who couldn't bear silence and felt they must drown it out with noise, any noise. To people like this, silence is something alien, something to be regarded with fear and hostility. Silence is acceptable only, the convention goes, as a mark of remembrance, but then only for a minute at most, after which relief breaks out and chatter can recommence. It appeared that the people in the hide that afternoon couldn't *not* chat about what they saw (or didn't see) from the hide, or their camera lenses, or some previous birdwatching trip. Writing in the 1990s, the Benedictine monk

Cyprian Smith had a forthright opinion about this: *Our spate of words and highly-developed communication techniques are simply a mask for our inner emptiness and poverty. They are like the fig-leaves Adam and Eve wore to cover their shame.*

I once went to a concert by the pianist András Schiff, who started playing Brahms to the disregard of the professional coughers who carried on coughing. He stopped playing, sat in silence for a while, then walked off. He did come back, but he'd made his point about the inessential coughing that so often wrecks the experience of the concert hall. Miraculously, the coughers (none of whom had coughs) remained quiet for the rest of the performance—and even more miraculously, for that *stillness scooped out of the heart of sound*, the silence after music as described in 'A Time to Keep Silence' by Patrick Leigh Fermor. Leigh Fermor describes the blessed relief from talk he encountered in the monastery at Solesmes: says the Abbot to him about the quiet, 'Oui, c'est une chose merveilleuse. Dans le monde hors de nos murs on fait un gros abus de la parole' (Yes, it's a marvellous thing. In the world outside our walls, people greatly abuse words).

As Origen wrote, *the wise man is known by the fewness of his words.*

Maybe the fear of silence has something to do with thinking it's boring. John Cage has a riposte: *In Zen they say, If something is boring after two minutes, try it for four. If still boring try it for eight, 16, 32 and so on. Eventually one discovers that it's not boring at all but very interesting.* I was on his side, but the birdwatchers in the hide clearly weren't. There would be no point in saying anything. Here was a place to practise Montaigne's 'back room'. I had to wait patiently (impatiently) until tea or cocktails lured the chattering classes away, and I could claim the reedbeds with the evening birds to myself, and re-enter the silence of the marshes.

By now it was cloudless. There was no wind, only the sound of a reed bunting singing. A curlew called a wistful evening trill. A Cetti's warbler rang out a burst of notes—a skulking bird named after an eighteenth-century Jesuit priest Francesco Cetti whose life was touched by birds: zoologist and professor of mathematics, he wrote a 'Natural History of Sardinia', where the Cetti's warbler was first identified and named after him, *Cettia cetti*, little warblers seldom seen but easily identified by a sudden brief explosion of song from somewhere in the reeds. Out of the stillness a pair of marsh harriers flew up over the reedbeds, male and female sundering the transparent sky. They began hunting, the low clear light catching maroon-chestnut backs and wings, creamy-pale heads. Flocks of small birds showered out of the reeds, startled by the harriers: in a gust of silvery underbellies, reed buntings flying up from their secret lives below. Flurries of little birds sprinkled the sky as a flock of lapwings flopped past, black and white and loose-limbed, on their evening route to roost.

The silences of unpeopled places.

Stillness again. The piping and whistling of invisible redshank. Nothing moved. I waited. I'd come to watch Bewick's flying in, but as always in the nature of waiting for birds, the experience is unpredictable: as T. S. Eliot said, *And what you thought you came for / Is only a shell, a husk of meaning / From which the purpose breaks only when it is fulfilled / If at all.*

Above the ruined abbey on the shoreline a mile away, a

murmuration of starlings gusted over the winter trees. At full stretch it must have been half a mile long. A Möbius loop of birds swirled over the skyline, contracting into a dark raincloud mass then extending and stretching out again. The black shoal elongated, retracted, transparent then opaque, drawn this way and that as if by invisible fingertips, thrown one way and then the other. Expanding then shrinking, the speckled mass swallowed vagrant birds into itself like iron files to a magnet. The cloud of starlings dropped momentarily into treetops behind the reedbeds until, as one in heart and mind, they billowed into the sky again, darkening it above the dusky trees.

The cloud of starlings continued spooling, gathering up from palest nothingness into black being, gusted by an invisible impetus in the windless evening as if that giant hand were casting a net back and forth. A family of mute swans stood preening by the silver water, settling to roost, the light of the sinking sun gleaming on their porcelain-white feathers and burnishing the feathery reeds. Gradually the sky deepened to blue in the west, in the east fading to an apricot glow where the starlings danced. Eternity caught in moments of time.

It's impossible to imagine how such perfect curves can be formed by a flock of birds, the coiling and unfurling of contoured helixes. Murmurations remain a puzzle to scientists: how do a hundred thousand birds swirl around in such intricate patterns without colliding? Nobody has fathomed the exact workings of these massings. It's been shown that grouping together offers safety in numbers, because predators—such as peregrine falcons—cannot target one bird in the maelstrom of movement. A murmuration of starlings moves as an intelligent cloud, as it were, thousands of them changing direction simultaneously. But how do the birds on the edge of the swirl sense the shift in the centre of the cloud, and move in unison with them when the timing is different by only a split second? How do the birds create perfect curves? How do they change direction so incredibly quickly? One theory goes that one bird's movement only affects its seven closest members, and each of those neighbours' movements affect their closest seven neighbours and so on through the flock: a pulse of movement. Thus the flock looks like a twisting, morphing cloud, some parts moving in one direction at one speed and other parts moving in another direction and at another speed. It's mostly mathematicians and physicists who have carried out the research looking at these patterns, trying to work out how thousands of birds avoid smashing into each other. Clues lead them to find the closest statistical fit in the physics of magnetism, how electron spins of particles align with their neighbours as metals become magnetised. Which seems apt, since that is actually what a murmuration looks like, iron filings playing to the draw of a cosmic magnet, following universal principles yet to be understood.

Unimpressed by the celestial drama, two otters were hunting in the centre of the mere. One of them had caught a fish, and for a few moments there was a friendly skirmish while the other wrestled for the catch, but when the victor swam off triumphant, turning on to his back and swimming away holding the fish in his front paws to nibble his prize, the other returned to hunt, diving, snaking down into the water, long tail lashing the water like an eel as a nearly full moon rose in a navy-blue sky.

And the murmuration went on. And on. For nearly an hour I watched the birds gusting into the sky as dusk folded into darkness. Unprepared, I had witnessed one of the wonders of the natural world: a murmuration of starlings, a quasi-religious experience which left me struggling for the words that are the prerogative of poets. As so often, I turned to R. S. Thomas: *I will simply say that I realised there was no such thing as time, no beginning and no end but that everything is a fountain welling up endlessly from immortal God.*

Those February days in the woods brought with them a feeling of light emerging slowly from darkness. Tiny signs of spring were appearing on the woodland floor, arum leaves spearing through the leaf litter, dog's mercury unfurling into leaf. Silence and space in the depths of winter had worked something unknown: a kind of *Winterreise*, a winter journey of solitude, stillness and silence had led me to discover that, as Meister Eckhart said, *there is nothing so like God as silence.* Silence, he posited, links us to the universal, to the mystery of life around us, to the perceptions of mystics and physicists alike that there is nothing in nature that is only matter, no division between matter and spirit: matter is merely light transformed, light imprisoned, nothing made into something.

I had begun to realise that silence has to be learned: but like learning music, just as nobody could be expected to play the violin in a weekend, or a week, or a year even, keeping silence, enjoying stillness, would take practice: as contemplatives of the past bear out, the struggle with the chattering mind is ongoing, but the practice of silence and stillness can reveal the true self

beyond the little 'me' with its desires and demands and opin-
ions. A space beyond language, beyond thought even.

On my last day at the cottage in the woods I drove down
to Boyton marshes. Parking my car in a deserted lay-by, I
walked into what seemed immeasurable vastness at the edge
of Suffolk. The depopulated land sinks ever lower and flatter,
receding into sky where a vista of reedbeds and marsh grasses
meets the sea wall. On the shore of the tidal River Ore, winter
remnants of sea lavender tint the mudflats of the estuary
which curls away to the horizon. In three hundred and sixty
degrees of sea-level flatness the only sign of human activity is
a Second World War pillbox and distant arable fields. Pockets of
faraway woodland, trees in leafless silhouette, merged with the
beige mist of wintering reeds. Lines of dykes led through tidal
pools of blue-grey water reflecting the sky. It reminded me of
the monk in the Caspar David Friedrich painting, isolation but
not aloneness in the vastness of an empty landscape.

Piping of redshank echoed from the mudflats. The bubbling
cry of curlews punctuated long silences. I had never felt so far
from anywhere in England, so alone in open spaces with no
human habitation in sight. It was something to do with the
flatness. Lapwings were flying around with starlings, feeding
by a distant stretch of water along with Canada geese and
greylags. As I walked I could make out gadwall, wigeon, teal,
cormorants, egrets and mute swans in this unspoiled place. A
single curlew was stabbing at the ground with downcurved bill
before taking off towards a tidal pool with a *wheep wheep* cry,
the trembling minor key floating over the marsh. There is no
equivalent sound in nature: haunting, plaintive, wistful. A flock

of lapwings flew in to join him, crying the *peeoooo peeeou* call that gives them the peewit name.

Walking on for miles, there was no sign of human life apart from the tiny bump of Orford Castle in the far distance. Not a power line in sight, or house visible. In this place on the edge of things, out in this wide, open, uninhabited landscape, there was no separation. In the spaciousness, alone with nature, even the experience of breathing was different. The immensity of the stillness. I had no sense of myself at all. It was as if the membrane of the self had dissolved into the vastness.

I sat by a stile to eat my sandwich. *The resting place of the mind is the silence of the heart,* wrote Thomas Merton. At that moment, that felt like an absolute truth. The natural silence of the world around me drew me into the *be still and know that I am God* from the Psalms that even non-religious people are familiar with, and understand—the peace experienced in the silence of a garden at evening, of a dawn landscape, of a serene sunset. Numinous silence. Absorption into what we can never understand as mirrored by the beauty of the natural world. Alan Watts, a Westerner drawn to Zen and the Buddhist tradition, discovered through his practice that stillness and silence are *the purest gold of mystical religion.*

Sitting there I was looking at distant swans to see if there were whoopers or Bewick's among them, migrants from the far north wintering among flocks of our native swans. One pair in this flock of mostly mute swans stood out: I watched them for a while, hoping, but they were too large to be Bewick's. Whoopers, possibly? I was searching for a patch of yellow on the beak, but as far as I could see the beaks were pure black. These two swans had very long, slim, straight necks which, as I watched, they stretched up to full extension, parallel to each other, eye to eye, beak to beak. A rendezvous of two white waterbirds whose graceful deportment and extreme dignity expressed a purity, a natural pride with no suggestion of arrogance. The extremely long neck, the heavy, teardrop-shaped body. After a while the two swans settled into the marsh grasses, purest white in the watery green, in tandem one behind the other, heads erect, shiny black eyes alert, big body half hidden in foliage. Then one moved slowly to its feet and opened its wings momentarily, huge, heavy wings with long-fingered pinions. Curling its neck as if in a dance, communicating something intimate and unknown to human language, it folded its wings to settle again.

There is no word for the whiteness of a swan.

Imagining that it was simply the distance that prevented me from seeing the hallmark yellow of a Bewick's beak, and so assuming them to be whoopers, I continued walking. Absorbing the silence of the marshes was like a return from exile, my true habitat for which I get regularly homesick. So much of the earth must have been like this unspoiled place before predatory humans started scrambling all over it. I felt how we have lost the ability to be in nature without commodifying, commercialising or colonising it. Or chatting over it, deaf to its sounds and silences. Watching the swans that day in that quiet place satisfied an urgent appetite. *Man cannot live by bread alone.* Out on the marshes I was a world away from a culture disconnected from the natural and the wild. I had no wish to return to it. I thought again of that favourite book, Patrick Leigh Fermor's 'A Time to Keep Silence' (an uncompromisingly forthright author, along with some of the monk-writers I like so much) as he unwillingly leaves the healing peace of the monastery at Wandrille: *the outer world seemed afterwards, by contrast, an inferno of noise and vulgarity entirely populated by bounders and sluts and crooks.*

But return I must. On my way back I saw the only two people I met that day, and although loath to break my silence, I was in luck. A gentle man with a gentle wife, birdwatchers both, were looking through a scope. These birds are never seen in Britain, the man said. Found only in North America, he went on, and non-migratory, they don't move far in winter and certainly not across the Atlantic, so in England they are found only as escapes from captivity. What I had been looking at earlier were trumpeter swans, he told me. What I had been responding to as something special, but not believing it, was a pair of rare and unusual waterbirds. The most regal, the most perfect of all the swans, trumpeters are the largest of the world's waterfowl, and one of the heaviest birds capable of flight (the largest recorded male was six feet long with a wingspan of over ten feet and weighing thirty-eight pounds, second only to the condor). Its neck can be twice as long as the neck of a Bewick's, and the call sounds like a trumpet. They mate for life, and if a partner dies the male may never pair up again. Trumpeter swans were almost extinct by the late twentieth century, hunted heavily both as game and as a source of feathers for everything from bedding to powder puffs, but they have thankfully recovered their numbers. Apparently, the man with the scope continued, the twitchers of Britain had come rushing down earlier in the year to see them, then discovered they were escapees so went away again disappointed (how could they be?) and left them to the silence of the marshes, natural denizens of a place whose boundaries dissolve into the space–time continuum.

The sight of the swans on a drab February day in the middle of nowhere, doing nothing much except what swans do, is imprinted on my memory as a simple, uncluttered moment in time and out of time. The eternal moment. It was, and still is, enough to make me happy, proving (to me, anyway) Einstein's perception that *the distinction between past, present and future is only an illusion*. In Plato's cave, some watch the shadows of dancing flames on the wall, while others, turning to the source of the light that cast the shadows, are dazzled by a direct perception which strikes the depths of the psyche. Watching a pair of trumpeter swans stretching their necks, settling in stillness, then opening heavy, pure-white wings in language only they understood, felt like that. The swans imparted the thusness of pure being. In those moments of self-forgetfulness I inhabited their silence, and they fed my soul. It was as if the cacophony of living had been in danger of eroding my humanity, and the silence of the swans restored it.

My hibernal retreat was coming to an end. Spring was on its way. Out on the reserve bitterns were booming, afternoons were lengthening, the mornings no longer dawned with frost. Making the transition back to 'the world' after being a hermit for those weeks was hard. It was painful to leave. I had been reading Aldo Leopold: *Solitude, the one natural resource still undowered of alphabet, is so far recognised as valuable only by ornithologists and cranes.* That gave me an idea. To soften the blow I decided to stop off at Lakenheath Fen on the way home. James had told me that a pair of cranes had bred there the previous spring, and that February was a likely month of the year to see these secretive, shy birds who would be increasingly visible as they prepared for the mating season.

I had never seen a crane. Maybe this would be the day.

Aesop wrote of the crane's ability to rise above the clouds into endless space, to survey the wonders of the heavens as well as of the earth beneath, with its seas and lakes, mountains and rivers. Playable flutes dating from 7000 BC, unearthed at a neolithic settlement near the Yellow River in China, were made from wing bones of the red-crowned crane. In the 'Iliad', Homer describes how the sound of armies approaching in battle was like the sound of cranes gathering for migration. Their bugling call can be heard up to four miles away, produced from an elongated, convoluted trombone-shaped trachea fused along part of its length with the sternum, making a series of plates that vibrate and amplify the sound.

Cranes are sacred in the Orient, messengers of wisdom often depicted in Japanese art transporting the recently departed to heaven, a bird symbolic of connections across space and time. The immortals were seen riding on the back of cranes, messengers of wisdom and harbingers of good luck. One of three mystical or holy creatures in their culture, along with the dragon and the tortoise, the crane was thought to live for a thousand years. Aldo Leopold wrote that the crane *is the symbol of our untameable past, of the incredible sweep of millennia which underlies and conditions the daily affairs of birds and man.*

They used to be a familiar sight in England: in the Middle Ages cranes would appear regularly, roasted, on the banqueting menus of lords and kings. By the early seventeenth century they had died out in the UK as a breeding species, and were subsequently seen only as a scarce passage migrant. The Industrial Revolution, and subsequent draining of waterlands to harness more soil to feed an ever-growing human population, did nothing to encourage them back, until in the early 1980s they returned to breed at Horsey Mere near the Norfolk coast. They are now slowly making a comeback in East Anglia, and a reintroduction programme in the Somerset Levels has proved highly successful.

When I arrived at Lakenheath Fen the sky was leaden, grey-brown, sluggish, and it was bitterly cold. A weak sun skulked behind a veil of cloud. Torpor prevailed, slowing the pulse of life. I walked my dog along the footpath surrounding the reserve. It was deserted. Blasts of wind knifed across the flat fields. The bank was slippery, thick with mud. River water stretched out to a group of little egrets glowing white through the gloom that hung over the mere. A pair of Egyptian geese were feeding on the bank, a great crested grebe floated aimlessly, mute swans drifted on the freezing water. The shivering wood beyond was a black smudge in a trail of mist. Greylag and teal flew in, followed by three oystercatchers sleek and plump in black and white livery with carrot-orange bills. Nothing else was stirring. I walked along the dyke towards the reedbeds where a pair of resident cranes were said to be prospecting for a nest-site, stopping from time to time to scan with my binoculars, but nothing appeared. It was silent, and very still.

Then suddenly, beyond the ghostly poplar wood, a crane flew out of the marsh, long neck outstretched, hugely wide-winged, stilt-legs trailing, toes pointed back, the tiny red cap on the head clearly visible. With effortless wingflaps it sailed towards the trees, elegant and graceful beyond anything I'd ever witnessed. This ash-grey bird was enormous, almost white in the dark day, with sooty throat and long blue-black flight feathers. I heard the cronking call as it was chased off by its parents, the trumpet sound that Dante calls 'clangourous' (Aldo Leopold describes it as *the trumpet in the orchestra of evolution*). I caught a glimpse of the three of them sparring in a clearing under pewter skies before they disappeared from view: the adolescent had outgrown the nest and the parent birds were unequivocally claiming the territory to bring up another brood.

As it began its adult life, the crane I saw that day conjured the prodigious cycles of time. *The Crane is wildness incarnate* (Leopold again), a large bird capable of a non-stop flight of two thousand miles (not that this youngster would go further than the edge of the reserve, probably). In those few moments I witnessed a creature of poise and beauty, artefact of a divine imagination, a miracle of the diversity of life. And like so much birdwatching, serendipitous: I'd been lucky to be in the right place at the right time, and happened to be looking in the right direction—yet every time I walk that path on Lakenheath Fen I half expect to see one again, remembering how the first crane I ever saw moved me with its soul-stirring beauty.

The eternal is bonded on to us, wrote Saul Bellow, *it calls out for its share.* There's nothing rational about how a place is changed by seeing a bird: but that spot on the reserve will forever be the place where I saw my first crane flying.

MARCH

Spain, Wales, the Suffolk coast, Essex

music

March arrived, month of winds and awakening and change. It was time to make plans. James and I were sitting on his sofa looking at an atlas, his finger moving over Europe. Sweeping eastwards, it stopped at Macedonia, land-locked between Albania and Bulgaria, bordered to the north by Kosovo and Serbia and to the south by Greece. Until that moment I'd had only a vague idea of where Macedonia was on the map. It looked so far away. But then he said, 'Why don't we go, later in the spring or early summer...? I have a bird-guide friend who can show us the best locations. Would you like to come...? Fantastic birds—and the wild flowers and butterflies...' Then he turned the pages of the atlas to the northerly British Isles. He pointed to the Outer Hebrides and said, 'There's somewhere I've always wanted to go, too. Wild, with wonderful seabirds...'

Even Scotland looked very far away. But I had to break out of my winter cocoon, it was time to move and adjust and embrace new opportunities. I knew that the trips James was describing would be arduous, trekking for hours at a time every day, and although I was walking-fit, he was younger and stronger than I am. There would be relentless schedules of early mornings (and, knowing his sociable tendencies, late nights). But the seeds had been sown. I decided to take no notice of my reservations. I refused to listen to them. We made an outline plan:

looking ahead, we would go to Macedonia in April, and then to Scotland in late May or early June. Like a bird on passage preparing for flight, I was ready. The migration-rivers had me in their flow. I would follow where they took me.

The first of these 'migrations' came sooner than I had imagined; it began on an impromptu birding trip to southern Spain. At the last minute James had been engaged as a guide, and ignoring my Garbo-tendencies he insisted I join the group. 'You've got to come.' *Carpe diem,* I thought. After all, migration isn't running away, nor is it a one-way street. Migration in the bird world is about survival, it's part of the purpose of life. So I did. I seized the day.

We flew to Almería in southern Spain, and the next day we were exploring the Cabo de Gata-Níjar *parque natural* where, perched on a boulder high above us, singing under a burning sun and cloudless sky, a blue rock thrush was silhouetted over a dried-up riverbed meandering across the valley. Cradled by hills verdant with Mediterranean spurge, asphodel and tamarisk, the track led higher and higher to the crater of a volcano that fifteen million years ago had spurted fire and molten rock from beneath the earth's crust. We walked up into the hills through a landscape of prickly pears, agave, rock-roses and wild herbs, past a deserted house and an abandoned car chassis, to where clouded yellow butterflies flitter along the path, and where the ocellated lizard makes his home with grasshoppers and stick-insects. Corn buntings were piping their jangly-keys song, crested larks whistled, black wheatears flew from rock to rock with giveaway flash of white tail feathers. Aromas of wild thyme and lavender wafted over phlomis in full yellow flower, and a black-spotted blue butterfly settled on magenta convolvulus that thrives everywhere on this terrain.

After climbing for a mile we came to the now grass-covered crater. Seeking the shade of a solitary almond tree, we lay on the baked ground surrounded by mountains. Looking up into the shiny green leaves I could see a nest—a large, wide raft of coarse twigs and dried mud. Within minutes, a female red-backed shrike fluttered into the far side of the tree, creamy fronted with a greyish-brown crown and eyestripe, chestnut winged. She hopped along a branch for a few moments, balancing with a flicker of her long brown tail bordered with white, showing surprisingly little sign of agitation at our presence.

As we walked back down from the crater, something was moving in an even greener and shinier almond tree. Blending with the leaves, a couple of wood warblers were hopping from branch to branch, perching briefly before darting on: two plump yellow-green birds on passage from West Africa where they had overwintered in the dense tree cover of Ivory Coast and Congo. On a three-week-long flight these tiny bundles of feathers had travelled for two and a half thousand miles across the Sahara and up into Spain. From here they would fly on to Wales where, at the culmination of their journey, they would nest and breed in the oak and beech woods of Wales and the West Country, spending the summer living alongside pied flycatchers that frequently share territory with them. A dead branch was sticking out from the far side of our almond tree, and perched on it was, indeed, a pied flycatcher in smart black and white livery: even during their short stay in this valley, the two birds had sought each other out.

Spanish marbled-white butterflies, vivid black and white, flickered over the grasses. The wood warblers hopped around in and out of the leaves, looking for beetles, flies and aphids, sometimes visible, sometimes not: *Phylloscopus sibilatrix*, 'whistling leaf-explorer' or 'leaf-watcher' searching for insects on the undersides of leaves. The tree seemed alive with these 'yellow wrens', sylvan sylphs with lemon throat and eyestripe, olive-green back, long wings folded over the tail, ivory underparts blending into the dappled light of shifting leaf shadows. From time to time we could make out the white trim of the wing feathers. Green Wrens some call them, others Wood-Wren or Barrow-Bird—and Shaking Pettychaps from the trembling voice.

We continued walking down the mountainside to the parched riverbed, under an afternoon sun so scorching it was easy to believe that in billions of years' time the earth will burn out and morph into a diamond the size of a massive meteorite. Passing the wreck of the 1960s car that had driven up the track some fifty years ago, we heard later how the driver had broken down and abandoned the vehicle while he went to seek help. Overnight, flash-floods tore rocks and boulders from their moorings higher up, hurling them on to the car, smashing the windows and crumpling the chassis. Over the years, walkers had added more stones to the cairn over the ruined chassis as it rusted away. Someone had placed a goat skull there. Golgotha in the sierras.

The wood warbler is a bird more often heard than seen, its passionate trill trembling the tiny body as it makes music that's been called 'the song of the woods', a silvery piping trill fol-lowed by a whistling *zzzzip*. It's been compared to the sound of a coin spinning on marble, or to raindrops scattering through the leaves—*a woodland song like no other*, in the opinion of

W. H. Hudson. *Its ways and movements and general happiness*, wrote Sir Edward Grey in 1927, *animate the beauty of young beech leaves [with] shivering and sibilant sound.* Wood warblers, spirit of the oakwoods since the Holocene.

Why does a wood warbler sing so sweetly? Why do birds sing at all? Why such beautiful music? Is beauty a principle of natural selection? Why is it that in most cases it's the male who sings? Do birds sing for pleasure and pure joy? Does self-expression or emotional release come into it? If so, why doesn't the female sing? Darwin's initial response to these questions was to equivocate: *Naturalists are much divided with respect to the object of the singing of birds.* Until his time, the beauty of birdsong was seen as the ultimate expression of God's creative powers, early ornithologists opining that it was God's gift to mankind. But Darwin's further observations led him to the conclusion, in parallel with sexual selection and territorial defence, that *It is probable that nearly the same emotions [tenderness, love, devotion, as well as the sense of triumph and ardour for war], but much weaker and far less complex, are felt by birds when the male pours forth his full volume of song, in rivalry with other males, to captivate the female.*

As time went on, Darwin proposed that the softer, more musical notes of birdsong are designed to woo a prospective breeding partner, that harsh sounds denote aggression for defending territory, and plaintive tones express fear when threatened by predators. *The sounds uttered by birds offer in several respects the nearest analogy to language, for all the members of the same species utter the same instinctive cries expressive of their emotions.* Certainly the cry of a bird being attacked sounds like panic, and some birdsong is domestic communication: a pair of bullfinches foraging in dense vegetation keep in contact with constant piping calls, some pairs even singing antiphonally, creating duets that sound like a single bird.

Following Darwin's lead, the ethologist W. H. Thorpe, working in Cambridge in the mid-twentieth century, thought it plausible that birdsong is *often an expression of irrepressible joy*. He concluded that birds do sing for pleasure or happiness, as part of their communication with a mate. *The songs of birds can be regarded as a first step towards true artistic creation and expression,* he wrote. A colleague of Thorpe's, Joan Hall-Craggs, concluded that birds share musical intelligibility with humans, a privilege she considered exclusive to birds and mammals. Hall-Craggs' observations on blackbird song in a Cambridge garden show how the bird will repeat ('practise') musical themes until it achieves a song with shape and balance which has a beginning, a rise and fall, and an ending. For which there may be a purpose: in the early twentieth century Henry Eliot Howard showed how the melodic elaboration of birdsong followed rather than preceded the act of sexual union, intensifying when the female was laying eggs, a very different song from the assertive territorial song of earlier in the breeding cycle.

Darwin became convinced that birdsong has an element of sexual selection in competing for females, borne out by an early twenty-first-century observation that a nightingale stops singing once the brood hatches, but resumes if breeding fails, hoping to attract a female again. Studies show that females respond to more elaborate songs by building nests more quickly, and in research on canaries in the 1960s, some rapid two-note trills, inaudible to the human ear at seventeen times per second, were found to stimulate the brain of the female bird and cause her to solicit for copulation.

These sounds are difficult to make. The entire respiratory

system of the bird is engaged in the production of song, as are the testes (fraudsters used to inject female canaries so that they could sell them as caged songbirds). Castrating a cockerel ends its crowing, and in a 1960s study a castrated chaffinch stopped singing but two years later, on being given testosterone, it began to sing again. The vocal centres in the brains of songbirds are larger in males than in females, only a very few of whom sing, and are larger in bird species that have better repertoires. Studies show that males with larger song repertoires are preferred by females: the better the song the higher quality the potential partner. Song serves as a keep-out signal to other birds as well as a mating invitation, so a superior song ensures better territory as well as better partners.

For centuries nobody could work out how birdsong was produced. From Aristotle onwards it was thought the tongue must be the main organ of sound, but although all birds have tongues, they play no part in vocalisation (except in parrots, another bird fact to delight me). In 1600 Ulisse Aldrovandi observed how a bird whose head had been removed could still sing while reflexes remained, proving that the source of the sound was below the head. Long before the days of endoscopes Sir John Hunter, working from dead specimens in the late eighteenth century, observed that the 'muscles of the larynx' were more developed in birds with the best songs, like the nightingale, and were larger in males than in females. He speculated about the role of 'air sacs', an extension of the avian respiratory system, that are now known to act as bellows in producing song.

Eventually it was discovered that birds produce song not with vocal chords at all, but with a syrinx, a pair of bilaterally symmetric valves at the base of the trachea where it forks into the lungs. Vibrations off the walls of the syrinx (Greek for 'pan pipes') create oscillations with the flow of air through a bar of cartilage called a pessulus. Adjoining air sacs resonate with sound waves that are made by connective tissue inside the syrinx past which the bird expels air, controlling both pitch and volume by increasing the force of the exhalation. The structure of the syrinx enables it to produce more than one sound at a time: muscles altering the tension of membranes and bronchial openings (whose action may close off airflow) allow the opposite sides of the trachea to operate independently, producing two notes at once. High- and low-frequency sounds are produced by right and left sides of the syrinx respectively, at a rate of seventeen times per second. To the human ear this sounds like a continuous trill, but the female bird hears the finer detail of a language that eludes us.

Back in the 1960s Bill Thorpe pioneered the use of sound spectography for the detailed analysis of birdsong (a spectogram is a graph which measures frequency over time). It enabled ornithologists to analyse the range of bird notes and scales so different to our music, to track frequencies inaudible to the human ear, and to trace harmonic intervals unique to birdsong. Although Gilbert White was convinced an owl hoots in B flat, human music terminology being the only vocabulary we have, those terms and descriptions are inexact when it comes to birds. We talk of pitch and tone, scale and consonance, transition and sequence, we assign a minor or a major key to a particular song, we use words like chorus and cantata, fugue and symphony, ensemble and cadenza. But these definitions can only be rough equivalents for bird music. The earliest attempt to notate birdsong in written music was the *Musurgia universalis* of 1650 when Athanasius Kircher had a go at transcribing songs of the nightingale, chickens, a cuckoo and a quail, with each bird illustrated singing their heart out, quaintly but inadequately represented in musical notation. Where that doesn't succeed, birdsong is more easily interpreted by mnemonic rhymes: the 'cock-a-doodle-do' of the fowl, the 'little bit of bread and no cheese' of the yellowhammer, the 'to-wit-to-woo' of the tawny owl. But the fact is, the music of birdsong is not our music, it's a language belonging to another world, one so captivating that the Sufi poet Hafiz, on hearing the cry of the golden plover, wrote, *if after a thousand years that sound should flow over my tomb, my bones uprising in their gladness would dance in the sepulchre.*

Birdsong is both innate *and* learned. It was observed by Aristotle early in the history of ornithology that *Among small birds some have songs that are different from their parents, if they have been reared away from the nest and have heard other birds singing.* Bill Thorpe took this a step further: he found that every species has a distinctive song, which is partly acquired, but invariably with an innate core characteristic. His experiments on chaffinches kept in auditory isolation show that they sing with a tonal quality recognisably unique to the species, even though the song itself may be unlike that of the usual chaffinch. A bird has to *learn* the song of its species, even the supreme songster the nightingale does. A fledgling nightingale, starting to warble in late spring, begins with a 'subsong' as it sings to itself, refining and developing the song gradually until it achieves full throttle.

Birds learn to mimic, too. It's not just the starling that sounds like your car alarm going off or a mobile phone ringing: caged birds can learn to whistle tunes taught to them, and repeat words as well as regular household sounds. Captive birds have been trained to talk, pipe and whistle since Roman times. Mozart kept a pet starling to inspire him (allegedly it could whistle its owner's compositions back to him). He gave it an elaborate funeral when it died, and his divertimento 'Musical Joke' has the imprint of the starling repertoire on it. Birds kept in auditory isolation from other birds copy the sounds of tape-recorder switches, or the stridulation of crickets. In the 1960s researchers noted that blackbirds regularly incorporate calls of other species such as greenfinches, nuthatches, great tits and goldfinches, as well as mechanical sounds, in their range. There's biological purpose to this ability, in that it's been shown that male birds with a larger repertoire enjoy greater reproductive success.

No wonder learning to recognise birdsong is a minefield. It makes me feel infinitely better about being a beginner—a permanent one probably, in the case of birdsong.

A visitor to Planet Earth from another galaxy might find music the most puzzling of human activities: how is it that music, including birdsong, appears to have the ability to restore humans to themselves, even to transport them beyond themselves? When human music and birdsong come together, a further dimension is created. The Finnish composer Einojuhani Rautavaara's 'Cantus Arcticus', a triptych subtitled 'A Concerto for Birds and Orchestra', uses the cries of birds recorded by him near the Arctic Circle on the bogs of Liminka in northern Finland. Rautavaara was by nature a romantic, a mystic even, and his composition conjures the medieval worldview of a cosmos revealed in musical ratios, the music of the spheres, musical harmony mirroring the harmony of creation. Merging birdsong with orchestral instruments he creates a mysterious beauty as a flute duet opens the piece before other woodwinds join in, followed by the birds. The bird cries gradually become more distinct, and the orchestra finds its motifs in birdsong while the birds sing in the background. A slowed-down recording of the song of the shore lark is followed by the sound of whooper swans migrating in a long crescendo for orchestra until both birdsong and orchestra fade into the distance.

Schopenhauer regarded music as the key to ultimate reality, portraying the flow of life more directly than all the other arts. Nietzsche maintained that music helps us transcend life's essential tragedy. Listening to a Bach cello suite played live by a friend in a small room in Italy once, I had the experience of my body *becoming* the music. There was no separation, as if it was being played deep inside a 'me' that had merged with the music and disappeared inside it. Some musicians achieve this crossing of time into timelessness, Arvo Pärt one of them. He took his inspiration from love of nature, its sounds and its silences, and his compositions express the purity of a lost paradise: his music has been called 'one big prayer'. St Augustine wrote that *when you sing you pray twice over*, and the anthropologist Claude Lévi-Strauss concluded that *the musical creator is a being comparable to the gods, and music itself the supreme mystery of the science of man*, a secret we share with the birds, its effects remaining obscure despite vain attempts at analysis.

Could it have been that same wood warbler I'd seen on passage in Spain when, a year later in spring, James and I were walking through the Welsh hillsides? Fanciful perhaps, but I liked to think so. The collective noun for wood warblers is a 'cord', and it pleased me to imagine a chain of connections linking that little green wren on its regular annual migration near Almería, to a wooded ravine at the southern edge of Snowdonia. We were climbing through Coed Garth Gell where a ravine drops down steeply to a torrent of white water tumbling and roaring over giant boulders below. In the bed of this deep cleft in the earth, gold used to be mined from under the rushing river where a grey wagtail was hopping around on fallen rocks to the roar of the water. Underfoot, wood sorrel with delicate purple-veined petals and heart-shaped leaves covered patches of ground between mossed tree roots. Bilberry was in early fruit, hanging like orange lanterns in the understorey. Ghostly lichens gave off silver light, crusting the weathered bark of trees contorted by wind, the branches cloaked with unearthly bryophytes of grey-greens and shades of dark emerald. Through birch trees we could see across to Cadr Idris, a mist of blues and purples under cottonwool clouds in an azure sky. The oaks were still almost leafless, tinged with green where leaf buds were bursting, but it was among the new leaves of a beech tree that we caught a movement, a flicker: a wood warbler within easy binocular view. He was so near he must have seen us. We waited, hardly breathing as he let forth a heart-stopping song that filled the woods, a musical trill interspersed with plaintive, penetrating calling notes. It was spellbinding. The lemony-primrose throat of this tiny bird swelled with sound, little feathered creature of greenish plumage merging with the translucent spring leaves of the woodland around it.

We were all too briefly in the presence of one of the holy trinity of the Welsh oakwoods—the wood warbler, the pied flycatcher and the redstart—and were lucky enough that day to see the other two as well. Further along into the trees we caught sight of a pied flycatcher, restless little bird with large eyes, black and white in dappled woodland light flitting among lichens and mosses. Later we were granted a glimpse of a male redstart whose orange-red tail gave it away, smart firetail with robin-red breast and slate-grey back, dark face and head with a white streak on its forehead, uttering his sweet melancholic *hweet* notes into the hillside.

Back in Coed Garth Gell, our wood warbler had been singing over the sound of rushing water, which was considerable. It's been shown that noisy habitats affect the types of songs birds use: great tits, instead of singing louder against competition, change frequency or pitch, whereas city nightingales in Berlin sing louder by up to fourteen decibels than their rural counterparts, notching up the volume on weekday mornings during rush hour when traffic is at its loudest, reaching (according to laboratory studies) around ninety decibels.

Among the artistic hierarchy, the birds are probably the greatest musicians to inhabit our planet, remarked the composer Olivier Messiaen. Birdsong fascinated him from an early age after his teacher Paul Dukas encouraged him to *listen to the birds.* From boyhood Messiaen loved the sounds and rhythms of nature, the wind and the waves and the cadences and rhythms of birdcalls. With the help of ornithologists, binoculars and a tape recorder, he travelled through France notating on paper the songs he heard around him *like an exercise in aural training.* He learned to listen to nature in a way never previously done by musicians. Walking through France's forests and the bird markets of Paris, scribbling and transcribing the sounds he heard, he became a more accomplished ornithologist than any previous composer, and a more musical observer of birdsong than any previous ornithologist.

To Messiaen the world of nature was no less real—was in fact a more perfect reality—than the world of human civilisation. Messiaen's love of birds and his religion were closely connected: a devout Catholic, he gave creative expression to his faith through his music, often using birdsong in his compositions. His music-theology was not in the vein of sin and guilt: it was one of joy, divine love, beauty and redemption, and as such it came to his aid in darker times.

> In my hours of gloom, when I am suddenly aware of my own futility, when every musical idiom—classical, oriental, ancient, modern and ultramodern—appears to me as no more than admirable, painstaking experimentation, without any ultimate justification, what is left for me but to seek out the true lost face of music somewhere off in the forest, in the field, in the mountains or on the seashore, among the birds.

For Messiaen, birds manifested the music inherent in creation: *They are our desire for light, for stars, for rainbows, and for jubilant songs.*

Messiaen began to note down birdsong in the Aube when on holiday in his early teens. Taken prisoner by the Germans in 1940 at the age of thirty-one, and transported to a POW camp, he met among the inmates a clarinettist, a violinist and a cellist. He managed to obtain paper and pencil from a sympathetic guard who also helped acquire the required instruments, and Messaien wrote a short trio for his fellow musicians which developed into the 'Quartet for the End of Time', *Quatuor pour la fin du temps*. It was premiered at the camp to an audience of four hundred fellow prisoners and guards, using a decrepit clarinet, decrepit violin and decrepit cello, with the composer himself playing a decrepit piano. On 15 January 1941, outdoors in the cold and rain, the quartet which would become a modern classic had its first performance. *Never was I listened to with such rapt attention and comprehension,* remarked Messiaen afterwards.

He conceived the *Quatuor* as liturgy as much as music, writing in a preface, *Between three and four in the morning, the awakening of birds: a solo blackbird or nightingale improvises, surrounded by a shimmer of sound, by a halo of trills lost very high in the trees. Transpose this onto a religious plane and you have the harmonious silence of Heaven.* In the third movement, 'Abîme des oiseaux', he experiments with a solo clarinet for birdsong. *The abyss is Time with its sadness, its weariness. The birds are the opposite to Time.*

After the Second World War Messiaen had a house built south of Grenoble where he composed much of the rest of his music, using notations scribbled down in the open air. He continued to regard birdsong as divinely inspired. But birds do not sing in Western musical modes. Transcribed, their songs can sound dissonant, jarring, chaotic, and the unique harmonic system of Messiaen's music can on first acquaintance be daunting. In this composer's hands though it doesn't take long for the enchantment to work as birds flit in and out of the musical textures in the flutes, percussion and woodwind. His avant-garde creations are full of light, colour, song and joy. In his 1953 orchestral work 'Réveil des oiseaux' the entire piece is built from birdsong: a dawn chorus for orchestra, it's his only composition to make exclusive use of birdsong for all its material. Recorded by him in the Jura, it follows the birds from three o'clock in the morning, through the dawn chorus to the silence of midday, broken only by brief calls from two chaffinches (violins), a blackbird (violin), the drumming of a woodpecker (wood-block), and the call of the cuckoo (Chinese blocks). He dedicates the piece *to the blackbirds, thrushes, nightingales, orioles, robins, warblers, and all the birds of our forests.*

'Catalogue d'oiseaux', completed in 1958, perhaps the best known of Messiaen's bird compositions, is a collection of thirteen pieces in which, although birdsong constitutes the essential material, he combines it with other sounds of nature too. Golden oriole, tawny owl, curlew and short-toed lark are transcribed in the context of their ambient sounds: as he himself wrote, *In 'Catalogue' I tried to copy exactly the song of a bird typical of a region, surrounded by the neighbouring birds of its habitat. The compromise,* he acknowledged, was that *I am obliged to transcribe the song at a slower tempo . . . and even four octaves lower . . . I am obliged to suppress the very small intervals which our instruments cannot play.* Even in the hands of a genius, replication of birdsong remains elusive.

When I was a child, having proved to my despairing teachers that I had no talent as an instrumentalist, partly but not entirely because of a complete incapacity to sightread, I took up with a turntable instead. Listening to classical music became a lifelong passion, on vinyl and every medium since, including live performance. One enduring memory is of going to hear Peter Pears sing his last performance at Snape, his swansong fading over the marshes as Britten's 'Serenade for Tenor Horn and Strings' died away into the still evening. And afterwards, wandering out towards the reedbeds, seeing a curlew fly over the marshes, hearing reed buntings singing, sedge warblers grating, skylarks calling high above, and watching swallows swooping and flicking in the late-evening light. There's a changeless quality to Snape with its marshes, a timelessness untouched by its increasing popularity, although I am glad to have known the place in the early days of its simplicity when the outlying warehouses were derelict, the boardwalks almost deserted, and where I first heard Britten's 'Sinfonia da Requiem' not long after his death.

I was on my way back to the Suffolk coast to walk the footpaths around Benjamin Britten's old home near Aldeburgh. A keen birdwatcher and accomplished ornithologist (his favourite bird was the nightingale), Britten would walk every day—his 'composing walks' as he called them. During these strolls, he would mull over his morning's composition, returning to rework it: *I work while I'm walking.* The walking, the landscape, the birds were central to his creativity, and this part of Suffolk hasn't changed much since his time. Unsuitable for agriculture and left to its natural devices (more or less), the coastline is a mosaic of mature woodland and coniferous forests, heath and gorseland where nightjars, woodpeckers and stonechats—and even the Dartford warbler—can be found. Fen and marsh are wintering grounds of Arctic and subarctic wildfowl and geese, and the signature sound of reeds rubbing against each other in the wind continues to whisper and hiss as it has always done. It's the land of William Plomer's 'Curlew River' set to music by Britten:

> in our reedy Fens
> the Curlew River runs...

That night I stayed overnight near Woodbridge with my daughter, and slept in her garden studio looking out over arable fields and woods. I'd dropped off to sleep only to be woken after midnight by a very loud bird singing in the scrub outside the window. At first I was annoyed. I was tired and wanted to sleep, but as I lay and listened I realised what I was hearing. I fell under its spell. It was a nightingale. Back from his wintering grounds, the male bird was proclaiming territory and announcing his availability to a female. He sang, resting only for short intervals, until after three in the morning. I recorded some of the sequences on my phone, incredulous at my luck. By the time the nightingale finished singing I was ready to sleep. But daylight was breaking and the dawn chorus started up. It was the turn of all the other birds to make music. Never have I had such an enchanted sleepless night.

The next day the plan was to follow in Benjamin Britten's footsteps, walking from his home at The Red House on the edge of Aldeburgh to listen for sounds he'd listened to, to hear echoes of a life in music retrieved on a cold afternoon thirty-five years after his death. A spreading oak tree in front of the house was still leafless, giant branches stretching out to a clear sky. Chris Watson was to lead us, sound-man *extraordinaire* who earlier that year had been exploring Britten's well-trodden tracks with his microphones, recording some of the natural sounds the composer would have heard as he paced solitary steps from his front door across the heath.

A path leads over the edge of the gorse-strewn golf course and along a lane to an overgrown, single-track railway running north to Sheepwash Crossing at Thorpeness. Here at a nature reserve known as The Fens, marsh harriers roost in the reedbeds, nightjars clap their nocturnal dance as they churr in the clearings at midsummer. Britten would pause at the Meare with its tame swans and noisy seagulls, before turning south into the prevailing wind down the shingle beach, then make for home across North Warren marshes. His spirit lingers in the polyphony of wind, sea, shingle and birdcalls, heard in the places he walked until his death in 1976. Absorbing wordless inspiration. Resting the restless brain in the rhythms of nature.

What relief to stop the chatter. Walking to listen. Keeping silence. Stopping to hear. As we crossed the heath that dull March afternoon, a cold wind started to blow from the east. Pausing beneath an ageing pine, intent on ambient sound, could we hear the subdued roar of the distant sea? No, it was the sound of the wind moving through dense green needles, dropping to a whisper as it poured through the bare branches of a beech tree. Waves of wind. Through a line of poplars came a glimpse of the marshes across the fields where strands of water shone pewter in muted light. We walked to the disused railway line, a long tunnel of leafless scrub and native trees disappearing into an ever-receding vanishing point. The beauty of trees in late winter, when mosses and lichens come into their own, sudden brightnesses, rich greens glowing in a monotone woodscape. Bracket fungus on a beech trunk. A glade of silver birch on a carpet of dull gold bracken. A pond, glinting water.

MARCH

There's a gap in the thicket where a ditch cut into the reeds leads to stretches of distant water. Here wildfowl float and fly and feed. Near this ditch, Chris Watson had recorded the shriek of the water rail, a noise like a stuck pig issuing from a shy waterbird seldom seen but known by its unearthly cry. In May, when the footpath is a three-mile-long arbour of greens, he had recorded the chorus of summer migrants, as blackcaps and willow warblers, whitethroats and chiffchaffs, garden warblers and nightingales join with our resident songsters in the great symphony of the dawn.

That March day you would, if careless, if wrapped in your own thoughts, think it a quiet place. Once you are alerted to the task of listening, however, myriad sounds are layered into the wind. Frequencies beyond our musical notation with some, like radio waves, beyond the grasp of human hearing, manna to the imagination. The plaintive call of the curlew haunts these water-scapes, wistful music counterpointed by the whistling chorus of teal, the gargle of tufted duck, the piping of pintail. The wail of a lone lapwing. Silences. A great tit starts up from a hawthorn tree near to us, 'teacher teacher', changing its tune as we approach to a sharp territorial chatter. Long-tailed tits bounce among bare branches, *tseeptseep*-ing and clicking. A bluetit chitters and whistles in alarm. A pair of magpies rattle in the undergrowth. A sudden throaty squawk, rough edged: a grey heron beside a watery scrape where a pair of mute swans float.

We came to The Fens, where reedbeds wait for harriers to float in to roost as the light fades, seeking safety against dark-ness. In less clement weathers, to the patter of rain and in the silence of snow, the flatlands of *dyke, marsh and mere* of 'Curlew River' are places of plainsong where the solitary bittern booms, barn owls screech, kingfishers pipe and tawny owls hoot at night. As we neared human habitation at Thorpeness a robin hopped into full view on top of an elder and opened its syrinx, braving us to come any nearer, the melancholy winter music declaring strident ownership. A sudden wren tuttutted at full volume as we passed. A cloud of jackdaws and rooks flew overhead towards their evening roost, chakking and cawing, suddenly hectic, scattered by a sparrowhawk in a whoosh of wings. And beneath our feet, white feathers the remains of yesterday's kill, a black-headed gull.

We started back along the beach at Thorpeness, a bevy of house sparrows chattering and tweeting in the bushes, familiar passerines now returning after decades of decline, sounds Britten would have been familiar with in days when they were two a penny. From someone's front garden a parakeet screeched, foreign discord in this most East Anglian of coastlines. The sound of our feet crunching on the shingle bank masked the boom of the sea behind it, the muffled swish of waves rolling on to shingle. In heavier weather, the rhythmic roar and crash of the waves will drown out the raucous cry of the seagull—even the submerged church bells of Dunwich, the city under the sea a few miles north along the coast, whose bells fishermen hear ringing from under the water.

Antiphonal sounds of sea and wind serenaded the silent flight of a distant marsh harrier as it dropped into the reedbeds at North Warren. The buzz of traffic—always that, the weft of any soundscape in our age of noise—prevailed as we crossed the road. We entered the nature reserve through a track lined with bramble and blackthorn. A few wildfowl flew in, a skein of barnacle geese smart in black and white livery in the evening light. The softer profile of the larger greylags, honking over the marshes. Dark shapes of wintering ducks gathering in groups on the patches of water, preparing for nightfall. Sounds of dusking waterbirds filling the air, an orchestra of plaintive piping and chickering. A cygnet drifting past into the evening silence.

Driving home that evening, I listened to a talk by Will Self on the car radio. He convinced me that in 1922, the year the BBC started broadcasting, a machine related to a transmitter was invented: a 'remitter' with the ability to retrieve and remit (re-transmit) all past radio signals. There is nothing, he said, that it couldn't find, since radio waves retain their content no matter how widely dispersed or how long ago. He asserted that this remitter can retrieve signals from the entire history of broadcasting and from all corners of the earth. Re-collecting. Recollecting. The Recording Angel of our time. So plausible was he, and so enchanting the idea, that I was bamboozled into believing him—but who knows, maybe there's something in it: even if the remitter doesn't exist, maybe all sounds last for ever, beyond our hearing. In any case, the idea enriched my experience of recollecting Britten's footsteps, re-collecting the sounds he heard in nature. Were we retrieving them too? Those sounds of nature that had stirred his imagination and kindled his creativity as he walked, were they there in the radio waves around us, woven invisibly into the ether, harmonies in a tapestry of sound? The call of the curlew, the many voices of the wind in the trees, the distant percussion of the sea, the music of waves crashing on to shingle and the wistful, wintry trill of waterfowl still there, working their ways into his orchestral compositions as the final phrases of the 'Sinfonia da Requiem' fade into silence and the land of 'Curlew River' sleeps.

Back home, I walked down a track leading into woods not far from the village. The first dog violets dazzled purple from the verge, and golden stars of celandine shone in the grass. Hidden among trees is a secluded pond surrounded by larch and Scots pine, silver birch and alder where a badgers' sett undermines the bank in the shade of a willow. The water is thickly reeded and left to itself, just beginning to show green shoots among the beige fronds of winter, unmanaged anomaly in intensively farmed fields. Settling to sit on a log by the shallows, needing solitude that spring day, I disturbed a basking pike, long and grey and eerie. With a muscular jump it plopped into the mud and disappeared underneath circles of widening ripples. I lingered in the silence as the water turned to silk. Later in the summer I would return to this place often, watching skaters skating over the surface of the water, dragonflies darting, butterflies flitting, when the pure white of waterlily petals would be reflected upside down in the still water. For now, there was just the hurr of wood pigeons' wings, a branch creaking, collared doves cooing. The plop of a rising fish, ripples furrowing the water lightly, disturbing the mirrored sky. The weird unearthly call of a heron rasped the silence. A movement in the reeds was followed by a scratchy song, the unmistakable throaty trill of a reed warbler. Another rustle, then a warning call, a nasal screech followed by long silence. A little bird who had survived the long migration from Africa, making it back to his breeding ground, this unremarkable reedbed in Essex, to build a nest and raise a brood again.

A pair of moorhens dabbled in the water by the edge of the reeds. Suddenly a reed warbler darted out from the fluffy plume of a reed and clutched the stem sideways on, balancing and swaying. After a few seconds he flew nimbly to another and balanced again. Graceful gymnast, sleek and elegant. As I watched him, pale brown with slender bill and long tail, a bird seldom glimpsed but often heard from the invisible life of the reeds, my reed warbler flew like a miniature torpedo from stem to stem, lithe bodied, swaying and bouncing before flying on. Then he shot off into the jungle of reeds. Twice I saw him later in the summer as I returned to my secret spot where the heron soars to his nest in the towering willow.

Thomas Bewick wrote that the reed warbler's song *has some times been mistaken in the North of England for that of the Nightingale*. Emma Turner, hermit of the reedbeds, called it 'the Nightingale of the Broads', describing the nest of the reed warbler as

> suspended between four or five reeds, about three-parts down the stalks, in a dense reed-bed. The supports are so carefully interwoven that the reeds look as if they had simply been thrust through the nest. There it hangs like a carefully slung cradle—swaying as the reeds sway... The nest is deep for so small a bird; it bulges slightly at the sides, and the rim turns inwards as if it had been slightly drawn up with a bit of elastic; and it is so deep that when brooding, the reed warbler almost vanishes from view.

John Clare elaborates: *it is not much larger then the inside of an hens eggshell it builds the out side of dead blades of grass small water weeds and lines it in a very workman like manner with the down of the old last year reeds.*

The trouble is, the cosy nest invites a brood parasite: the female cuckoo, who never makes her own bed, lays an egg directly into the reed warbler's nest, and leaves the latter to rear the foundling (Gilbert White calls this a *monstrous outrage on maternal affection*). Along with reed warblers, meadow pipits and dunnocks—and even occasionally the tiny wren—are targeted. Every day that March I'd been hoping for the song of the cuckoo to proclaim spring, the one birdsong that nobody, surely, can fail to recognise. But for several years now there has been no cuckoo within hearing distance of my village. I've had good views of them flying over Lakenheath Fen, and heard them on my daughter's patch in Suffolk, but my home patch is barren of cuckoos, and I feel deprived of something irreplaceable.

It's an unlikely mix, the burly thirteen-inch cuckoo with the delicate five-inch reed warbler, a shy and solitary bird. Cuckoos are striking creatures, with yellow legs and feet, eyes with yellow rim and irides. At a distance, in flight, the sleek body with ash- and slate-grey plumage, long tail, strongly barred underparts and two-foot pointed wingspan, could easily be mistaken for a falcon. Dubbed one of nature's most notorious fraudsters, the invading cuckoo may remove one of the host eggs before laying her own, sometimes eating it (noted by Aristotle: *it lays its eggs in the nests of small birds after devouring these birds' eggs*). The male cuckoo will even imitate a sparrowhawk, to which it has a passing resemblance, to distract the host bird and allow the female to nip in and lay her egg. To deceive their victims, cuckoos learn how to mimic specific songs, plumage, species behaviour—even egg coloration—in what has been called an evolutionary arms race, each constantly developing new ways of fooling the other. The natural selection of a cheat.

The female can lay twenty-five eggs in a season, each invasion taking a scant ten seconds (although rare, there are records of a cuckoo laying two eggs in one nest). She and her mate prepare by making an intense scrutiny of the nest-site, judging its readiness for incubation. Within two weeks the hatchling grows to at least three times the size of the native babies, yet the host parent apparently can't distinguish a cuckoo chick from its own, devoting its energy to feeding the intruder which, in return, will mercilessly eject other nestlings. It's a bird without remorse.

As in the human world. Nobody has done a research study, as far as I know, on the natural selection of cheats. Dante had a stab, though, in 'The Divine Comedy'. He depicts duplicity as an indelible stain on the human soul. He stuck people who cheat and lie and betray those who love and trust them in the deepest darkest coldest part of hell, at the profoundest depths of the pit closest to the monstrous three-headed Satan, imprisoned for eternity in the everlasting ice of their own hearts.

As in the human world also, when making for prey, cuckoos fly in a dead straight line, predator to prey. The cuckoo's song has long represented the coming of spring, but this popular favourite is underwritten with a lie: it's the song of the siren. The cuckoo employs vocal trickery (the honeyed smooth-talk of the human cheat) to stimulate the care it requires from the host bird. Starting up as winter passes into spring, the seductive sound of the trickster, a descending minor third in the key of C, lengthens to a longer interval as summer comes. *In April the Cuckoo comes, In May she'll stay, In June she changes her tune, In July she prepares to fly, Come August, go she must.*

*

Dwelling on human beings who cheat and lie and betray their loved ones would achieve nothing. It so happened that during March I was reading Proust's 'Time Regained', and he had words for me: *The whole art of living is to regard people who cause us suffering as, in a degree, enabling us to accept its divine form and thus populate our daily life with divinities.*

APRIL

Essex, Cambridgeshire, northern Greece,
wild Macedonia

joy

Through my sleep I hear a distant church bell chime the hour. Silence. A single bird awakens. A lone song floats into the dark, sleepy and faint. The solo grows gradually louder and more insistent. A bird answers. Another joins in. Over the next half-hour a crescendo builds up as birds of many voices add their sweet strains, until a symphony floods the early-morning light. John Clare's *hymn to sunrise*, music of another world. I cannot resent being woken up by the birds at daybreak: through April as the chorus grows fuller and louder until it reaches top volume in May, it's become a habit to listen to the dawn chorus for an hour or so, dozing off as the music fades. I've noticed how different the morning music is from bird-evensong with its more plaintive and reflective tone—in my garden dominated by thrush sounds, of the blackbird, the mistle thrush and sometimes, at the beginning of the month, even a lingering fieldfare—whereas the morning chorus sounds like one of pure joy, optimism and unadulterated hope.

As the days grew longer I became restless, a stirring of wings. For many months I'd had the idea of walking in John Clare's footsteps in what was once Northamptonshire, now Cambridgeshire, following his poems and natural-history prose across the habitats he haunted in his free time. April was the perfect time to find many of the wild flowers he loved, and the nesting birds of early spring he observed so closely. The weather was set fair for several days, the trees were in bud and nightingales were arriving back in England, so I decided to make the most of it before we left for Macedonia. I settled into a rented cottage I found in Glinton, opposite the church whose spire Clare could see from the fields at Helpston, and to whose church schoolroom he walked every day and back as a boy. I unfolded the Ordnance Survey map and traced my daily itineraries—my pilgrimage—marking a series of walks where I would explore places he loved and wrote about: Swordy Well, disappeared as he knew it but now a nature reserve with rare butterflies and chalkland wild flowers, the open sweep of Emmonsales Heath, and the woods at Castor Hanglands where Clare found nightingales' nests. I wanted to find the early spring flowers he describes with such affection, and to watch out for the birds that were his companions on his *soodlings*, his saunterings. I would spend the days in the company of a man I had come to love: following in his tracks by day, and reading his words by night, he became a living presence.

I was rewarded, finding many of his favourites including an early purple orchid in exactly the spot he described in Royce Wood. Cowslips were growing just as he found them at Lolham Bridges, and the first pasque flowers were peeping through at Barnack Hills and Holes. I heard and saw many of his birds, but the peak experience would be listening to nightingales on Bainton Heath. Every evening as I returned home from my ramblings, driving past his cottage next to the pub in Helpston, I imagined him sitting there with his drinking mates, downing the ale of which he was perhaps over-fond, telling his nightingale joke. When

walking with a friend in the fields of Shaklwell we saw
a gentleman and lady listning very attentive by the side
of a shrubbery and when we came up we heard them
lavishing praises on the beautiful song of the Nightingale
which happend to be a thrush but it did it for them ...
such is the ignorance in large Citys that are nothing less
then over grown prisons that shut out the world and all
its beautys ...

The minstrel *par excellence* of the bird world is, of course, the
nightingale. It's pretty much a consensus: two thousand years
ago Pliny declared that *there is not a pipe or instrument in all the
world that can afford more musick than this pretty bird doth out of
that little throat.* In his day nightingales could sell for as much
as a slave, and over the centuries there are stories of caged
nightingales beating themselves to death against the bars. The
seventeenth-century author of 'The Compleat Angler' Izaak
Walton wrote that the nightingale *breathes such lowd sweet music
out of her littel instrument that it might make mankind to think
miracles are not ceased ... Lord, what music thou hast provided for the
saints in heaven, when thou givest bad men such music on earth!* Yet
the nightingale—just a plain brown bird with buff underparts
and a longish reddish tail—does not have the looks to match
its song: *it is not remarkable for the variety or richness of its plumage,*
commented Bewick.

Nightingales still sing on Bainton Heath near Helpston
where Clare heard them as a boy, his *clod brown* bird, *plain as a
sparrow* with *sweet melodious song.* Passionate birdwatcher before
the days of binoculars (he must have had exceptional eyesight),
Clare saw and heard nightingales often, and the descriptions
of them by a man who knew them from first-hand experience

and observation are hard to better. *Nightingales are very jealous of intrusions and their songs are hymns to privacy,* he wrote, and Thomas Bewick agreed with him that this bird of legend and mythology is a bit of a Garbo: *The Nightingale is a solitary bird,* he writes in 'British Birds', *and never unites in flocks like many of the smaller birds, but hides itself in the thickest parts of the bushes*... But fame sought the nightingale out: in the 'Odyssey', Homer tells the story of Philomel who, after being ravished by her brother-in-law, wreaked her revenge by being transformed by the gods into a nightingale, forever singing a lament—thereby embedding the poetic fallacy of the female songster. The legend passed into taxonomy: the French know the nightingale as *Rossignol Philomèle*, the Irish as *Filiméala* and the Hungarians as *Fülemüle*. In Persian literature the love of the nightingale for the rose is legendary, where the bird—female again as opposed to nature's, always the male—sings with its breast pierced by a thorn, so poignant is the outpouring music.

Clare would creep into dense undergrowth and sit for hours near an *old prickly thorn bush* hoping to see the bird on its nest—*one of them is of a darker brown then the other but I know not wether it be the male or the female.* But he wasn't always successful: *even their nests are very difficult to find as they are seldom found but by accident being hidden among the tall weeds that surround the roots and cover the woods undisturbed recesses.* The bird will resent discovery, to the point of abandoning its home: *The Nightingale keeps tweeting churring round / But leaves in silence when the nest is found*... When Clare did find a nest, he noted that it was made of oak leaves lined with moss, and scraps of grass, down and hair: *an hermit's mossy cell* he called it, envying what he coined the *pathless solitude* of *Luscinia megarhynchos*.

*

APRIL

Bainton Heath. I splashed through puddles as chill rose off the wet paths, swishing through water alongside gravel pits dug out for recreational fishing. It had been raining heavily that April afternoon, month of sudden showers, and there was no guarantee that the clouds wouldn't open again, nor that night-ingales would sing now the evening had turned cold. A willow warbler started up. The yaffle of a green woodpecker echoed from woods surrounding the heath. A train rumbled past to Peterborough, drowning out the underlying moan and swish of traffic on the A1. I stumbled across uneven land bordered by pylons, a site once a quarry and now a nature reserve, infilled with London rubble by the electricity board after the Second World War and used as a dumping ground for refuse. Lumps of coal, bricks, scraps of rusty wire. In this unlikely place, unrecognisable to Clare who knew it as open fields before the Enclosure Acts, I was nonetheless hoping to hear nightingales sing just as he had. As I glooped through the mud I thought of another place he loved, the woods at Castor Hanglands where I'd walked earlier in the day. It was midday. I'd passed into the solitude of this magical woodland, fresh and green in April sunshine, trees in new leaf where the light of spring filled a silver-birch glade. A carpet of bluebells radiated blue light, a bank of primroses glowed where a bumblebee hovered. Two nightingales had started singing and for several minutes the world seemed drenched in liquid music as the sweet song poured out of the thicket.

Her wings would tremble in her extacy
And feathers stand on end as twere with joy
and mouth wide open to release her heart
Of its out sobbing songs

—the song Clare captures in words, penetrating and stirring the heart with joy as it has done across time. 'Joy', one of John Clare's most commonly used words, finding joy all around him in the beauty of nature. *I love wild things almost to foolishness,* he wrote as he wandered these parts, this sweet suffering man who loved all things natural: *bees trees flowers all talked to me incessantly louder than the busy hum of men and who so wise as nature out of doors on the green grass by woods and streams under the beautiful sunny sky—daily communings with God and not a word spoken.*

Back at Bainton it was after nine o'clock and the light was failing fast. A nightingale started singing from one of the copses that dot the heath. Then another. Then four of them, pouring out music across the heath, quadraphonic, dominating all other sound with Clare's

> Chew-chew Chew-chew – and higher still
> Cheer-cheer Cheer-cheer – more loud and shrill
> Cheer-up Cheer-up cheer-up – and dropt
> Low Tweet tweet tweet jug jug jug . . .

The sky turned from dark blue to dark behind the trees. The evening shimmered with song echoing from the scrub, liquid gold notes—silver perhaps—a melody that defies language, music on a frequency from infinity, coming for reasons unknown to man from the syrinx of a small brown bird who flies into our countryside from tropical Africa each summer to pair, nest and rear its young before disappearing again to warmer places.

Every year I watch for the *bird that comes last and retires the earliest*, as Clare puts it, waiting for the avian aeronaut whose squealing lifts my gaze above the medieval rooftops of Saffron Walden a few miles from where I live. But I would have to wait: even though spring had been unseasonably warm that year, with many migrants arriving early from wintering quarters, swifts don't usually arrive until May. Once they do, I stop whatever I'm doing to watch them playing over the town, glinting in the early-morning sun, soot-brown, pale-chinned, silvery under-parts gleaming. Sickle-shaped long-winged fliers, gusting and playing, they are never still for an instant, spiralling high into the skies where they vanish from sight, preferring space to gravity, heaven to earth. Their generic *Apus*, 'without feet' (of course they have feet, but legs too weak for lift-off), came to swifts representing in heraldry the arms of a fourth son who is unlikely to inherit land: footloose, fancy free perhaps, certainly with no foothold: for a grounded swift is a dead swift unless helped back into flight (John Clare describes one he found: *its legs was very short and muffled with feathers like a bantum*).

How fast they fly as they rise, arrows in a never-ending dance, rising on thermals until they are tiny specks high above the roofline, disappearing from sight and leaving the blue sky empty. Later, as I return to my car in the quiet street after early-morning Mass, there they are again over the rooftops close to their nests in the eaves, chasing insects to feed their young.

*

Swift facts are among the most arresting of the bird world. They have absorbed me in hours of reading: member of an order (*Apodiformes*) of only three members, one of which is the hummingbird, they fly on average five hundred miles a day, clocking up two million miles in a lifetime that can span thirty years. That's four times to the moon and back, reaching a top speed of sixty to seventy miles an hour and flying as high as two miles above the earth. For three years the juveniles remain on the wing without landing, from the moment of fledging until after mating. Then they stop to nest, lay eggs and incubate. Swifts feed the young from a bolus, a saliva-bound ball of anything up to five hundred insects, gathered into a pouch situated just below the beak of the flying parent bird. Site-faithful, they pair for life, and sleep on the wing by closing down one half of the brain at a time.

They are adorable-looking birds, with large eyes and a small beak that opens into a wide gape. Their stunted legs have four toes, good only for clinging to vertical surfaces and shuffling about in the holes or crevices where they nest, often in buildings under the eaves, nests made of feathers, insect matter, butterflies' wings, grasses and straw, all caught on the wing and cemented with saliva. In spite of bird conservationists' best efforts, the number of swifts arriving in the UK has halved in a few decades. Re-roofing, over-assiduous restoration of old buildings and the predominance of modern house design devoid of swift-friendliness have caused their numbers to plummet. We could learn something from the Dutch: in Amsterdam it's illegal to re-roof or new-build without access for swifts.

Some cultures call swifts Rain Birds or Rain Swallows, since they fly in front of a storm feeding on insects caught in the updraughts (and avoiding stinging insects which, it's thought, they can identify by the sound they make). Swifts have learned to dodge rain by moving clockwise around low-pressure systems, even if it means flying an extra thousand miles. Returning home on the warm air that rises as the front lifts, at forty miles an hour with wingbeats at eight per second, decelerating to approach their nests and braking only at the last moment. The collective noun for swifts is a 'scream'—although in his book 'Nature Cure' Richard Mabey suggests it should be a 'hullaballoo'. John Clare thought them creatures from another world. He called them *develings*.

At last, the day had come, and the plans we'd laid in March were about to materialise. Flying to Thessaloniki for an overnight stay before driving on to Macedonia, I felt I had arrived in another world. We found our tiny hotel down a narrow street, squeezed between tall buildings. Taxis and trucks strained through double-parked cars as traders and pedestrians dodged slow-moving traffic. At the top of a winding stairway with cast-iron balustrade and snaking mahogany banister, my room faced the street. French windows opened on to a mini-balcony looking down over stalls selling fruit and vegetables. Sitting on a wooden chair outside his olive-oil shop, an old man was reading a newspaper. Two women in black were standing talking, laden with shopping bags. Constant cheeping of sparrows penetrated the din of scooters and honking horns in the humid evening heat. Antique bells clanged for Vespers.

A tunnel of sky above the street led my eye out into the

square where, in open spaces high above the setting sun, a volley of hundreds of swifts hurtled into vision, squealing, screaming, swerving, wheeling and diving, streamlined scimitars in flight with beaks agape for insects, a gyroscope of birds sky-racing, veering, skimming, banking and tumbling, falling vertiginous into long sailings on swept-back wings, floating and gliding on thermals. I was watching birds which have the ability to shoot like an arrow or turn on a coin, birds which fly three and a half thousand miles a week, week after week, catching raindrops in the air or skimming over the surface of water to drink, and mating on the wing in a split-second action.

Over this town, cradle of the Ancient Greek and Roman civilisations of western Europe, flew creatures that have been around for fifty million years, Ted Hughes' *mole-dark* swifts winnowing the air with shrill squeals. The priest, poet and birdwatcher R. S. Thomas loved to watch them in his adopted Wales as the day ended, finding relief from the world's follies as he followed their *unseen ribbons ... trailing upon the air*:

I have shut the mind
On fools. The 'phone's frenzy
Is over.

There in Thessaloniki, swifts scribbled the sky with aerodynamic gambits, plunging and roiling against the white sun as they have done for millennia on passage to their breeding grounds. They appeared to own the sky their kingdom, but when I walked out into the street twenty minutes later, all had disappeared apart from one lone acrobat looping and scything the sky.

Crossing the Greek border into southern Macedonia, first impressions were of a landscape of gentle hills and river valleys, rolling lowland foothills swathed in thick forest against a backdrop of mountains melting into blue-grey distances. Pastureland covered the green gorge cut by the Vardar, arterial river of Macedonia that rises above Skopje, bisects the country and flows through northern Greece before draining into the Aegean. We travelled through an underpopulated countryside dotted with rocky outcrops, meadows and smallholdings. Passing small pockets of subsistence agriculture we saw women in black in the fields, stooping over the weeding and hoeing and vegetable-picking, headscarved. Gnarled donkeys and skinny ponies pulled hay carts along the roads, slowed by the heat.

On our first full day we drove out of Prilep under blue skies to what felt like a vision of the Auvergne. Flower-filled fields at Mariovo folded into foothills whose meadows were ankle-deep in buttercups and orchids, creamy rock-roses and blue bellflowers, lemon mullein and ivory Star-of-Bethlehem. I nearly trod on a wild tortoise ruminating in the shade of feather grass, half hidden by asters and potentillas. She was a youngster, inquisitive and unafraid, with a glossy shell of gold and chocolate-brown markings. I held her, entranced. The sunshine had warmed her carapace. Flocks of parent starlings were flying around to the buzzing of bees and hum of insects, raucously finding food for their noisy, insatiable young. We watched a lesser grey shrike, a female, darting in and out of her nest lying low in a shrub, feeding her babies before settling down to brood. A long-legged buzzard flew over the ridge of the hill, and we heard quail calling. Calandra larks were flitting around, chunky larks with wing feathers white-edged, the full wingspan trimmed with a white frill. More shrikes—red-backed and woodchat—were busily feeding, often pausing to perch on top of a bush, exhibiting sleek outlines and stubby bills, immaculate markings and sturdy shrike-shapes. A cuckoo called. A hoopoe flew into the bare branches of a distant tree where it perched in crested profile. Just being there in that meadow was to be profoundly happy, an unforgettable and timeless experience of beauty.

Leaving the meadow, we took a narrow road winding up into the mountains. We stopped to talk to an old man resting against a stone wall with his sheepdog, looking down from the verge to pastureland where his sheep nibbled. He was uncommunicative, telling our Czech guide and friend Martin that it was a rotten job ('it stinks' was the translation). We continued towards the village of Stavica where Milcho Manchevski shot his haunting film 'Before the Rain', a picture of life in Macedonia just after its independence from Yugoslavia in 1991. The Communist past is most evident in the towns with their utilitarian, brutalist architecture, practical but run down. Tito left Macedonia an important legacy: he banned goat-grazing because it was denuding the land, and ever since then the countryside has recovered its diversity. Macedonia is enviably species-rich, boasting thirty-seven thousand different plants (several of them endemic), two hundred species of butterfly and an impressive list of lizards and snakes and turtles, mammals from brown bears and wolves and martens to the almost extinct Balkan lynx, pretty well every raptor and a wide range of birds both migratory and resident.

Houses nestled in the valley below us, scattered homesteads of local stone with roofs of terracotta tiles, a medley of dwellings and barns punctuated by grassy spaces, surrounded by deciduous trees and presided over by the open-arcaded belfry of the village church. Below us down the slope, a young shepherd was grazing his sheep. He made his way slowly up the hill, stabbing at the long grass with his crook. He had a shock of dark curly hair and sun-darkened skin, prematurely wrinkled by the outdoor life. Warm brown eyes, a friendly face, clean shaven. His flock straggled below, lambs and sheep with thick woolly coats and long wagging tails roaming over the lush grass, iron bells clanging. The scene was biblical. As was he, young shepherd with his crook. He approached, curious about us and what we were doing, but without a common language we made do with smiles and body-language. We were bird-watching, we gestured with binoculars. And taking pictures. Which appeared to puzzle him. He sat down not far away and watched as his dog settled placidly in the shade halfway between us and the sheep and lambs below. Silent but friendly, the shepherd stayed with knees drawn up, crook beside him, as we scanned for wheatears, turtledoves and an elusive wall-creeper James had spotted from the road.

All of a sudden a rosy starling flew into an acacia at the edge of the village. Stunningly smart, it perched high on an outlying branch, displaying the pink mantle, the rosy underparts, the pink legs and feet, the pinkish-orange bill. Sunlight caught the lilac iridescence of the black head feathers, and as the bird began to sing, shuffling its wings, they glistened too, greenish-black. The song belied the beauty of the bird, a squeaky jingling, short and harsh with rattling sounds—but no matter. Its beauty excused it. I discovered later that flocks of rosy starlings have been used to exterminate locusts in China: in Xinjiang, the use of insecticide has been almost eliminated as colonies of up to three thousand birds regularly harvest two or three tons of locusts in one day. The Orientals hold it to be a sacred bird for this reason, since it appears to offer divine deliverance from a plague of insects. We were to see, further along our journey through unspoiled Macedonia into northern Greece and the pelican lakes at Prespa, small flocks of these rosy starlings, elegant in pink and black plumage, every time a delight.

Although it was economically poor, there was a sense of plenty in the natural abundance of this landscape: the wealth of flower-filled meadows, the richness of colours and scents, the myriad sounds of insects, the ubiquity of butterflies and birds. Land of beekeepers and shepherds, it was the countryside of dreams, of bucolic films and visions, a glimpse of a world untouched by the culture of the profit margin, unstained by the shabby sideshows of human consumerism. The contrast with the impoverished habitats of my homeland soil could not have been more vivid.

Our Czech friend Martin who'd organised our itinerary in Macedonia had enlisted the expertise of a raptor-man who knew the nesting site of every vulture in Macedonia. Emil, whose life is devoted to their protection, is responsible for the wellbeing and protection of some of eastern Europe's rarest birds, in tandem with a national vulture-conservation project. Burly and strongly built, in his middle years, affable and with the weathered face of a man who spends much of his life outdoors, Emil agreed to take us on an expedition that would be more than likely to give us a sighting of Egyptian vultures—and with the promise of much more besides: a river trip along the shores of Lake Tikveš.

It could have been a scene out of 'The African Queen': a flat-bottomed boat with iron railings and tarpaulin roof, plastic chairs on deck around a rusty steel-framed table, moored up with a frayed rope. An outsize captain, all belly, squeezed into a tiny cabin behind a worn metalwork lever for forwards and backwards, his fat hands clutching a wheel painted old blue with gold tips to the handles. The wide water was a sheet of glass, the lake—a reservoir created in the 1960s—deserted. Forested mountains sloped down to the lakeshore on either side, increasingly lovely the further we sailed from human habitation. A lone rock partridge perched on a crag high above us, a Levant sparrowhawk soared over the trees. We passed herons and cormorants as we scanned the hillsides for buzzards both common and long-legged. Two short-toed eagles circled overhead, their nest clearly visible in a shrub growing out of a crevice on one of the escarpments. We spotted alpine swifts and kestrels. Then, to Emil's great excitement, a pair of Egyptian vultures soared into view.

He hadn't see them since the spring, he exclaimed, and had assumed this pair to have been killed (he recognised all his vultures by sight). Local farmers were illegally baiting wolves with poisoned meat to protect their sheep, but it was often taken by vultures. Part of Emil's mission was to intercept this criminal practice, he told us with the air of a gentle man who has no time for the stupidity and cruelty of the human race. For centuries the bird that so impassioned him and consumed his spare time, the Egyptian vulture whose nearest evolutionary ancestor is the lammergeier, used to be seen perched on the pyramids at Giza and was known as the 'white-plumed sage'. It has lived alongside mankind since the beginning of history, celebrated in legend and lore wherever it makes its home, sacred to the people who revered it ever since the time of the Ancient Egyptians. Pharaoh's Chicken, others called it, this two-foot-long bird whose stance is, it is true, faintly chicken-like. But *Neophron percnopterus*, smallest of the vultures and by far the prettiest, is a good-looker, predominantly white but with dramatic black flight feathers. A punk hairdo haloes its wrinkled yellow nares and orangey-yellow, black-tipped beak.

As we watched, a raven started harrying the vultures and was energetically chased off by one of them which turned on the potential predator, twisting in the air with surprising agility for its size, seeing it off. Emil's sunburned face became animated as he pointed to where one of the parent birds had swooped to the nest, almost hidden on a ledge, carrying food for a now visible chick with fluffy white feathers. We watched enchanted as the boat sailed slowly past, a rare sighting of a pair of breeding Egyptian vultures, flying together and feeding their youngster. It was a thrilling sight, made all the more memorable by Emil's joy.

Because, in spite of being protected by law, and crimes against them punishable by due process, the life of the Egyptian vulture is beset with hazards: habitats have been lost to ploughing or quarries, solar parks or windfarms. Roosting trees have been felled in places where the birds have bred for generations, forcing them to leave for good. In addition, intensive farming causes disease in livestock, and vultures who feast on their carcasses become prone to infection. Agricultural rodenticides and pesticides affect the food chain: vultures eat the poisoned mammals and insects which are a natural part of their diet, and die. Vultures are victims of poaching, procured for taxidermy, egg collectors or wildlife trafficking, lucrative trades all. Egyptian vultures are sensitive to human disturbance, and the nervous parents may leave eggs unprotected. The birds use electricity poles and pylons as resting or roosting sites, and may be electrocuted, or crash into cables. Windfarms constitute a lethal hazard—a case of 'green energy' costing the lives of thousands of birds (and not just Egyptian vultures).

On the other side of the lake a golden eagle floated into view over the skyline, mobbed by ravens and jackdaws: this gigantic bird, despite its seven-foot wingspan, found itself nevertheless outnumbered, and eventually flew down out of view behind the mountain. We sailed on through a landscape of hillsides mirrored in blue-green water, under a brisk sky with feathery white clouds. As we chugged along, Emil told me the shocking story of black-market trading in goldfinches, how the birds are attracted to a double cage, in the outer one food, in the inner cage another goldfinch to lure the visitor bird who takes the food and is trapped. These birds are exported in tens of thousands to Italy and Spain where they are sold on as caged birds. He went on to describe a cruel technique of trapping small birds for the table, smearing lime on to branches of trees, where they become stuck.

Rounding a bend, we came to where thirteenth-century painted caves nestled in the rocky shoreline, overgrown with greenery. Through the entrances we could make out a row of haloed saints frescoed on the walls, and a pair of angel's wings. The skeleton of a hermit had been found in one of the caves, measuring more than six and a half feet long, remnant of a life lived here long ago, bones of a lean ascetic. Here you could picture a bearded holy man, stooped from the bending he had to do living inside a cave, incredibly thin, gazing at the Madonna of his frescoes, living a life of adoration and prayer in the mountains by the river with its changing moods and colours, its raptors and waterbirds his companions. All this for years on end, then dying alone, his skeleton remaining undiscovered until eight centuries later, bones picked clean by the vultures he had watched and knew—as in traditions of sky burials where the role of certain birds is to transport the soul of the deceased to the next world.

Returning homewards we had a brief view of a griffon vulture, and we saw kestrels mating on a rock, a black stork on its nest and two hobbies. Three honey buzzards floated in; we spotted a hooded crow, a white wagtail and a distant—and rare—glimpse of a sandwich tern. And a short-toed eagle, also known as a snake eagle. With a snake in its beak.

At the end of its river journey the 'African Queen' pulled in under the trees, back where we'd started at the ramshackle pontoon. Before parting for the evening, we sat drinking mint tea in the shade of a tiny café next to the water. Sensing our enthusiasm, Emil came up with an idea for the following day: if we had been captivated by the Egyptian vulture with its long history, perhaps we should see a member of the oldest surviving hierofalcon species on earth, traceable back to the Late Pleistocene over a hundred thousand years ago. *Hieros*, Greek for sacred, a bird virtually synonymous with holiness. *Falco biarmicus* was a member of this tribe, and this was the bird he was hoping to show us.

We drove to a remote place called Gradsko—meaning 'castle' in Czech, Martin told us. West of where the Crna meets the Vardar river in southern Macedonia, steppe unfolded under a cloudless sky, wide and blue, flooding the landscape with evening light. Scarlet poppies splashed the ripening barley fields, silvery green and ruffled by a light breeze. The verges tumbled with wild flowers, the plateau rippled towards mountains smokey blue with distance. We stopped by a newly ploughed field where calandra larks were displaying on chocolate-brown clods. We watched them showing off, chunky, vigorous and playful, the markings on their backs streaking against the dark soil as they hopped and flew. Black shoulder patches and vivid white trim to the wings were clearly visible as they rose high above us, hovering, hanging and drifting over the field with slow wing-beats, singing a dry fizzling song—a good deal less musical, disappointingly, than their cousins the skylark.

Emil led us to the brow of a hill. In the distance we could see a line of electricity pylons stretching across the land, and this was as near as he was willing to take us. He set up the scope. There, perched on the upper echelons of the pylon with his back to us, was a lanner falcon. Unmistakably the falcon, proud head turned in profile: hooked beak, black moustachial stripe, large dark eye rimmed with yellow under a light chest-nut supercilium. The peregrine glare. He remained motionless for a long while, then swivelled his rufous head to look in the other direction. He was completely, utterly beautiful. It is hard to say why. I can't explain it, but this majestic bird was in a league of his own.

And rare. There are just twenty-five pairs of lanner falcons in an area of Macedonia the size of Norfolk, of only three hun-dred or so pairs in Europe. This one had taken over a deserted raven's nest built high inside the pylon, a crude raft of twigs and branches into which a colony of Spanish sparrows had woven grassy nests. They were buzzing around like wasps, and although the lanner lives on a diet of small birds—including those calandra larks that had been entertaining us—it leaves the sparrows alone. Emil explained the mutual benefit involved, how the sparrows' grass-weaving insulates the raptor's nest and holds it together, while the proximity of a top predator protects the passerines and their young.

Serenely poised among the hectic sparrows the lanner, perched in silhouette, was drenched in clear light that picked out every detail of his plumage. He resembled a strongly built kestrel, but with shorter tail feathers, and rust-red head. Slate-dark wings folded over his back quartered by diamond patterning of subtle blue-greys, each feather trimmed with white, marbling the plumage. When he eventually turned to face us we could see the darkly mustachioed cheek, the creamy cinnamon-spotted breast feathers, the pale streaked 'trousers' canopying the strong yellow feet. The savage black talons.

What was it about this handsome bird that made him so unforgettable? I can't honestly say, only that looking at the lanner falcon surveying his patch from on high on an electricity pylon on the steppes of Macedonia, I felt I was in the presence of the most beautiful of all the raptors. And that he gave me something of himself. And that I was able to receive it because I had begun to learn how to look, and how to see. My weeks of hibernation had created a stillness somewhere inside, a calm that enabled me to experience the world in a different way, and to engage in it as never before. Travelling to new places and meeting new people was opening up new horizons both literally and inside my head.

Towards the end of the week we drove through the night towards the mountains of northern Macedonia, through rolling landscapes swathed in thick forests where brown bears and lynx, chamois and red deer, wolves and foxes and martens roam far from human habitation. At the end of a remote track curling up the hillsides we arrived at a guest-hut in the depths of a conservation area. Through thick darkness I heard the call of a scops owl before falling asleep, dimly aware of pulses of rain gusting across the night between the profound silences of a remote mountainside.

At the time, I had no idea there were eleven species of woodpecker in Europe, and two hundred worldwide. Just a handful of facts about woodpeckers induces awe. The head-pounding drilling, at a rate of about twenty times a second, produces ten times the G-force sustainable by even the best-protected human head. Luckily, nature designed the woodpecker to prevent it inflicting severe brain injuries on itself. A thick bone with a sponge-like mesh construction, extending like a sling designed to minimise vibration, protects the brain by distributing the G-force while also acting as a safety belt. This hyloid bone starts at the underside of the beak behind the tongue, loops through the nostrils, goes under and around the back of the skull, and over the top of the brain to the forehead. The brain is longer top to bottom than front to back, which distributes the G-force over a larger area. In addition, the subdural cavity is minimal, reducing the shaking of the brain on impact. Also, the woodpecker turns its head slightly as it drills, influencing how the forces are transmitted, and the hard beak is slightly elastic, softening the impact. The upper and lower mandibles are of unequal length, an asymmetry that lowers the load on the brain. The finishing touch: a third inner eyelid is provided to prevent the eye popping out.

Walking along the River Treska, marvelling at the intricacy of this divine engineering, I caught my first ever glimpse of the middle spotted woodpecker, whose banal name belies its good looks. Wandering through the Matka gorge, a limestone canyon soaring three thousand feet above us, James and I stopped to sit on the grassy bank. On a tiny spit of land in the middle of the fast-flowing river, a gnarled willow leaned steeply over the water, trunk bark deeply fissured. Its canopy cast shifting light and shadows as a gentle breeze moved leaf patterns over the bank. The movement was more than the wind: pecking for invertebrates around the mossy roots, a middle spotted woodpecker emerged from behind the willow. This pretty bird, slightly rounder and plumper than the great spotted, compact and a little smaller, had similar black and white wings, but a coral flush to its belly, softer than the vermilion vent of its cousin. A vivid scarlet crown capped the top of its head, and without the severe black moustache of its relative, it had a sweeter look. As it disappeared behind the tree, pecking for food, I could see that the bill was noticeably smaller than that of our native woodpeckers. A few moments later it flew out with a *kik-kekekekek* call, down to the next island in the wide river, leaving me thrilled to have seen a bird I will never see at home.

The following day we drove in an ex-army jeep to a tributary of the Treska, the River Ocha, where fresh bear-prints in the track bore witness to its remoteness two thousand feet above sea level. Tall, light-seeking trees grow from the bottom of an escarpment dropping down to the river, rising high into the sky and sheltering the valley under a canopy of beech and birch, box and willow and maple—and copious flowering ash, *Fraxinus ornus*. We walked through a Macedonian oak forest to the sound of water tumbling over stones in the river below. Where a beech tree towered out of the sheer bank, dominating a natural clearing with several dead trees, we heard a piercing call, a long shrill penetrating note. Looking up we saw, on a topmost naked branch, a black woodpecker. His powerful bill was silhouetted against the sky, opening and closing as he called. This blacker-than-black bird, with streak of cardinal red crowning its head, is twice the size of the great spotted woodpecker. Immediately there was a sense of a creature with a pronounced out-there personality, whose loud call reflected his size and attitude. For several minutes we watched enthralled, engrossed by clear views of this bird, this character, high up in the dead branches, in profile, calling, then taking off and flying around.

Gilbert White, describing our green woodpeckers, says they fly *opening and closing their wings at every stroke, and so are always rising and falling in curves*, but the trajectory of this bird wasn't undulating and dipping like most woodpeckers: instead it was a straight, flappy flight. Through binoculars we followed it to the trunk of a beech tree where dead wood had been drilled with several large holes and masses of small ones. Bird village. Losing sight of the black woodpecker for a moment, we saw a great tit pop in and out of what had to be our woodpecker's nest hole. Not for long: he reappeared and settled in typical pecker-profile, stiff-tailed against the trunk, and started to drum a musical message with his chisel-bill. The soft, full-bodied resonance surprised me not just by its pitch but by how different it sounded. I had assumed woodpecker-drumming was just drumming, the same noise the world over: but no, bird drumming is well named, it's music just as percussion is, individual to each species and to each individual's instrument, as is the human voice. A woodpecker-voice.

And then he flew off, calling, dramatic, distinctive, dark, into the forest.

Not far from where we were staying at Selište in the heart of the Karadzica mountains, the rare Balkan lynx has been seen. It is critically endangered and almost extinct, its habitat a range of mountainsides and forests in a government-protected area. There was no chance of seeing one during the day of course, but nonetheless climbing the steep path up one of the escarpments was to imagine it prowling for food at night, spotted cat of the mountains with whiskered pointed ears and secretive habits. Up in these mountains brown bears and wolves roam, martens make their homes, and red deer populate the woods. On the lower slopes, a drift of pollen from flowering ash dusted aromatic grasses and wild herbs, and mists of blue ajuga glowed in the grasses. The higher we climbed, the more dramatic the panorama in early-evening light and, through the trees, we could see chamois in the far distance resting on the snowline. Underfoot grew lily-of-the-valley and lady orchids, and the exquisite, rare mauve *Raymonda nataliae* peeped from crevices in the rocks.

The narrow track took us through thickly wooded terrain to an opening overlooking a natural amphitheatre miles wide, dominated by the call of a cuckoo which was perched in full view on top of a tree overlooking the plateau. We continued through a pine glade where a forest fire long ago had created a clearing of scattered tall trees, filtering light like the pillars of a Gothic cathedral. We heard a sharp, penetrating, low-pitched *kik-kik* call, scratchy, persistent. We froze. Silence. Suddenly we saw, angular head and long bill in profile against a thin pine trunk, a woodpecker. It started drumming, an echoey sound like a pingpong ball bouncing to a halt on a hard surface. Incredibly loud. The sound belonged to the place, just as Gregorian chant belongs in a church. This recital continued, and in the clear evening light we were treated to a prolonged view of a black and white bird with light-red cap, white face with black strap running across the cheek, conspicuous white patch across the back and dramatic black and white wings. A vivid flush of salmon-rust-pink with hint of carmine on the belly faded like a blush into the ash-streaked breast. Speechless, we watched as it flew off, the openness of the trees making it easy to see as it disappeared. Another one called, possibly even two. Spellbound, we waited, but the show was over. We had been looking at a threatened bird, increasingly rare and seldom seen. The exquisite white-backed woodpecker.

That night, in the black and velvet darkness, in a place where the silences are deep and different, rain came and went with ferocity. Some time after midnight a massive thunderstorm shook the mountainside, sheets of lightning tore the dark apart, and the percussion of the rain hammering the corrugated roof of the lodge drummed with the anger of the gods. Mountain weather. Woodpecker weather.

MAY

Essex, the Outer Hebrides (Lewis and Harris)

the consolation of beauty

Tawny owls hoot from the wood on the hill at the edge of the village. I often hear them as I drift off to sleep, birds of Morpheus, presences of darkness, gods and goddesses of the night. Owls belong to the 'other worlds' of dusk, of ill omen and superstition, but also of ambiguous wisdom, ghosts of the departed or spiritual guardians facilitating the transmigration of souls. The night before Kafka died of tuberculosis in a sanatorium in the Wienerwald in 1924, his lover Dora Diamant saw an owl perched on the windowsill outside the sickroom: was it waiting for him to give up the ghost? The owl, receptacle of our projections almost more than any other bird, bird with front-facing eyes and binocular vision like ours, bird with a face, bird of hidden nocturnal habits.

From early spring to summer owls will be busy courting and mating, nesting and laying eggs, then hunting to feed their young—mostly at night—but for the rest of the time they hang around doing very little. Apart from in autumn, when young tawny owls get busy establishing territory and are super-vocal, owls generally have a habit of dozing for all but two hours of every twenty-four. They don't go out in the rain, because their feathers aren't waterproof: flying becomes difficult in wet weather, and hunting impossible. But on a good night their noiseless flight enables them to stalk prey without being heard, using their acute hearing to locate voles and shrews. The facial disc, acting as an amplifier for ears concealed asymmetrically to either side of the face under a ruff of feathers, receives different information from the same sound source. This enables the bird to locate precisely its strike in total darkness: a great grey owl has such fine hearing it can pinpoint a mouse in deep snow. What with that, and with eyesight more than twice as light-sensitive as ours, owls are a fearsome threat to their prey: hunters with killer talons and a meat-hook for a beak.

It's difficult to imagine what it must be like to be a bird, although mankind, forever envious of the ability to fly, has never quite given up trying. From Icarus to aeroplanes to space travel, the human imagination strives to reinvent itself as a creature of the air. But we have no idea what it feels like to have a heart that, in flight, beats a thousand times a minute, or to have a skeleton that weighs less than the feathers it supports and makes up only five per cent of total body weight, or to have hollow bones with respiratory sacs in them supplying the oxygen essential to maintain metabolism for flight. What's it like not to have a diaphragm, and to breathe actively only on exhalation? To mate with (in most cases) split-second timing, or to have eyes that measure more than half the volume of the skull? In the case of owls, the tubular eye socket takes up seventy per cent of the cranial space, a design that prevents it from rolling its eyes to look around—which is why owls evolved rubber necks to rotate the head (a snowy owl can achieve an almost complete circle).

Their world must appear quite different from ours. With heightened hearing that picks up the minutest detail—an auditory equivalent of slo-mo, with high-speed sensory and nervous systems providing sophisticated touch receptors, and visual acuity beyond human dreams, they live in a world that moves ten times faster than ours appears to. Surrounded by the constant activity of life we can hardly see, from microscopic invertebrates to elephants, birds inhabit a surreal visual kaleidoscope, a vortex of movement, a tumult of sounds, a miasma of smells. And they navigate it with skills unique to them.

The skull of a bird constitutes only one per cent of total bodyweight, yet the ratio of brain to bodymass is markedly more than that of *Homo sapiens*, indicating an advanced and complex intelligence beyond our comprehension, which is partly why they appear in our myths and legends and literature. The medieval Persian poem 'The Conference of the Birds' (a kind of Sufi 'pilgrim's progress' of the birds through a divine comedy) hints at this: in an allegorical journey to free themselves from earthly things—*seek out the wine-press of the infinite*, as the poet puts it—the chief of the birds, the hoopoe, exhorts his aspirants to persevere against all odds in the quest to experience what is beyond human reach: *the oneness in diversity, / Not oneness locked in singularity*. Some of them succeed, and for those who make it through to the end of the journey—*your soul should not submit*—the hoopoe inspires them to recognise their essential affinity with God.

The mad plan James and I had made back in March, to go birding in Scotland only a few weeks after returning from Macedonia, was about to unfold. We took a flight to Glasgow where we boarded a twin turboprop plane ferrying passengers to the outlying Western Isles. In what felt like a precariously small aircraft, we flew so low over the sea we could see every detail of the breakers below, unnervingly close to outlying rocks of an island formed of the oldest mountains in Europe, a jaw-dropping two and half billion years old. Touching down unsteadily in a headwind on Stornoway's runway, we arrived in Lewis with its wild hills, its sweeping landscapes of mountains and bog moorland punctuated by lochs and heathland, sand dunes and grassy headlands. Grand territories of seemingly limitless horizons and grey winds. I thought of R. S. Thomas, poet and priest, who spent hours in similarly wild landscapes in west Wales watching for birds, never knowing whether he would see any or not.

> It is beautiful and still:
>   the air rarefied
> as the interior of a cathedral
> expecting a presence.

It is exactly the same, he writes in his autobiography, *with the relationship between man and God that is known as prayer. Great patience is called for, because no one knows when God will choose to reveal Himself.* The thrust of much of the poetry of this anguished cleric is the absence of God, and his search for our relationship with the infinite. He often felt like giving up. Once, alerted by local twitchers of an albino dunnock seen on the Lleyn Peninsula, he muttered, *Waiting for birds is like waiting for God, but I don't think I'd wait three hours for God.*

We stocked up with the week's provisions at the Co-op in Stornoway. Our tiny stone cottage on Lewis, whitewashed with a slate roof, nestled into a remote hillside on the eastern side of the island overlooking one of the South Lochs which drain into the Minch. Winding down a narrow road into the village, we were greeted by the wafting scent of coconut from gorse in full flower by the gate. The view from the kitchen window looked over deserted cottages to cloud-obscured hills beyond, grey as the granite they are made of. Marsh marigolds shone bright gold among mossy boulders on the banks of a stream running gurgling down the hillside into the bay. Over the days a family of robins befriended us, the youngsters coming to the back door every morning from their nest in the hedge. On a nearby fencepost, James saw a great spotted woodpecker, a very occasional visitor to Lewis and a rare sighting on the island. He was so excited he contacted the local bird recorder (who was equally excited).

The wild flowers on Lewis are small, with an intimate and intricate beauty—specialised moorland plants. The season for everything on the Outer Hebrides—wild flowers, birds, trees— is late at this northerly latitude. The heather wasn't in flower yet, but walking the lonely hills was to discover bright gorse, clumps of ruby lousewort, the spotted heath orchid and start- ling blue milkwort exploding from dark peat soil like azure jewels. In damper patches a litany of wild flowers flourished in their ideal habitats—ragged robin, flag iris, bogbean, water forget-me-not, butterwort, sundew, cotton grass.

We drove through Lewis to Harris past increasingly verdant landscapes, the hills becoming softer and more tree-covered near Northton where pasturelands stretch sea-level-flat along the Atlantic coastline. Here cattle graze as they have done for centuries on the machair, speciality of the Outer Hebrides. Windblown shellsand, formed by powerful waves crushing the shells of sea creatures, combines with peat to make calcium- rich grassland. With its rich lime content it harbours up to forty different species of wild flower per square yard, a rich and diverse flora unique to this coast. Pink seathrift carpets the saltmarshes in summer, and marram grass—the only grass that can grow in pure sand—stabilises the ever-moving dunes. The great yellow bumblebee is found here, and the elusive corncrake can be heard at dusk. The machair is famous for its many different orchid species, its numerous grasses and three heathers, the ling, the bell and the cross-leaved.

The place is a haven for birds. Framed by dark hills against a pewter sky, lapwings and dunlin were flying around, females on eggs and males feeding. Skylarks and redshank were calling their plaintive songs, oystercatchers roamed (with carrots in their beaks) and rock doves fluttered. A sedge warbler squeaked lustily from a hedge. The walk to the headland at Toe Point followed a steep path winding up the hillside to the remains of an Iron Age fort. Next to this primordial habitation of the Outer Hebrides, the ruined stones of a fifteenth-century chapel stand overlooking the sea, silent witness to a later Christian settlement. Ravens were flying around, perching on boulders of granite embedded in the hillside, streaked with geological time, sparkling with crystals of pink feldspar, whitish quartz and flaking mica. We stood on the edge of the cliff looking across to Harris, the Uists distant contours of deep blue hills beyond Taransay. Great northern divers, resplendent in black and white summer livery, bobbed on the water, and a pair of eiders in Mr and Mrs plumage were swimming around, glinting on the diamond water. Below us on a promontory, under banks of rain-full clouds lit by the sun, a shag was ruminating, prehistoric statue on a rock.

Out at sea, gannets were diving. At that moment I thought them the most stunning birds I'd ever seen: streamlined and elegant, sleek and strong, gods of the seas. Born to fly, aero-dynamic *par excellence*, one was swooping tail-splayed over the sparkling sea, playful, energetic, torpedo sharp, purest-white plumage glinting in the sunshine. Folding back its wings, it plunged the waves with surgical precision, Exocet missile entering the water leaving a plume of spray. This Concorde of the seas, strong-winged, bright white with long pointed black-tipped wings and yellow-blush head, has an ice-blue eye bespectacled with black lines that outline its dagger of a bill. Bewick, endearingly, refers to the gannet as a Spectacled Goose, whose *eyes... like those of the Owl, are set in the head so as to look straight forward, and the extreme paleness of the irides gives them a keen wild stare... These features of its countenance, altogether, give it somewhat the appearance of wearing spectacles.*

We watched it high, high up, seventy or eighty feet, before suddenly, in a nano-second, it performed a vertical stoop in a dive for fish, folded wings cleaving the air in a breathholding plunge, dividing the waters at over sixty miles an hour. I was to learn that a special adaptation prevents injury to the bird on this colossal impact: gannets have no external nostrils (these are located inside the mouth), and they have air sacs under the skin of head and chest which act like bubble-wrap, cushioning the impact with the water and allowing them to dive for fish to depths of seventy-two feet (they also have glands near the eyes that eliminate salt, enabling them to drink sea water). Underwater, they use their wings and webbed feet to swim in pursuit of fish. These adaptations, evolved over millions of years (fossil gannets date from the Pliocene, when the diversity of seabirds was much higher than it is today), may well give the gannet the last laugh on a race that came along consider-ably later, called them morons, ate their babies and borrowed the gannet's name to describe those of their race susceptible to gluttony: excessive eating being more characteristic of the human race than of this wild bird of the oceans. Mankind's contempt is evident in the taxonomy, *Morus bassanus*: the Greek *Morus* meaning 'silly'—even worse, moronic, because gannets are so easily predated by man.

The French call the gannet *Fou de Bassan*, madman of Bass Rock, the specific *bassanus* naming gannets after the rock in the Firth of Forth where between February and October their numbers peak at over a hundred and fifty thousand, making it the largest single-island gannet colony in the world (although the St Kilda archipelago comprises twenty per cent of the entire world's population). In 1518 a visitor to Bass Rock described it as *an impregnable stronghold. Roundabout it is seen a marvellous multitude of great ducks that live on fish.* The site of an important castle subsequently used as a prison, Bass Rock is currently uninhabited by humans, but the Bass Rock Lighthouse built in 1902, and ruins of a chapel on the site of a very early Christian hermitage, remain as traces of past habitation. After roaming the seas during the winter, gannets return to the Bass Rock gannetries for the breeding season, each greeting their mate with a display of bowing and head-pointing and ritualised preening while seals haul themselves up on to the rocks below. Gannets pair-bond faithfully, sharing the incubation of the single, chalky-blue egg which they place under webbed feet on nests of seaweed, feathers and plant stuff. The rock ledges are divided territorially into tightly packed ghettos of razor-bills, shags and guillemots. The gannets usually colonise the flatter areas on the top, and readily attack birds which land too close. It's a busy, teeming place: Bass Rock is a visual phenomenon beloved of birdwatchers, one of the wonders of the ornithological world—and an olfactory phenomenon too, the reek of ammonia assaulting the nostrils from afar.

Gannets were once classified as *Sula bassana* and are still 'Solan' to the Hebrideans, with other names too: Solan Goose, Soland Gose, and Sula (the Old Norse *sula* means a cleft stick, after the crossed black wingtips). These seabirds provided a valuable harvest for the locals, and their eggs were taken too, traditionally preserved in beds of peat ash for months, eaten raw. Sulasgeir off the north coast of Lewis, not far from where we were staying, supports an historic gannetry where an annual cull of birds is taken for food. Over a period of two weeks, two thousand young gannets are captured by ten local men from Ness, using traditional methods dating back to the sixteenth century (up to fifteen thousand birds a year used to be culled for food, until the practice was restricted in 1885). 'Gugas', recently fledged young gannets with smoky-grey plumage, their garb for the first four years of life, were eaten during the Second World War under the disguise of 'Highland Goose'. They were plucked and wind-dried in stone cleats, and hung like biltong to preserve them through the hungry months. Gannets had other uses as well: the feathers were once used for stuffing pillows and furnishings (but it takes feathers from three hundred birds to fill a single duvet), and their copious guano provided a natural fertiliser, rich in phosphates and nitrates.

Gannets are the largest seabirds in the North Atlantic, longer in body than a golden eagle and almost as heavy, with a six-and-a-half-foot wingspan. Their eyesight is formidable, their binocular vision enabling them to judge precise distances. Flocks of gannets can number a thousand strong following in the wake of ships, picking up flotsam and scraps, feeding on mackerel and herring, making mass attacks on shoals of fish, raining down like a shower of missiles (as Bewick puts it, they *fall perpendicularly*) in what is known as a 'herring-gant' or 'mackerel-gant'. These unforgettable seabirds prompted one of the earliest poems in the English language, 'The Seafarer', from the tenth-century 'Exeter Book':

> There heard I naught but seething sea,
> Ice-cold wave, awhile a song of Swan.
> There came to charm me gannets' pother
> And whimbrels trills for the laughter of men,
> Kittiwake singing instead of mead.

The following day, early-morning sunshine danced on silky waters in the Sound of Taransay. Tiny waves rippled over the shallows. Clouds hung motionless in a blue sky, reflected in sea-shades of turquoise and aquamarine. The serene stretch of sand, rated one of the ten most lovely in the world, was deserted as a light breeze waved marram grasses on the dunes behind the beach. Great northern divers drifted far out in the bay, so far away it was impossible to imagine that this stunning black and white seabird is the same length as a golden eagle, and heavier. Scoter, eider and oh-so-elegant red-throated divers were feeding leisurely in the balmy seas of Luskentyre—Losgaintir in Gaelic—on the west coast of Harris.

Harris, world famous for its tweed whose dye-colours reflect local plants and minerals of the hills and moors, is one of a chain of islands of the Outer Hebrides or *Innis Fada*, 'Long

Island', grandest and most lonely of Scotland's outlying isles, land of sea caves, of lashing Atlantic breakers and rugged hills. The Hebrides archipelago—of two hundred islands only fifteen are inhabited—used to be, in its prehistory, one long island. A Viking legend tells how they wanted to take it back with them to the Norse Kingdoms, but when they flung a chain around the top isle to pull it back up through the sea to the north, the land broke up into little pieces, where they remain.

Over millennia, sinking back into the seas from which they once erupted, the mist-laden islands lie mostly alone but for the sound of the sea and the cry of the seabirds. *The language of birds is very ancient,* wrote Gilbert White, *little is said, but much is meant and understood.* Waves sweep milk-white over granite rocks as they have done since prehistory, grey winds scour hills and moors of a now all-but-treeless terrain. Glens lined with debris from retreating glaciers are punctuated by deep-gashed lochs and lochans. Too demanding for mankind to make his home, these windswept islets have become the territory of seabirds and waders, a landing platform for migrating birds, and a safe nesting place for those who spend summers in the circumpolar north.

Arctic terns were racing over the blue-green waters of the bay, elfin, diving like arrows into the gentle waves, plunging for fish. A pair were wind-dancing, skipping and flicking over flat expanses of sand and sea—all bright white rump, streak of ashen wing and flash of red leg. Sleek-headed with sharp, blood-orange bill as long as its head (a weapon that can inflict a serious head injury on a predator, including human), black-hooded and white-cheeked, *Sterna paradisaea* of the pointed silvery wings and tail streamers is a bird of paradisal beauty and grace, a sea-swallow, snow white and river-pearl grey with sheen of ice. A heart muscle enclosed in a wing muscle, seem-ingly fragile but not, migratory bird of the oceans.

In Italian *Sterna codalunga*, the tern with the long swallow-tail has a delicate streamlined look, with resolute shoulders that plough the air with graceful wingflaps across the face of the planet and back, not just once but as many times as the years they live—and they can survive for over thirty years. As they played over the Sound of Taransay, ethereal, dainty, adroit fliers feeding and diving and dancing, it was hard to believe the relentless destiny of this enchanting fairytale seabird, which during its lifetime makes the ultimate Odyssey known to crea-tion, visiting almost every shoreline on earth.

The Arctic tern is a bird of the light, flying through nine months of perpetual day as it travels from northern breeding grounds in summer—the Hebrides among others—to winter on the Antarctic coast. If it flew direct, it would cover twelve thousand miles, the shortest distance between the two poles as the crow flies (not that it does). But the Arctic tern chooses a more complicated route: birds nesting in Iceland and Green-land make a round-trip of more than forty-four thousand miles, and birds nesting in the Netherlands nearly fifty-six thousand. The Arctic tern flies twice as far as the distance from Britain to Japan, twice a year, for up to thirty-four years. From the Antarctic where it winters to the Arctic where it breeds, it can cover a staggering one and a half million miles in its lifetime. There is no comparable migration, or anything close to it, in the animal kingdom.

Later that week I stumbled on the remains of an Arctic tern lying on bog moorland on a headland looking out over a lonely loch. Just one wing had been left intact by a predator. I picked it up: it's an astonishing construction, this component of an avian machine that weighs less than four ounces, defying gravity, weather and distance to travel further than any other creature on earth. The underside of the wing is of the softest, whitest down, feathers that have no weight, the top side silver-grey. The longest pinion feather, spearlike to cut through the air, has a narrow, soot-black stripe only marginally wider than the pure ivory shaft, slimline and haute couture (Arctic terns were hunted to near extinction for the millinery trade in the late nineteenth century). The other side of the vane is a single, wider stripe of soft grey and ice white. Handling this wing is to touch the intangible, to sense something of the stamina and endurance of these timeless navigators of the globe.

Not far from where we were walking at Taransay lies the mountain range of Harris with the highest density of breeding pairs of golden eagles anywhere in Europe. That year, there were twenty pairs resident on the island and it was our hope—part of the plan, it goes without saying—that the legendary *Aquila chrysaetos* would float into the scope of our eager binoculars. *This noble bird*, writes Thomas Bewick in 'British Birds', has a *bill of deep blue; cer yellow; eyes large, deep sunk, and covered by a projecting brow; the iris hazel, and sparkles with uncommon lustre… Quills chocolate* [sic], *with white shafts.* He describes the legs feathered to the toes, and remarks that the claws are *remarkably large; the middle one is 2 inches in length.* In January 1735, he goes on, *a very large one was shot near Warkworth, which measured from point to point of its wings, eleven feet and a quarter.*

But the weather turned on us: that day there was no chance to explore those hills of Harris for golden eagles because the rains set in chased by grey Atlantic winds, large wet rain shed by gigantic black clouds. We retreated to the cottage, consoling ourselves with the memory of a sea eagle we'd seen on our arrival. That this had been our first sighting of a bird on the Outer Hebrides (apart from a few waterbirds) still felt like something we'd dreamed up or invented. We'd been driving towards South Lochs after picking up the shopping in Stornoway, and turned left off the main road heading for the virtually unpopulated east coast of Lewis. The road dwindled to single track, a thread winding along the edge of Loch Erisort on one side, deserted moorland and rock-strewn hills on the other. We had entered a world of drifting salt mists and soft light.

Like a mirage we saw a dark shape on top of a rocky ridge beside the road. In profile against a leaden sky, an eagle. Incredulous, we stopped the car: unmistakably a sea eagle with ochre head and pure-white tail, bulky, broad shouldered, vulture-like, aquiline profile displaying the ferocious yellow beak, hooked to savage prey, feathered legs, talons the size of a man's hand. The haughty stare, the stillness. For several moments the eagle remained motionless, ultimate avian aristocrat looking down in our direction. Then it lifted into the air with powerful movement of chest and shoulders, opening eight-foot rectangular wings with long fingered pinions and, with slow wingflaps like an outsize heron, floated down behind the ridge, wings held flat, pinions splayed, and disappeared from view.

This welcome to Lewis had seemed unbelievable. Although the chances of seeing eagles there are good, birdwatching never guarantees anything even in these remote unpeopled hills: eagles are wild creatures, not performing monkeys. The weather on Lewis is wild, too, and eagles fly only in certain conditions. Or you can be in the wrong place at the wrong time, or looking in the wrong direction. We couldn't believe our luck.

*

Curled up under a blanket on the sofa in the cottage I watched rainwater sliding down the windows and decided there was no alternative: if I couldn't go looking for golden eagles I'd immerse myself in finding out more about these spirits of the mountains. *When thou seest an Eagle, thou seest a portion of Genius. Lift up thy head!* wrote William Blake. Standing for power, wildness and freedom, across cultures eagles represent all the superlatives: aspiration, inspiration, faith, loyalty, freedom, courage, ascension, immortality, vision, majesty and splendour. In Norse mythology the golden eagle sits atop Yggdrasil, the great ash tree that canopies the universe. Eagle-gods feature in Ancient Babylonian legends, the double-headed eagle appears in Mesopotamian art from Sumerian to Hittite, it's a symbol of victory in Deuteronomy where the warmonger Sennacherib, self-styled King of the World commanding vast Assyrian armies, is described swooping down on Jerusalem *as swift as the eagle flieth*. Universally admired for speed, physical prowess and apparently endless endurance, the eagle is a symbol of light and sky powers in Arabic poetry. It's the personal emblem of Saladin, and as sacred to Zeus in Greece as to Jove in Rome. Sometimes this great bird is depicted with a snake in its bill, the snake representing earth (in Christian iconography the Devil), the eagle symbolising heaven. Emblem of John the Evangelist, mystic apostle, the eagle of the lectern represents transcendent wisdom. In the holy trinity of biblical symbols—eagle, raven and dove—Constantine the Great chose a double-headed eagle to symbolise for Byzantium the twin sovereignty of Church and state. Ancient Greek coins depict eagles, and Roman soldiers carried eagle standards, the *Aquila* being the most prominent symbol of the Roman legions. When a Roman emperor died, his body was burned in a funeral pyre and an eagle was released above his ashes to carry his spirit to the heavens.

Eagles are the commonest national emblem in the world. The eagle of Saladin is an emblem of Arab nationalism, the bald eagle the national bird of the USA, and in its least fortunate historical representation, Adolf Hitler used the eagle as a symbol for the Nazi Party perched atop the swastika, prominent on monuments and statues, buildings and bridges as well as on pins worn on Nazi officers' lapels.

In falconry, eagles were traditionally reserved for emperors and kings, which is why common names for the golden eagle in different languages roughly translate as 'royal eagle'. With an ability to spot prey from well over a mile away (an eagle can see a hare twitch in the grass from three thousand feet), their eyesight endows them with such prowess they have been regarded with almost religious reverence (one of my much-loved bird facts is that if we had eyes that large in terms of ratio to our face size, they would be the size of oranges). Falconers have trained golden eagles for hunting since well before the Middle Ages, and in the barren landscapes of the Altai mountains in Mongolia, they still do. There are about a hundred eagle hunters active in Mongolia and Kazakhstan today: in places where nomads eke out a living from unyielding plateaus, a handful of men still train eagles to hunt the deer, antelope, foxes, rabbits and wolves on which they rely for food and skins, creatures they could never hope to catch without the help of the top predator of the bird world. Here, man and raptors live closely connected—even to death and everlasting life: for this is the land of sky burials, where following time-honoured rituals a corpse is taken to a remote spot in the mountains and dismembered for griffon vultures and lammergeiers to feast on before its decay transmits disease. In the locals' worldview, the birds which eat the body transport its soul to the next world, recycling the body into the eternal cycles of life in a transmutation of life that benefits birds and people equally.

Involving a hazardous climb down a sheer rock face by the would-be trainer, an unfledged golden eagle is taken from the nest. The young bird spends the next five months bonding with its master into adulthood, and is trained in falconry to become a working animal with an active life of fifteen years or more. Riding on horseback with reins in the left hand, the falconer carries his eagle on the right arm protected by a sturdy leather arm-glove, wearing a wooden brace to support the eagle's considerable weight. Reaching the highest peaks, the bird can spot movement of prey from the height necessary for a stoop. In a single season it's possible for one eagle to catch between thirty and fifty Mongolian foxes. These are lightning-fast creatures, but, said one of the trainers to a documentary film crew, 'With an eagle you can hunt anything, they are the best hunters on earth.' He also admitted that some remain truly wild and untameable. Not all birds can be trained: 'Some are like people—silly and stupid—so we release them back.'

After a day and night of rain, the weather lifted. We walked into an expanse of wild beauty where the hills drop into a valley of bog moorland and lochs, territory of the golden eagle where otters fish in the waters and the rare (twice as rare as the golden eagle) black-throated diver makes its nest. Leviathan cloud shadows swept over us, followed by bird shadows: high above, a pair of sea eagles were flying over the moor, scanning for carrion, white tailed, flat wingspan wide as a London bus, yellow beaked and vulturine, more ragged in flight and slightly bigger than the 'goldie' as the locals call them, tumbling, untidier in outline and longer fingered, thrilling sightings that left us incredulous at our luck. They were flying low enough for us to make out the long-fingered wings, the rich brown plumage of the back, the white feathers of the wedge-shaped tail, the pale nape and prominent head, the yellow beak. To my delight one of them did a talon-touching roll, a split-second aerial somersault characteristic of—at about ten pounds—the fourth-heaviest eagle in the world.

Later, making our way homewards, we crossed a bridge where a wheatear, sleek with smart dark eyestripe, pearl-grey back and black-edged wing, stood sentinel on a post. As we walked on, two more pairs of white-tailed eagles soared into view over the hills, long pinioned, soaring over the glen before disappearing over the ridge. We were jubilant: we joked that to see this number of sea eagles was probably the closest we would ever get to seeing the collective for eagles: a 'convocation'. We were thrilled. No golden eagles appeared that day, but watching their cousins the sea eagles in flight over the wild mountains was more than compensation.

Eagles are superlative fliers, despite their size. For the few humans on the planet fortunate enough to watch eagles fly regularly, they will observe a variety of behaviours: some flights by solitary birds—or between well-established breeding pairs—appear to be acts of playfulness. In courtship, the pair soar spirally over their territory and plunge earthwards with half-closed wings, sometimes rolling over in mid-air so close that their talons appear to touch. Or they glide into headwinds, hardly flapping, with occasional wingbeats which appear laboured, head prominent and wings held in a shallow V, long fingered—wings that would knock a well-built man over. Hunting flights consist of a high soaring at least a hundred and sixty feet above the ground, before gliding to attack. When it spies prey, the eagle partially closes its wings and enters a long, low-angled glide which can carry it over distances of more than half a mile, the speed increasing as the wings close. Just before the attack, the wings open, the tail fans and the feet are thrust forward. Apparently the wings whipping against the wind create a sound like a clap of thunder in the instant before the strike: I would give anything to witness that.

Alternatively, the golden eagle may perform a vertical stoop to attack birds in flight. One of the two fastest-moving creatures on earth when performing a full stoop, wings folded tight against body, feathered legs flattened to tail, it can reach nearly two hundred miles an hour, second only to the peregrine falcon. The eagle's most common hunting method however is a low-level quartering flight, hugging the contours of the land fifteen to twenty feet above the ground, leaving the skyline unbroken when observed from below by the small mammals or ground-nesting birds he is hunting. He will land on the back or neck of his prey, huge talons gripping and piercing vital organs, the crushing hold causing fatal shock (the force exerted can be fifteen times the power of the strongest human hand). The eagle may then ride his victim for several minutes with wings outstretched, flapping to maintain balance until it collapses either with exhaustion, shock or internal injury.

The wide world of the glens had awakened hushed after another night of rain. The single-track road from the cottage wound through the open hills of eastern Lewis, deserted on a windless day. In soft light under a veil of cloud, a lone swan drifted near the shore of the local lochan, wild and shy, delicate outline of its slim neck mirrored in the water, gamboge bill the only colour in a steel landscape: a whooper serenely swanlike in his whiteness.

Further inland, a curlew trilled from a stretch of bog moorland, a lapwing cried, redshank piped—signature sounds of the landscapes of Lewis. A snipe was drumming, dancing in the skies high above us, outer tail feathers percussing the wind, a spectacular, relentless display ending in a bleat so like a lost lamb I was convinced it was until James persuaded me it wasn't. A flock of golden plover flew in with two dunlin and started feeding among heather on the rocks. Passing Loch Erisort we spotted a pair of red-breasted mergansers, several Arctic terns darting like arrows over the water, and many gulls.

We turned up a narrow track leading through deer-stalking country to Eishken, a hunting lodge half hidden by trees presiding over a rushing stream and small loch. The land of the Pairc is carved out of the oldest exposed rock on earth, Lewisian gneiss formed deep inside the earth between three and four billion years ago. Rounded hills and craggy bluffs loom over boggy glens littered with boulders and pebbles. Rust-brown heather in winter garb punctuates the rock-greys and grass-greens of grazed moorland. Hidden among the contours live red grouse, raven, mountain hare, red deer—and golden eagles. Ancient colours reinforce a sense of prehistory in this windswept place, the colours of Harris Tweed, colours of myriad minerals billions of years old, the first colours: iron-oxide reds, greens of malachite and olivine, blue of azurite, creams and ochres of mica, and the whites and pinks of quartz and feldspar. Butterwort and lousewort spangle the heather-strewn rocks, the spotted heath orchid grows alongside stunted royal-blue milkwort, and otters play freely in the lochs.

The great silences of these hills.

Suddenly above the skyline of a sheer crag a golden eagle appeared, soaring, floating, circling, broad wings held in a shallow V, strong fingered. The head neat, tail slender in silhouette. Through binoculars we could make out the dark-brown plumage and golden nape, the proud aquiline profile with hooked beak that tears flesh apart. The vast wings spanning seven feet, unbelievably for a flying creature, holding this huge bird on invisible air-currents with effortless grace. The golden eagle, *Aquila chrysaetos*, godlike winged creature which disdains the company of man and his activities, bird of silence which for ten thousand years has been flying over the hills of Lewis witnessing the course of human history. Golden eagles have elected silence for their habitat—and even for their habits: this more-than-bird hardly speaks even to his own kind, seldom vocalising. He's a creature with a predilection for few words, setting him apart from the penetrating calls of smaller raptors over whom he rules, let alone the cacophony of the human world. Imperious top predator, bird regarded with reverence throughout human history, symbol of untamed wilderness.

Stopping to scan the skyline, we continued along the

winding road towards hills grey with mist, where gorse grew thick flowered and honey-gold along the rushing burn, and where violets nestled in the banks. Further along where the hills slid into a loch, under leaden clouds reflected in the water, dark with unshed rain, we saw a black-throated diver. Although indistinct, we could see the pointed head, the white underside, the black throat, the so-smart black and white stripes on the neck, the pied panels on the wings. On the far shore of the wide water, circled by open hills where two otters played under an ever-changing sky of swirling clouds, this rarest and shyest of waterbirds was feeding while his nesting female remained hidden in the shoreline grasses.

As we returned, to our excitement a pair of golden eagles soared above a ridge, two adults—a monogamous couple paired for years for all we knew. We saw even more clearly than before the golden head and nape, the rich brown plumage with lighter touches of the same gold catching the light, the broad, long wings with finger-like tips spread open, immense arms held in a slight, upturned V, the patches of paler feathers on the undersides as, soaring and gliding with occasional wingbeats but mostly floating on the wind, they circled above us, amber eyed and yellow footed. The ferocious talons were visible in clear light, for the sun had emerged briefly from wind-driven clouds, chasing shadows across the glen.

These eagles, royal bird in so many languages, rulers of the skies since neolithic times, surveyed their terrain, this their kingdom, with defiant indifference, just as they have done since long before the nearby standing-stones of Callanish that we call prehistoric were erected four thousand years ago. In that wild place, in the sweep of hills, in open spaces away from human crowds with their noise and machines, this archetypal bird defied the passing of millennia. Transcending all languages, it appeared changeless on an ever-changing planet, the third rock from the sun evolving to its unknown destination under the gaze of the golden eagle, eternal bird of wild territories and limitless horizons.

Our time on Lewis was coming to an end. Looking back, that journey was a watershed. The impact remained vivid for years afterwards, a landmark that changed me in indefinable ways and affected my perspective on life. Something to do with real wildness, perhaps, real life in all its uncompromisingness: nothing like the managed farmlands of my home county, nothing like a nature reserve, nothing like anything I had ever experienced. Nothing safe.

After a final day of birdwatching, driving back to our cottage in Arctic winds and wet rain (it was hard to remember it was May), we'd been compensated by a sighting of turnstone feeding on the machair at Barvas along with dunlin and ringed plovers, and by watching red-breasted mergansers and oyster-catchers on the loch. We joked on the way back that maybe our sea eagle from Day One might be waiting for us to say goodbye. He wasn't there on the rocky bluff where we had seen him the day we'd arrived (how often we expect to see a bird where we saw it before: it almost never happens in wild places, yet they remain defined by the memory). We continued to a stretch of bog where we'd been watching moorland waders all week, with regular views of golden plover, dunlin, lapwing, snipe, redshank and even a merlin torpedoing across the moor. Just as we were about to leave, James spotted a shape on a distant ridge.

A sea eagle. *Our* sea eagle? Waiting for *us*? (Of course not, but we liked to think so.) He perched on the contour for several minutes, clear through binoculars, a fantastic view in late-afternoon light. A snipe started to chip-chip, a lapwing put up an alarm call, and the eagle turned his head, lowering it, twisting his neck to locate the sound. After a few moments he lifted off on massively wide wings (no surprise he is likened to a barn door in flight) and with the contemptuous takeoff of the monarch of the raptors, flew with graceful wingflaps over the moors in the direction we were heading, and disappeared behind a ridge.

Late sunshine was breaking through the grey day. We followed in the car, glimpsing him again in the distance floating over the hillsides, the moorland terrain his domain. He was a mature adult with bright white tail, pale head and beak. As he flew over a contour we thought we'd seen the last of him, but when we came to the swan-lochan near our cottage I spotted a large shape in the skies over the water. James was concentrating on the driving, didn't see it, but then I said words he has never allowed me to forget. 'There's something big over there.' There was indeed. Three birds were involved in a skirmish over the water: our white-tailed eagle was being harried by a raven and a herring gull—two birds of significant size made to look totally insignificant by this aristocrat of birds. As if he couldn't be bothered with them, he shrugged them off and flew low over the road in front of us, directly above our heads as we watched through the windscreen: a supreme view of a huge white-tailed eagle, clear every detail of plumage in the light, each feather etched on the broad wide-fingered wings. He flew over the hill and out of our lives, master of the skies, effortlessly imperious, majestic bird of majestic landscapes.

For years to come I would revisit the Outer Hebrides in my memory. They affected me more than any other place I have ever visited, even Monte Oliveto in Italy or the unpeopled expanses of Russia seen from the trans-Siberian express years before. The days on Lewis and Harris remain deeply imprinted. The uncompromising wildness of their landscapes and weathers, the untamedness of the moors and mountains, have a savage beauty which isn't always beautiful, but is ultimately true. I wonder if it contains the true meaning of joy—the joy John Clare hung on to—not a noisy kind of joy that delights in superficial gratification but something more akin to the truth encountered through the natural world in the depths of stillness, beyond itself, unnameable and indefinable. An elemental truth that is what it is, relentlessly indifferent, a ruthless dimension providing, paradoxically, the consolation of beauty that isn't always recognizable as beauty but is the consolation of truth. What is, is. The prehistoric rocks of these Atlantic islands in the sea are too harsh and unyielding to be simply 'beautiful': beyond beautiful, a place where birds belong, they have a special place in my heart.

JUNE

Skye, the Cairngorms, north-west Essex

the uncommonness of the commonplace

The following day we headed back to the mainland by way of the Isle of Skye. Crossing the Minch by ferry from Harris, prehistoric mountains divided sea from sky, indifferent to things that pass. If we were lucky on Skye, James said as we watched the surf breaking from the wake of the boat, we would hear corncrakes, golden and white-tailed eagles, maybe twite—and ravens, my particular obsession at the time. There would be all kinds of seabirds and, once we got up into the Cairngorms, even dotterel and ptarmigan, if we were really lucky. And really lucky we were: the first bird we saw on Skye was yet another golden eagle. After picking up a hire car, we had stopped in a lay-by to stretch our legs. James was scanning the skyline and, high above a ridge, too distant to see in any detail, floated a golden eagle, just as members of its kind have done for aeons. It seemed a good omen, and maybe, if we were that lucky, we would get to see the most elusive and tricky of birds, the corncrake.

Arriving at our rented cottage in Uig we could see Lewis and Harris shadowed across the Minch. Through a wide picture-window, the meadow outside the living room was a mass of gold buttercups. Across the lane, a river rushed over mossy boulders under the shade of thick-branched, large-leaved wych elms. Crossing a bridge where the Rha cuts a gorge through sheer basalt rock and plunges into a series of waterfalls, we entered a canopy of jade light. The fissured bark of the trunks, pocked with velvety mosses and silvery lichens, towered over a carpet of bluebells, wild garlic and water avens. In the 1970s, the people of Skye saved their elms: they closed the bridge to the mainland, prohibiting the import of any elm whatsoever, from saplings to carpentry timber. Consequently the Isle of Skye escaped Dutch Elm Disease. To walk under these huge trees was to realise the tragic loss to the English landscape.

It had been raining all afternoon. Stillness hung over the harbour in Uig bay. It was nine in the evening and wouldn't be properly dark until midnight. The water in the bay lay like silk.

Hearing from a local birder that there were several corn-crakes calling in the grassy fields that border Uig bay, we set out through the buttercups, passing a sedge warbler hopping around in a clump of wild raspberry bushes. A bullfinch perched on top of an elder, clear in profile against the sky, pink and plump. Down in the bay a common sandpiper piped, and we heard the mystical wail of a red-throated diver out at sea. On the far horizon stretched the Western Isles, dove-grey shadows in the soft light. A distant fishing trawler ploughed a furrow through the smooth water, followed by a flock of flustering black-backed gulls, raucous, eager for scraps.

We knew how rare it is to get a sighting of a corncrake: *The bird is seldom seen,* writes Thomas Bewick in 'British Birds', *for it constantly skulks among the thickest part of the herbage, and runs so nimbly through it, winding and doubling in every direction, that it is difficult to come near it.* He describes how the corncrake will play dead if caught, or drop suddenly immobile while being chased by a dog, which will pass over it and run on. John

Clare thought its existence was *a sort of living doubt.* Neverthe-less he managed to see one, sitting patiently for hours before *accidentally as it were we started it up it seemed to flye very awkard and its long legs hung down as if they were broken it was just at dew-fall in the evening.* A strange creature unwilling to take off, a clumsy flier according to those who have glimpsed it in flight, the corncrake is unwieldy and ungraceful in the air, grey legs trailing (although for longer migration flights it will tuck them up), frequently crashing into things yet succeeding somehow in flying to East Africa every year. A solitary corncrake can sometimes be seen migrating with a group of quails, its larger size giving it its French name *Roi de Cailles.*

Long grasses along the shoreline were wet underfoot. We found yellow sea sandwort cradled in star-shaped sepals, a maritime goosefoot with fleshy leaves, and clumps of wild mint. We picked some to make tea with later. Walking along the pebbly shore where nesting sandpipers were whistling and eiders sheltered on the rocks, we crossed the narrow coast road to the edge of a meadow of midsummer grasses. We waited. After a while, a sudden craiking, a sound like a loud cricket. The rasping, throaty, insistent echo of the corncrake, the *crex crex* that gives it its name. The sound came from somewhere close, almost next to us. We stopped and listened. It called again, then again, this time from the iron-grey shoreline, seemingly from rough grasses between the road and the shore. We crept along to flush it out, one of us going along the beach, the other along the tarmac, following the disembodied call. It stopped. We waited. Suddenly it called from the meadow on the other side of the road. How? It had outwitted us, this impossibly elusive bird who can apparently cross an open road without being seen, winged magician, will-o'-the-wisp, John Clare's *farey thing* who taunts the bird-lover with its call but never reveals itself—ventriloquist throwing its voice to deceive, just when we think we know where it's calling from, teasing us with its invisible presence.

> Ive listend when to school Ive gone
> That craiking noise to hear
> And crept and listened on and on
> But neer once gotten near . . .

So what *does* the corncrake look like? Related to coots and moorhens, it's slightly smaller than the latter, a dumpy bird with moonstone-grey flush on its head and breast, mottled brown and beige wings and patch of rust on the flank. William Turner (1562) called it a bird of bad omen, describing how *in spring and early summer it makes no other cry among the corn and flax than* crex crex, *and moreover it repeats the sound incessantly.* In days when the scythe was used to harvest hay meadows, nesting birds survived, but their numbers have been decimated by the use of mechanical cutters and tractors, along with the wide-spread loss of grassland habitats. The corncrake is in danger of disappearing from the UK: this shy bird with its blue-grey and russet plumage has been exiled to the margin of our lands by intensive farming practices, driven to near-extinction.

We focused on the long grass as it continued to craik, the call the female hears as 'come in', the male as 'keep out'. We continued homing in on the sound, which infuriatingly would suddenly appear to come from the opposite direction altogether. This bird is not afraid of being heard: at close range the call of the corncrake registers a hundred decibels (an ambulance siren registers a hundred and fifty) and can be heard up to a mile away. But would it grant us a sighting? We scanned the grasses for movement as it called. Nothing moved. There was no sign of any living creature in the meadow, and the corncrake is a chunky creature which lifts its head to stretch its throat as it calls. This one was managing to move without causing movement, like a ghost. *A very spirit to my wondering thoughts*, wrote Clare as he waded *knee deep the downy grasses among*.

The perplexing bird which used to inhabit the wild-flower meadows beloved by John Clare has all but vanished from our fields. I wondered if Thomas Aquinas ever saw a corncrake. It would have been common in his day, and with its elusive presence the corncrake almost more than any other bird fits his theology of the unseen. In 1273, while celebrating Mass, the Doctor of the great age of faith received a revelation that so affected him he wrote no further, leaving his *magnum opus* unfinished as he realised conclusively the impossibility of defining the invisible with words: *I can write no more. I have seen things that make my writings like straw.*

Ever since reading Heinrich's book on ravens, I'd longed to see one. There were ravens on the Isle of Skye, James had told me, finding it amusing that the highlight of our days on the island was, for me, the ravens. They were my holy grail. I went on about them a lot.

On our second day on Skye we drove to the rugged north coast of the island. To my excitement, below the road winding into the hills, some ravens were gathering in the drizzle. A few perched on fenceposts, others were flying up and along, settling again, floating down on to the moor to feed, turning and twisting before landing. Their amphibian croak echoed across the moors (according to Heinrich these would have been unmated juveniles, nomadic and covering large distances for food— they'll eat almost anything—and roosting together). Beyond them stretched, jagged and sombre against an agate sky, anvils of rock: the Quiraing Pass, black landscape of basalt pinnacles. Freak of nature, *Quiraing* means 'pit of rock pillars': fifty million years ago a mass of basalt lava landed on even older Jurassic sedimentary rock, bringing it to breaking point. It split into giant shards under immeasurable weight and shattered into a catastrophic landslip. The pass cascaded into labyrinths of towering blocks and pinnacles, leaving the hilltops scattered with ruined sphinxes of frost-shattered rock.

A bank of cloud rolled in behind a fleeting patch of sunshine, hiding the Western Isles in mist. Harris became a shadow as light rain veiled the view across the loch below. We started along a stony path uphill, past boulders weatherbeaten by millions of years of wind and rain. The track was lined with tiny white bedstraw, cushions of creeping thyme in bright pink flower, miniature alchemillas, wild strawberry and delicate ferns and mosses. Rooted in a crevice, a stunted wind-sculpted hazel leaned out of the rock face. Looking down towards a freshwater loch, we saw a pair of ravens pick-axing invertebrates on a rock slope, just as they have done for aeons before man appeared on the planet. When he did, he took immediate note of the raven: reckoned to be the bird represented in the Death of the Birdman, the paleolithic cave painting at Lascaux in south-west France, the raven was the first creature sent out from Noah's ark to find land after the Flood.

Its descendants, the two we were watching on the Quiraing, were male and female. (Once mated—and they mate for life— ravens generally separate themselves from juveniles and establish a territory over which they preside.) Relaxed and peaceful, they were doing an early-evening *passeggiata*, strolling, stopping to look around, walking on again. At one point the male flew up on to a rock and perched above his partner. Meditating over the prehistoric landscape, the ridged brow, the powerful talons. Archetypal the powerful profile, the strong shoulders, the thick, strong beak with curved upper mandible, 'horny-beaked one' of the Old English sagas. And so black, dark as starless midnight, glossy black with gleam of blue. A bird that rolls and dives like a thunderbolt, or flies with liquid gliding strokes showing wide, fingered wings that span four and a half feet, and handsome wedge-shaped tail. Regal bird—*Corvo imperiale* in Italian—that makes within its croaking range, according to Heinrich, a greater variety of sounds than any other creature apart from man. A bird of language, then, *Corvus corax*, Greek for a croaker, a bird which can be trained by humans to imitate voices and words. A playful, clever bird which will use twigs as toys and go sliding on snow slopes for fun.

We were to see and hear ravens again, often, on Skye, but nothing so thrilling as the sight of a raven flying up suddenly from a ridge to mob a sea eagle in Portree bay. The eagle was floating across the harbour high above our boat, casting an eight-foot shadow of long-fingered wings. The powerful head, aquiline beaked. It was making towards a ridge behind us, when suddenly, as if out of nowhere, a raven shot up and started to chase it, mobbing it and worrying at it until the two almost touched. The eagle did a complete roll in the air from right side up to upside down and right again, talons flailing, before disappearing over the hilltop. Even this king of birds, at twice its size, is a respecter of the blue-black bird whose only predator is man.

It was with a feeling of wistfulness that we left Skye after only a few days, taking with us memories of the wild hills with their flowers and birds. No visit could ever be long enough. As we drove south through the island, the hill shapes softened into gentle contours opening to wide vistas dotted with mostly deserted crofters' cottages, a sense of history and landscape merging in time and place. Under melodramatic skies looming over the jagged line of the Cuillins, we drove over the bridge linking Skye to the mainland, and passed into a rain-fed land-scape of forest-covered hills where trees tower over carpets of bracken and long grasses. Weather-beaten oaks, mature ash, tall beeches and hornbeams were coated with mosses and bryophytes, the papery bark of silver birches smothered with grey-green lichens which bathed the woods in verdigris light. Walking under these trees through undergrowth and sedges, feeling part of a life beyond my small self, I could understand what John Muir meant by *going out is going in*.

This remote, wind-clipped woodland of the west coast of Scotland, known as the Gaelic rainforest, has evolved a species known as Atlantic hazel. Many of the lichens, bryophytes and mosses that flourish in the clean air and damp climatic condi-tions here are new to science, encrusting hazel branches with mosaics and creating a forest of unearthly beauty. Hazel grows so abundantly in Scotland that the people named their country after it: Caledonia comes from 'Cal-dun', Hills of Hazel. Our Caledonian days included a trip to the reedy oasis of Loch Ruthven to glimpse the Slavonian grebe, gorgeous in breeding plumage. We went out at midnight to watch pine martens, the most endearing of small mammals (immediately my top favourite ever), red deer and badgers. We walked along a broom-bordered stream, the butter-yellow blooms reflected in mirroring water, to watch crossbills in the fir trees, and we sought (and found) crested tits up in the Caledonian pine forests.

Nearing Aviemore, our final port of call, evening light turned the uplands pink, and dusk covered the slate-blue hills in mauve shadows.

The next morning we started from base camp of Aviemore's ski runs, climbing a steep scree path punctuated by boulders and stepping stones helicoptered in to create a track to the top of Cairngorm. It led uphill through bog and moorland gouged with streams, lined with native shrubs struggling against harsh conditions: cowberry, blaeberry, cloudberry, bearberry, and tiny, stunted juniper bearing a few small berries which gave out heady incense when crushed. Our guide pointed to tormentil, its yellow petals miniaturised by the cold—tor*men*til as he pronounced it, used to cure torments of the stomach, known locally as red-root, its dye used for tanning. Intricate lichens and mosses, specialities of eternally wet Scotland, covered the tiny wind-formed trees, some of them morphed into eighty-year-old dwarfs by the elements.

For an hour we climbed, stopping occasionally to take in the views encircling us, all the colours of Scotland and tweed: heather-green slopes tinged with tawny rust and dun browns, granite-dark rocks, and purple cloud-shadows drifting across the lavender-blues and greys of distance. Streams poured off the hillside, water rushing noisily over the rocks. It was a long, steep climb requiring regular pauses to inspect the mountain flora and catch the breath. Demanding on legs and lungs it was, but as I stopped to rest and look around at this wild land-scape I thought, it's when we experience beauty that we are the most fully alive—an idea the poet who wrote the twelfth-century 'Conference of the Birds' was familiar with:

> If you could glimpse the beauty we revere
> Look in your heart—its image will appear
> Make of your heart a looking glass ...

Banks of cloud were building up, mist swirled in over a sheer ridge above us. We continued for another hour, the wind increasing the higher we climbed, and after a rugged scramble of two and a half hours we reached a plateau at three thousand five hundred feet. A three-hundred-and-sixty-degree vista of the Scottish Highlands stretched away into a haze. We could see across the Moray Firth in one direction, towards Ben Nevis in another: a circular view of the top of Scotland. It was here that we hoped to see a bird which lives and breeds in remote places around the Arctic Circle—quite commonly in Greenland and Iceland (where it used to be hunted for food) and northern Scandinavia, but sparsely in the Scottish Highlands, the Alps and the Pyrenees. The ptarmigan.

We stopped to rest briefly (as far as rest is possible in a fifty-mile-an-hour wind). I sat with my back to the elements, glad of a long waterproof coat and shrouding hood that did nothing to turn me into a fashion icon but did something to protect me from the soaking cold. After a while we set out across rough moorland and squashy bog, scouring the terrain for ptarmigan among limestone rocks mixed with granite, the same colouring and mottling as the birds we were looking for (in winter snows finding them is just as hard, since the male ptarmigan turns pure white, surviving Arctic temperatures in the shelter of forest trees and revealed only by the fanning of black tail feathers). We were looking for dotterel too, for males sitting on eggs or feeding hatchlings—their wives having flown off to Scandinavia as soon as they'd finished the business of mating rituals and the laying of eggs (the emancipated females of the avian world). I picked up a ptarmigan feather from the ground, minuscule and down-light, insulating the feet, toes and nostrils of this bird of cold climates. Stowed in my camera bag for safety, it eventually found a home in a tiny frame on my study table.

We came to a stony slope of whitish, black-pocked boulders blotched with lichen. Something was moving. A few yards away, a pair of ptarmigan had seen us, but they continued pottering around gently, seemingly unbothered by our presence (ptarmigan have few predators and are generally trusting of man: it's the seven-foot wingspan of the golden eagle that strikes terror into their hearts). Another appeared, a male with more white in his plumage than the females, showing the distinctive fanning of the tail as he turned, and the brilliant red eyebrow, the comb, near the top of the head. There was something very lovable about these birds. Relaxed and self-contained. The females appeared and reappeared among the stones, dappled granite-grey and brown with white front and neck, white flanks and feathered feet, the 'hare's foot' of the ptarmigan's generic name *Lagopus*, from two Greek words for hare and foot (the Gaelic *tàrmagan* meaning 'croaker' had a 'p' added to it in the seventeenth century, as in the Greek for feather, *pteron*).

We left them and continued over the ridge. Turning to the left, we saw three more ptarmigan scuttling uphill away from us, clear sightings against the sky in the rinsed light. One ran with long neck outstretched and we could make out the rounded grouse-like body, the smallish head, the mottled grey-brown plumage which in close-up is vermiculated black edged with white. The ptarmigan's specific name *muta* suggests an unvocal bird, and we didn't hear them call, although apparently a strange croak—a cross between a snore and a belch—is sufficient for their communication needs in these deserted places. Birds looking and sounding like granite.

On the leisurely stroll down, still hoping for dotterel and looking out for wild flowers, I reflected that we were among a very small percentage of the human race ever to set eyes on a ptarmigan. These birds have chosen to live in virtually inaccessible places, to endure the coldest climates on earth through the severest of winters, in habitats inhabited by very few creatures. Far away from the human race, they live on the margins of creation: *I know all the birds in the sky, All that moves in the field belongs to me,* wrote the Psalmist. Here tiny Arctic saxifrage grows bright pink on a moss of vivid green leaves, and wild azaleas flower with petals smaller than a baby's fingernail.

Our days in the chilly north over, the time had come to make the journey home from some of the remotest and most challenging places in Britain, to the cosy dimensions of a cottage in East Anglia where blackbird song fills the summer garden. As I hung out the holiday washing I thought of St Augustine, who had his moment of conversion, of clarity, of certainty, in a garden. It changed his life and the life of many who have followed his inspiration for over fifteen hundred years (and it would come as no surprise to discover that a bird was singing at the time). The revelation came to him in his older age: *Late did I love thee, beauty ever ancient and ever new.* He had been looking at beauty without seeing it, or looking in the wrong place, and finally (but not too late) discovering something that had always been there.

As I returned to domestic chores, I thought about how late it was in my life, too, that the birds had flown in, effecting conversion of a kind. They had certainly changed my life in the course of that year. Wandering into their world I'd learned, thanks above all to my mentor, more about birds than I could ever have believed possible. The birds themselves had taught me the value of a beginner's mind, helped me discover freedom in solitude, stillness and silence, and shown me the consolation of beauty. I'd glimpsed transcendence through birds, birds as both kindred and other, birds as uber-phenomena yet completely grounded in the everyday.

Socrates said that *the secret of happiness is not to be found in seeking more, but in developing the capacity to enjoy less.* Like hanging out the washing in the garden in summer and listening to a blackbird singing.

That signpost at the crossroads as I started out had pointed to a change of direction, the choice being to allow myself to be overcome by personal loss and unhappiness, or not. The mirror the birds held up to my small self helped me see how I should live. The details of what happened to me are for self-pity to indulge in, or prurience to revel in, but what the birds showed me was the 'I' beyond the personal self, and how the little 'me' in all of us plays its tiny part in the divine comedy in which we all participate. If we are grains of sand in the scheme of things, the great paradox is that we are no less significant for that. The story of love and betrayal and pain is a universal one, and at the same time deeply personal. The languid song of the blackbird floating across the lawn was imbued with freedom from the small concerns of the ego, its fluting conveying ease at being in the world, a lazy quality of contentment at what is, of pure being. Blackbirds don't have egos, they just live according to the necessities of life, in all its glory and difficulty. The careless beauty of this bird's music sang of the uncommonness of what we take for granted (in a moment of genius G. K. Chesterton called it *the starry pinnacle of the commonplace*). Simply pegging up washing on the line in a garden on a summer's day, I was struck by how the beauty of the ordinary is in fact completely extraordinary.

Clare describes the familiar sound: *The rich Blackbird through his golden bill / Litters wild music when the rest are still*, a hymn of praise like the *Sanctus* sung for thousands of years ever since the eighth century BC when Isaiah wrote *Holy, holy, holy is the Lord Almighty, the whole earth is full of his glory*, words of the daily liturgy heard throughout the globe by millions of people in many languages down many generations. Somewhere in the warp and weft of sound on earth the *Sanctus,* held in the radio waves which retain it, needs only that imaginary remitter to retrieve the accumulated dream of a perfect world. *Heaven and earth are full of thy glory* sung by a blackbird in a sun-filled garden at midsummer one afternoon. In those moments, Augustine's lines floated into my head: *the world is a beautiful poem . . . My questioning with the heavens and the earth was my thought, and their answer was their beauty.*

As William Blake said, *everything that lives is holy*. That blackbird's song was nothing out of the ordinary, but also it was.

Later that week, under a blue June sky, I went walking among all the greens of midsummer. A short car journey from where I live there's an organic farm, brave anomaly in the prevailing agribusiness, where no chemicals are used on the land, pest control is left to the birds, fertilising the soil is left to natural processes, and crops flourish under the stewardship of a farmer who is an expert in soil science and ecology. It was one of those rare moments when the world seemed flawless, the *Sanctus* dream emerging from its nebulous existence and becoming, for that hour, real. Lines of dark trees divided the fields into seas of blue-green wheat. A yellowhammer wheezed its 'little bit of bread and no cheese' song from an oak tree. Bindweed scrambled underfoot, brilliant white. I wandered along grassy lanes where butter-yellow bird's-foot trefoil peeped through the long grasses, the swollen capsules of bladder campion hung their heads among red campion under flowering brambles, and viper's bugloss splashed the verges with indigo. Tiny field geranium and cheerful herb Robert dotted the grasses with pink, the yellow of lady's bedstraw tangled with purplish hedge woundwort and greater knapweed, startlingly magenta, stitching a wild-flower tapestry along tracks which could never thrive under the impact of chemical farming. Yet this is a farm that produces food at a profit, organically. The place was full of birdsong. It was like walking through a lost Eden.

Back home I opened the picket gate, disturbing a fledgling blackbird on the gravel, plump and chocolate brown with a heavily speckled breast, and a much shorter tail than an adult blackbird. In alarm it took off and crashed into the one of the conservatory windows, dropping stunned to the ground. After a few seconds it staggered off into the foliage of a flowerbed and took shelter under some leaves. I tiptoed past and watched it from indoors. Eventually it hopped away and disappeared into its native hedge. Not the brightest of blackbirds, I reflected. Bird-brain? Surely not. The fact that birds have a large brain-to-bodymass ratio reflects their advanced and complex intelligence—and the epithet 'bird-brain' was in any case invented by a race that hasn't got the auditory sophistication to hear the thirty-six notes in one second of a skylark's song, and which in its ignorance banished diminished fifths as 'music of the devil' at the Council of Trent in the sixteenth century.

Blackbirds used to be common country fare, trapped or killed with a catapult. Famously, four-and-twenty blackbirds were baked in a pie: in medieval times, a live bird or birds were put under the pie crust just before serving, and flew out when it was cut: 'a surprise pie'. Now they are (in the UK at least) free of that kind of predation, and can regard a garden as a protected place (apart from cats who kill millions of baby birds every spring and summer). The mellow fluting of the blackbird's song is one of the commonest sounds in our English gardens, *nearer to human music than any other birdsong*, in W. H. Hudson's view, a melodic purity counterpointed by the scolding *tchook tchook* of the alarm call with its urgent 'pinking'.

My blackbirds return to the same nesting site in the hedge by the gate year after year. And year after year, the song of the blackbird, Beethoven of the birds, fills the garden. Here was another musician whose life was touched by birds and the beauty of birdsong: in his Pastoral Symphony you can practically hear blackbirds singing. To Beethoven, the woods were *a holy of holies, a Home of the Mysteries*, as he wrote in his journal. Out in nature he became naively happy, transposing its beauty to his music. The manuscript of his Spring Sonata looks like an uninterrupted flow of dreams transposed on to staves, a transport of joy: *Nature is a glorious school for the heart! . . . Here I shall learn wisdom.* Beethoven, a passionate agnostic, copied into his diary words from unidentified Eastern wisdom: *God is immaterial, and for this reason transcends every conception. Since he is invisible he can have no form. But from what we observe in His work we may conclude that He is eternal, omnipotent, omniscient and omnipresent.* Gerard Manley Hopkins felt the same way, speaking of *God's immanent revelation of himself through the world. The Sacrament of the World . . . Everything is sacred.*

I had plenty of opportunity to watch my 'ordinary' garden birds that summer after the dramas of the Scotland trip. Every time I opened the door or came home through the gate, my proprietary robin sang loudly from high up in a boundary tree, *tutling* (John Clare's word) his song. The birds we take for granted are just as special in their own ways as the corncrake or the eagle, the ptarmigan or the Arctic tern. Roger Deakin loved his resident robin: *It is good to feel the blessing of a wild bird trusting you like that,* he wrote in his journal. He was always one to see the uncommonness of the commonplace: *As a naturalist you hope never to lose your virginity, always to be looking with wonder, to remain innocent, wide-eyed.* Likewise Clare, who found beauty in the ordinary, in what he called *the refuse of nature*, the small things easily disregarded.

I spent much time that summer watching my robin in the garden. To Roger Deakin, *Robins are the angels of my vegetable garden. You turn round and they're not there. Then there they are, next to you.* Cock robins can become very tame—the hens are less confident—and can be trained to take mealworms from the hand. Tame they may be in Britain, but not so in eastern Europe according to Martin, our friendly guide in Macedonia, who envied us for our robins living among us. There, he told us, they are wild woodland birds, seldom seen but hunted to be eaten, roasted with breadcrumbs. That used to be the custom in medieval times in Britain too, when many wild birds were caught for the table: robins were still common fare in seventeenth-century England, eaten for what was claimed to be medicinal properties. But cats who eat robins have been observed vomiting them up, and never kill one again. Maybe there's pragmatism behind the traditional ditty:

> The Robin redbreast and the Wren
> Are God Almighty's cock and hen.

He's not designed for human consumption, this friendly character who makes his home in our gardens and nests in our sheds, in discarded wellies or an old jacket hung on the door, a rusting kettle or broken flowerpot. He sits on spade-handles while we weed, watching us with eyes like *black dewdrops*, as Frances Burnett put it in 'The Secret Garden'. Robins have always been special. William Blake famously wrote, *A Robin redbreast in a cage / Puts all heaven in a rage,* and to harm a robin was always thought to bring evil consequences: John Clare recorded *a belief (still current even fifty years ago) that to rob a Robins nest of its eggs would result in you breaking your leg.* As in the popular ditty,

> Kill a Robin or a Wren
> Never prosper boy or man.

Robins belong to the same family as the nightingale—with which their song competes for beauty, a music shifting to a mournful key in the winter when it sings, including at night, with the *plaintive sweetness* John Clare was so *fond of it may be calld an eternal song for it is heard at intervals all the year round & in the Autumn when the leaves are all fled from the trees there is a melancholy sweetness in it that is very touching to my feelings.* But although we think they are so sweet, robins are highly aggressive: the male will attack stray birds on its territory who are competing for food or a mate, fighting to the death in some cases. Or sometimes they'll skirmish just for the hell of it. With early mortality, a robin has an average life expectancy of only one year, although if it makes it beyond that it can expect to live significantly longer. One robin has been recorded as reaching nineteen: I have no way of knowing how old mine is. Nor of verifying another astounding robin-fact (of which there are many), that its little heart beats at a rate of 456 beats a minute.

One man who devoted himself to investigating robin facts was the evolutionary biologist and ecologist David Lack. He it was who, when involved in early work on radar, referred to the then inexplicable radar echoes of birds as 'angels' (and even got stiff-upper-lipped military personnel to do the same). Lack, a convert to Christianity after the Second World War, managed to integrate his faith with his science to his own satisfaction, and a fellow member of the Royal Society said of him, *David Lack was the only religious man I knew at that period who did not allow his religion to dictate his view of natural selection.*

He came from a family of tenant farmers, and spent part of his childhood in a palatial house in Devonshire Place run by a retinue of servants and a succession of nannies. When he was sent off to school at Gresham's, the Norfolk coast with its rich bird life was within easy cycling distance. While at school he did some original studies on the nightjar, finding it to be double- and not single-brooded as the books said. Lack was a devoted and outstanding member of the Cambridge Bird Club, as Emma Turner had been, and all but ran it when he was an undergraduate. On arrival at Cambridge at the age of nineteen one of his first actions was to visit the sewage farm where he saw his first wood sandpiper. His friend and Cambridge colleague Bill Thorpe—they were both elected FRS in 1951—wrote in his obituary that he found the David Lack of the birds an entirely different creature from the academic David Lack. Aloof and laconic in the latter, he bubbled over with enthusiasm on the subject of birds, and was outstandingly learned about them from an early age. His was a socially withdrawn character with a fierce manner, one that didn't tolerate fools: like the robin, he could be hostile on his territory. He had what he called *my irritating weakness*, namely his need for nine or even ten hours' sleep a night in order to work efficiently. Thorpe said he hardly dared ring him up after 8 p.m. But in the company of birds David Lack came alive in a different way.

Lack's work on robins resulted in the classic monograph that made him famous, 'The Life of the Robin', a bird he describes as one *whose life is devoted almost exclusively to fighting.* Begun at

Dartington Hall in January 1935, the four-year study lays out in detail the life of a robin throughout the year, telling you everything you could ever want to know about robins, in an accessible way that does nothing to undermine the science behind it. Lack balances his research findings with proverbs, among them *one bush does not shelter two robins*, poetry (Shakespeare, James Thomson, W. H. Davies, William Cowper, George Herbert, John Webster), history, philosophy and humour. One of several black-and-white photos in the first edition includes a picture of Lord Edward Grey with a tame robin perched on his deerstalker. A chapter title 'Food, Feeding and being Fed upon' conveys his light touch, an ability to write with a twinkle in his eye between quoting heavyweights like Darwin and Gilbert White and John Bunyan. Cervantes' 'Don Quixote' makes an appearance heading the chapter 'Adventures with a Stuffed Robin' which describes Lack's use of a taxidermist's robin as a decoy, in an attempt to test aspects of behaviour never examined before. It led the author to conclude that *the world of a robin is so strange and remote from our experience that into it we can scarcely penetrate, except to see dimly how different it must be from our own . . . [we] deceive [ourselves] into assuming that the mind that inspires them is not unlike the human mind.* He ends his monograph with a quote from the philosopher Francis Bacon: *It is strange how men, like owls, see sharply in the darkness of their own notions, but in the daylight of experience wink and are blinded.*

A triple-pronged feeder stands outside the studio window next to my garden hedge, providing cover for the birds as they wait their turn to feed. Among the shrubs a *Rosa andersonii* briar, gnarled with age, arches over the patio, providing a convenient launch-pad as the birds line up for seeds and suet balls. A white clematis, acanthus and hellebores mingle in this secluded corner of the cottage garden. A trailing nasturtium, self-seeded, scrambles over the terrace walls and under the feeder. The studio doubles as a bird hide, affording illicit distraction. The usual suspects—greenfinches, bluetits, great tits, house sparrows, chaffinches, dunnocks, long-tailed tits, a great spotted woodpecker—visit at regular times of day, taking turns, establishing pecking orders, always competing. My resident robin among them, of course.

I saw him on the suet balls one afternoon before noticing, perched on the briar, a brown bird. Pretty much just that, with its back to me, an LBJ, little brown job, plump with speckled head. As I watched, the robin on the feeder darted on to the branch and fed it a morsel of fat. Then again. The little brown bird hopped and turned sideways on to me: it was a young robin, fresh-feathered with streaked face and spotted thrush-chest, buff and chestnut wings handsomely marked with a yellowish wingbar, and grey underparts. It was joined by a second youngster, slightly smaller. The parent bird hopped to and fro feeding his offspring, then started to cajole them into having a go at helping themselves—to comical effect: it took one of the young birds most of the afternoon to get the knack of holding on to the wire frame of the feeder before inserting its beak to reach seeds. The second bird didn't get it at all, sat there on his branch looking abject and hopeful in turn. But before long the first juvenile was balancing confidently on the feeder and helping himself.

It was a while before I saw them again at the feeders. When

JUNE

they returned, the juveniles were still plump, strong looking, fresh and shiny. The older one's smart chestnut speckles were now freckled with scarlet. A splash of rust-red was beginning to spread like a blush from underneath his wing. Beyond him, through the shrubs, I glimpsed a pair of garden warblers on the lawn, flitting from flowerbed to apple tree with quick, nimble movements: delicate birds, small and mushroom brown with intricate marbling where their wings folded over the back, and sharp, thin beaks for insect hunting. They stood with skinny legs akimbo, pausing to cock the head to one side, listening, then flitting off again.

In the simplicity of those moments I was struck by how, in a Darwinian 'survival of the fittest' cottage garden full of 'ordinary' birds and bugs and butterflies and bees, everything is in timeless relationship. That the natural world is dependent on connected relationships is obviously not an original thought, but at that moment it wasn't a reflection, it was an experience of the unitive consciousness of quantum physics which observes there's no dividing line between things: a universe (us) in quantum entanglement in which one particle of an entangled pair 'knows' what is happening to another particle, even when separated by great distances, although there is no known means for such information to be communicated between them. The Great Chain of Being.

Beauty is ill and has a drawn face, lamented R. S. Thomas in one of his late poems. Humans continue to trample on beauty with industrial damage, greed and thoughtlessness, smothering what Rumi called *the great spirit in all things.* The poet-priest Gerard Manley Hopkins thought that part of human dignity is to know the land and its plants and creatures, and part of human intelligence to realise our dependence and our interconnectedness. Generations of readers of Gilbert White's 'Natural History and Antiquities of Selborne' (written in 1789 and never since out of print) have continued to read him because of the universal appeal of looking closely at the small, the local and the commonplace, and recognising their wider significance. White knew his patch intimately, and his is the perfect example: we can all start in our own back yard, and it seems we may have to. I started my bird adventure with the naive expectation that out there in the countryside was where they lived, in natural abundance. The arable heartland of East Anglia with its intensive farming, where the soil is cultivated to exhaustion and wildlife is marginalised, was far from wild. I had to go further afield, or to nature reserves, to see birds in any variety or quantity, apart from the usual suspects who have made my rambling cottage garden their home. As human populations increase, our own patch is all we'll have unless we start caring enough to apply joined-up thinking. Wild places will become tamed, and 'nature reserves' highly managed habitats, natural history farms busy with people and cameras, nothing much less than zoos.

The next time I saw my juvenile robin was in early September. His head and face were still speckled, and the rust-red blush had spread—he reminded me of a spotty teenager—and the underparts had turned whiter. I might never see him again, this unique, plucky little creature: he would be driven off my patch by his territorial father to establish his own, and if he survived village cats and the perils and dangers of being a young bird, perhaps I would hear him singing his autumn song on one of my walks up the lane into the fields.

Back home from my travels, sitting in the June sunshine listening to my robin *tutling* and thankful for my angel of the garden,
I thought of T. S. Eliot's lines from 'Four Quartets',

> We shall not cease from exploration
> And the end of all our exploring
> Will be to arrive where we started
> And know the place for the first time.

My first year with the birds had come full circle. New worlds
had opened up to me, I'd learned more than I could ever have
imagined about birds as physical and metaphysical beings,
their ways and their history and their beauty. The mirror they
held up helped me see my own life in new ways, teaching
me as much about myself as about them. Waiting for birds
and watching birds, I'd picked myself up and realised how
interconnected and part of a continuum we all are, and of how
beautiful and mysterious life is in its micro-detail and macro-
immensity. Brokenness had led to unanticipated resources. *To
get to the kernel you must crack the shell,* wrote Meister Eckhart
back in the fourteenth century. I'd found fulfilment living as
an integrated solitary, and as my knowledge deepened and my
experience with birds widened, I came to understand what it
means to be human in relationship to nature, how wildness is
embedded in the human psyche, and how the consolation of
beauty is central to our mental and emotional wellbeing. But
I also saw with distress the careless damage we are inflicting

on the natural world, on the Great Chain of Being to which we belong.

I often stop in the lanes on summer days to watch yellow-hammers or a family of long-tailed tits, and see them as if for the first time. Watching them darting in and out of the hedgerows or balancing on telegraph wires, I lose all sense of self. At any time of the year, seeing a heron lifting off the lake with stony glare and languid wingbeats, I find myself absorbed in the newness of watching a bird: it's always different, never the same, enabling—as R. S. Thomas put it—

> the heart
> to migrate, if only momentarily,
> between the quotidian and the sublime.

Epilogue

Several years have passed since the day in Greece when a window opened in my consciousness and the birds flew in. They have become part of my everyday life, changing and enriching it in ways I could never have dreamed of.

A dull, grey, windy July day—not much of a day for birdwatching, I thought (wrongly). Above the bridleway leading through the woods, a cloud of house martins was swirling and circling, chirping and volleying on neat wings, glossy blue-black backed, white rumps flashing above forked tails, torquing on the wind. There's something eternally cheerful about martins, *Hirondelles de Fenêtre*, Window Swallows, which so often choose our houses to make their homes, each nest a phenomenon of engineering taking ten days to construct using a thousand pellets of mud, and feathers gathered in the air to line it. The lane opened on to stubblefields where swallows were swooping, meteors of sloe-blue, terracotta and ivory. I walked across wet fields to the edge of the wood, and looking up through a lattice of ash leaves saw, against the light, a sparrowhawk hanging high over the field. Seeing me, it flew into a tree, yellow-eyed *spearhafoc* of the Anglo-Saxon world.

That afternoon the windswept reedbeds at Fowlmere were quiet, apparently deserted in the buffeting elements. A brief torrent of notes lit the gloom, a Cetti's warbler. The rest of the afternoon produced three mallard and a moorhen. And corvids of course—a carrion crow puffing his feathers and doubling his size as he presided over the shallows from his perch on a post. Rooks circled. A speckled-wood butterfly settled on water crowfoot, and I found a hornets' nest made of regurgitated wood fibres shaped into paper combs, the swollen sculpture of its buff walls nestling in the hollow of a dead tree trunk. But largely the hours were birdless. R. S. Thomas, waiting for his albino dunnock to turn up, was convinced in his priest's heart that *when He reveals himself, he does so through the natural world.* He also said, *The meaning is in the waiting,* the man of God refusing to, as he put it, domesticate an enigma: Thomas's God was a God of absence, of silence, a God of the gaps between, anguishingly unknowable.

> You have to imagine
> a waiting that is not impatient
>   because it is timeless.

God-and-birds comes up a lot in the bird business, an acknowledgment that birds don't quite belong to this world, mediators of the divine like Shelley's blithe spirit of the skylark, flying high in the skies, owner of the spaces between earth and heaven. Emma Turner, maverick bird-seer who sensed the interconnectedness of things, said that to try to explain birds was *tantamount to interviewing an archangel.*

Epilogue

*

Yes, you could call it ornitheology.

As I sit waiting-for-God-or-birds in a bleak bird hide, where the hush resembles the silence of an abandoned church, it doesn't matter all that much whether the birds turn up or not. One of the reasons I've come to love waiting for them (and it is a love affair) is that it continues to take me away from empty chatter, from the tentacles of technology, from the slow poison of the world's ways. I continue to discover how much I like—and need—periods of solitude and silence. The wildness of birds draws me to them, untamed creatures who prefer hidden places, keeping themselves to themselves, away from the human race, independent of us. Beings who sing an otherworldly music to communicate in ways we can only attempt to decode.

They live in the now, in their bird world, in their isness, among us but mostly invisible, like God—or what we falteringly call God for lack of words to express what lies beyond the limits of consciousness.

The serendipitous nature of watching birds, unpredictable and beyond human control, never at our wish or command, has taught me new ways of looking and seeing. I have come to trust the randomness of life, the certainty of uncertainty. The cycles of life and death have become familiar and natural. I now know the futility of expectation: I can only encounter what turns up, or doesn't. And that applies to my wider life. Trusting in that inevitability, I have grown to be happiest of all out in wild places where nature is left largely to itself.

*

We no longer dare to believe in beauty, writes Hans Urs von Balthasar in 'The Glory of the Lord'. Beauty, he declares, is the forgotten theme of metaphysics. Beauty, personal and subjective
as it may be, and ultimately indefinable, offers a glimpse of the
transcendent. It connects us, he considers, with the ultimate
mystery of being, answering our deepest spiritual and moral
needs. Passionately he pleads that, without stepping into the
crucible of beauty, we are impoverished, we cannot be whole.
As Agnes Martin, visionary painter whose delicate, minimalist
silence on canvas speaks to my soul, wrote, *Beauty is the mystery
of life. It is not just in the eye. It is in the mind. It is our positive
response to life.* Continues von Balthasar, *Beauty is a word that has
never possessed a permanent place or an authentic voice in ... the exact
sciences ... We can be sure that whoever sneers at her name as if she
were the ornament of a bourgeois past ... can no longer pray and soon
will no longer be able to love.*

Every year I return to my bolt-hole on the Suffolk coast, the
rented cottage in the woods I have come to love. I often book
a week in November, and spend much of the intervening time
dreaming about the place where I find refuge to recover from,
and avoid, *the strife of tongues* (Emma Turner's neat phrase).
Finally the time comes: depleted and exhausted by the chitchat
and busyness of what is loosely called 'life', I drop my bags off
at the cottage and set out. I have an urgent need to sit in a bird
hide and do nothing. Nothing but watch, in silence.

It was a damp, cold, steel-grey afternoon and soon it would
be dusk. But I went anyway. Walking the boardwalk through
the marshes, I didn't care if nothing turned up. The quiet and
the stillness would be enough. I sat for a while, waiting. Within
yards of the hide, a bittern appeared, and started to pick its

way along the edge of the reeds, carefully, slowly, placing one huge foot after another over the cut stalks. At each step, the stretch of its neck streamlined effortlessly into its long pointed beak, then released back into itself. The impetus seemed propelled from a spring coiled deep within, lengthening and retracting into the neck ruff which lay flat, only lightly rippled by the movement. The bittern's plumage melted into the reeds, streaked ginger neck feathers and brindled wings of many browns. Feathers becoming reed shadows. After standing motionless for at least a minute, this shade of the reedbeds made another long step with its enormous foot, and stopped. Watched. Stood still again and did nothing, pointed its long beak upwards, stood still again, then turned, slowly, deliberately, and took another step. It took at least a quarter of an hour for it to reach the uncut reeds, into which, with measured deliberation, it disappeared.

Above the ruined abbey on the shoreline a mile away, a murmuration of starlings gusted over the winter trees like handfuls of soot thrown up into the sky, clouds of birds coiling and unfurling, flung across the evening treeline before dropping into the land. In the foreground, two marsh harriers were hunting: commanding raptors, demigods of the reedbeds, chestnut-brown wing feathers and creamy heads catching the late light, floating over the reeds before falling like stones into the marsh. A brief cascade of notes from a Cetti's warbler. Twilight thickened. A line of Bewick's swans pierced the gloom, spears of white flying over the water, slender necked, chanting their chamber music as they flew in to land on the field beyond the mere.

Long silences. A tawny owl hooted from the woods. And then there was only the thin song of the wind in the reeds.

Ah, but a rare bird is
            rare. It is when one is not looking,
at times one is not there
       that it comes.
You must wear your eyes out,
as others their knees.
   I became the hermit
of the rocks, habited with the wind
and the mist. There were days,
so beautiful the emptiness
it might have filled,
       its absence
was as its presence: not to be told
any more, so single my mind
after its long fast,
       my watching from praying.

from 'Sea-watching' by R. S. Thomas

A Note on Albino Dunnocks

There's no evidence that R. S. Thomas, waiting patiently to catch sight of an albino dunnock, ever got to see one. In any case, if one had turned up it would have been more likely to be leucistic, not a true albino. Albinism is congenital and caused by a recessive gene which results in the absence of the enzyme tyrosinase in pigment cells, and goes with an inability to produce melanin (dark) pigments. The eyes are pink due to the absence of ocular melanism which makes visible the blood in the capillaries of the retina. Leucistic birds have white or whitish plumage, in whole or in part, but normal colouring in the eyes and soft parts.

The name dunnock comes from Middle English *donek*, *dunneck*, *dinneck*, from the dun of its plumage, and by 1475 the spelling was established as 'dunnock'. Dunnocks were referred to variously through the centuries as Dike-smowler, Swart Colemouse, and Dingie Dunnock. From the seventeenth century onwards they were known as hedge sparrows or hedge warblers (*Accentor modularis*) until, in 1951, ornithologist Max Nicholson called for a change in seven birds' names including hedge sparrow to dunnock. It was the only neologism to catch on: his 'throstle' remains a song thrush, the great spotted woodpecker did not, sadly, become 'pied', nor the common gull the 'mew gull' as he suggested.

Albino dunnocks are extremely rare: there's one reference in a 1962 article published in 'British Birds',* one in a list of albino birds recorded in the British Isles, but it lacks corroboration. Photographs online claiming to be the real thing are dark-eyed beauties, leucistic rather than albino: in true albinism the plumage is pure white, the eyes pink, the legs and bill yellowish-white to pinkish.

Waiting for the albino dunnock. As in the case of the all-but-legendary snow leopard, the waiting is more about the search than the result: what began as an expedition in the 1970s by George Schaller and Peter Matthiessen to find a rare creature on the Crystal Mountain in the Himalayas developed into a quest for the meaning of Being, and became as much an inner journey as a field trip. Likewise 'waiting for the albino dunnock' is not about the achievement of spotting a rare bird and recording it on a list, wonderful though that would be, but an intuition about what is mysterious and just beyond our reach.

---

* 'Albinism and melanism in birds', by Bryan L. Sage, 'British Birds', Vol. 55 No. 6, June 1962.

Thanks

I'm indebted to Matt Merritt at 'BirdWatching' who read my work at an early stage and agreed to publish it in the magazine as an ongoing series of 'Reflections'. This book would not have come about without his support over the years, and much of the material is based on pieces I wrote for the column. Thanks to my agent Felicity Bryan for championing the idea of turning these pieces into a book, and to Alan Samson at Weidenfeld and Nicolson for his enthusiasm, support and help in getting it into shape. I owe a huge debt to Jeremy Mynott for his close reading of the manuscript, for his editorial expertise and kindly advice. Thanks to Professor Eric Robinson for his permissions and help with John Clare, to Professor Tim Birkhead for his enthusiastic research on albino dunnocks, to Stephen Moss, John Fanshawe and all at New Networks for Nature who have inspired me over the years. And I owe special thanks to Father Ben O'Rourke at Clare Priory.

Thank you Carry Akroyd for your exceptional illustrations, and for your comments on reading the manuscript at an early stage. Thanks to the Weidenfeld team for their help and expertise: to editorial director Lucinda McNeile, designer Helen Ewing, publicity director Elizabeth Allen. To Peter James for his sensitive copy-editing, and to Christopher Phipps, bird-lovers both, much gratitude. I am grateful to Eleanor and Richard Barnes for being able to escape to the 'cottage in the woods' over a period of many years. It's largely due to the practical support of my daughter Emily and twin sister Juliet that I was able to finish the book, and I am indebted to the Cambridge doctors and nurses who helped me through the months of illness.

And thanks above all to James Parry for all the fun and friendship, and without whom this book could never have been written.

Select Bibliography

These titles are published in various editions, available through good search engines.

Attar—*The Conference of the Birds*
Augustine, Saint—*Confessions* (trans. Ben O'Rourke OSA)
Balthasar, Hans Urs von—*The Glory of the Lord*
Baker, J.A.—*The Peregrine*
Barrow, John D.—*The Book of Nothing*
Basho—*The Narrow Road to the Deep North*
Birkhead, Tim—*The Wisdom of Birds*
—*Bird Sense*
Blythe, Ronald—*Outsiders*
—*Aftermath: Selected Writings 1960–2010*
—*A Year at Bottengoms Farm*
Cage, John—*Silence*
Chardin, Teilhard de—*The Phenomenon of Man*
Chesterton, G.K.—*St Thomas Aquinas*
—*Orthodoxy*
—*St Francis of Assisi*
Cocker, Mark—*Birds and People*
Cocker, Mark and Mabey, Richard—*Birds Britannica*
Deakin, Roger—*Notes from Walnut Tree Farm* (eds Alison Hastie
    and Terence Blacker)
Eckhart, Meister—*Selected Writings*

—*Meister Eckhart* (ed. Halcyon Backhouse)

Eliot, T.S.—*The Four Quartets*

Flegg, Jim—*Time to Fly*

Ford, Emma—*Falconry: Art and Practice*

Gaddis, Thomas—*Birdman of Alcatraz*

Gordon, Seton—*Wild Birds in Britain*

Heinrich, Bernd—*Ravens in Winter*

Hesse, Hermann—*Steppenwolf*

—*Journey to the East*

Høeg, Peter—*Miss Smilla's Feeling for Snow*

Hopkins, Gerard Manley—*The Major Works*

Hudson, W.H.—*Birds and Man*

—*Adventures among Birds*

—*The Vision of Earth*

Huxley, Aldous—*The Perennial Philosophy*

Jamie, Kathleen—*Findings*

—*Sightlines*

Jefferies, Richard—*The Story of My Heart*

—*Field and Hedgerow*

—*The Notebooks*

—*At Home on the Earth* (ed. Jeremy Hooker)

Kerst, Friedrich (ed.)—*Beethoven: The Man and the Artist*

Kierkegaard, Søren—*The Lily of the Field and the Bird of the Air*

—*The Soul of Kierkegaard: Selections from his Journals* (ed. Alexander Dru)

Krishnamurti, Jiddu—*Krishnamurti's Journal*

Lack, David—*The Life of the Robin*

Leopold, Aldo—*A Sand County Almanac*

—*Round River*

Lopez, Barry—*Arctic Dreams*

Lorenz, Konrad—*The Year of the Greylag Goose*

Lutyens, Mary—*The Life and Death of Krishnamurti*

Maitland, Sara—*A Book of Silence*

Malcolm, Norman—*Ludwig Wittgenstein: A Memoir*

Mascaro, Juan (trans.)—*The Upanishads*

—*The Bhagavad Gita*

Merton, Thomas—*Seeds of Contemplation*

—*Thoughts in Solitude*

—*A Search for Solitude*

Monk, Ray—*Ludwig Wittgenstein: The Duty of Genius*

Montaigne, Michel de—*The Complete Essays*

Neruda, Pablo—*Art of Birds*

Niemann, Derek—*Birds in a Cage*

Proust, Marcel—*In Search of Lost Time*

—*Time Regained*

Ricard, Matthieu—*Mysteries of Animal Migration*

Selous, Edmund—*Realities of Bird Life*

Smith, Cyprian—*The Path of Life*

Storr, Anthony—*Solitude*

—*The Dynamics of Creation*

Stroud, Robert—*Looking Outward*

Sullivan, J.W.N.—*Beethoven: His Spiritual Development*

Thoreau, Henry David—*Walden*

—*Civil Disobedience*

—*Walking*

—*Thoreau on Birds*

Thorpe, W.H.—*Bird-Song*

Traherne, Thomas—*Centuries of Meditations*

Turnbull, A.L.—*Bird Music*

Turner, Emma—*Broadland Birds*

—*Stray Leaves from Nature's Notebook*

—*Every Garden a Bird Sanctuary*

—*Birdwatching on Scolt Head*
White, Gilbert—*The Natural History of Selborne*
White, T.H.—*The Goshawk*
Williamson, Henry—*The Peregrine's Saga*
—*Henry Williamson: The Man, The Writings*
Zweig, Stefan—*Montaigne* (trans. Will Stone)

JOHN CLARE
Clare, John—*The Natural History Prose Writings*
—*The Major Works*
—*By Himself*
—*Poems of John Clare's Madness* (ed. Geoffrey Grigson)
Tibble, W.N. and Anne—*John Clare: A Life*
Bate, Jonathan—*John Clare: A Biography*
Robinson, Eric— *John Clare's Birds*

R.S. THOMAS
Thomas, R.S.—*Collected Poems 1945–1990*
—*Collected Later Poems*
—*Autobiographies*
—*Selected Prose*
Wintle, Justin—*Furious Interiors*
Rogers, Byron—*The Man Who Went into the West*

GENERAL REFERENCE
Bewick, Thomas—*A History of British Birds (Vols I and II)*
—*Collins Bird Guide*
The King James Bible
Turner, William—*Turner on Birds: A Short and Succinct History of the Principal Birds Noticed by Pliny and Aristotle*

INDEX

INDEX

Index

Persian literature, 217, 242, 269, 304

pesticides *see* farming, use of chemicals

petrel, 46

pheasant, 100, 105, 107

phoenix, 91

photography, wildlife, 59–62, 80–81

physics, 156, 197, 317

pied flycatcher, 211, 220–21

pied wagtail, 50

pigeon, 38, 87, 105, 145, 149, 231

pink-footed goose, 169, 170

pintail, 155, 228

pipit, 62; meadow, 233

Plato, allegory of the cave, 203

Pliny, 73, 241

Plomer, William, *Curlew River*, 226, 229

plover: golden, 23, 47, 66, 217, 286; grey, 23, 170; ringed, 170, 289

'plover's eggs' (delicacy), 132

Portree, Isle of Skye, 301–2

Prespa, Lake, Macedonia/ Greece, 252

Prilep, Macedonia, 249

prisons and prisoners *see* imprisonment

Proust, Marcel, 8, 12, 38, 235

ptarmigan, 50, 295, 304–6

puffin, 73

quail, 35, 54, 217, 250, 297

Quiraing Pass, Isle of Skye, 300–301

Rauschenberg, Robert, 186

Rautavaara, Einojuhani, 218–19

raven, 69, 119–24, 135, 254, 255, 272, 281, 286, 290; on Skye, 295, 299–302; at Tower of London, 121, 123

Ray, John, 90, 188

razorbill, 274

red grouse, 176, 177, 286

red kite, 35, 188–92

red-backed shrike, 211, 250

red-breasted merganser, 286, 289

red-throated diver, 2, 276, 296

redshank, 103, 130, 151, 155, 195, 199, 272, 281

redstart, 35, 125–6, 221

redwing, 187

reed bunting, 52, 166, 195, 225

reed warbler, 231–3

Rha Falls, Isle of Skye, 296

ring ouzel, 1

ringed plover, 170, 289

robin, 100, 137, 229, 271, 311–15, 316–17, 318

rock partridge, 253

rock thrush, blue, 210

rock-hopper penguin, 66

Rome, Ancient, 218, 281–2

I've wandered the world in search of life:
bird by bird I've come to know the earth:
discovered where fire flames aloft:
the expenditure of energy
and my disinterestedness were rewarded,
even though no one paid me for it,
because I received those wings in my soul
and immobility never held me down.

Pablo Neruda, 'The Poet says Goodbye to the Birds'